JIMMY CARTER
RIVERS & DREAMS

THE BITTER SOUTHERNER

**FOREWORD BY
PRESIDENT JIMMY CARTER**

JIM BARGER JR.

—

DR. CARLTON HICKS

To Rosalynn and Jimmy Carter

"IT IS GOOD TO REALIZE THAT, IF LOVE AND PEACE CAN PREVAIL ON EARTH, AND IF WE CAN TEACH OUR CHILDREN TO HONOR NATURE'S GIFTS, THE JOYS AND BEAUTIES OF THE OUTDOORS WILL BE HERE FOREVER."

—

JIMMY CARTER, *AN OUTDOOR JOURNAL*

CONTENTS

FOREWORD BY PRESIDENT JIMMY CARTER   13
PREFACE BY DR. CARLTON HICKS   14
AUTHOR'S NOTE BY JIM BARGER JR.   20
—
ACKNOWLEDGMENTS   297
NOTES & SELECTED BIBLIOGRAPHY   300
BIOGRAPHIES   306

CHAPTER ONE
SPRUCE CREEK
P. 25

CHAPTER TWO
GOLDEN ISLES
P. 41

CHAPTER THREE
ROCKY MOUNTAINS
P. 59

CHAPTER FOUR
ARGENTINA
P. 85

CHAPTER FIVE
VENEZUELA
P. 105

CHAPTER SIX
HONDURAS
P. 131

CHAPTER SEVEN
RED HILLS
P. 147

CHAPTER EIGHT
BLUE RIDGE MOUNTAINS
P. 179

CHAPTER NINE
MONGOLIA
P. 203

CHAPTER TEN
RUSSIA
P. 217

CHAPTER ELEVEN
ALASKA
P. 239

CHAPTER TWELVE
YUCATAN
P. 257

EPILOGUE | P. 282

Jimmy Carter, Rosalynn Carter, and Carlton Hicks in the Black Canyon of the Gunnison River, Colorado.

FOREWORD

Dr. Carlton Hicks and I met in 1966 when I ran for governor of Georgia, and he quickly became one of my earliest supporters. After working together on my campaigns for governor and then president, we became close personal friends.

We started fly fishing together in Spruce Creek, Pennsylvania, when I was in the White House and continued to go annually. Along with Carlton and a few of our "fishing buddies," we fished around the world. These travels afforded Carlton, Rosalynn, and me ample opportunities to discuss politics, campaigns, and old friends.

I am pleased that you have chosen to read this book, which highlights our trips, conversations, and the adventures we had catching and releasing numerous and varied species over the years. It offers a unique look into our long friendship and some rewarding fishing stories.

I first met Carlton's co-author, Jim Barger Jr., when Jim was a little boy. We reconnected when Carlton and Jim visited with us in Plains. We talked about trips we had in common and environmental issues in some of the places we visited. He and Rosalynn had a common interest in the monarch butterfly. He even has a patch of milkweed for the monarchs at his second home in North Carolina.

—President Jimmy Carter
Plains, Georgia

PREFACE

I am an optometrist in the little coastal town of St. Simons Island, Georgia, in the southeastern corner of the state. I have lived here and served the local community as their "eye doctor" for going on sixty years. My wife, Jenny, and I moved here in 1964 because it seemed like an idyllic place to settle and raise our children and for me to build my optometry practice. As a native Georgian, I'd always enjoyed traveling to the Georgia coast with my family and thought it would be a nice place to live. Back then, St. Simons was just a sleepy little beach community among the string of barrier islands known as the Golden Isles. Historically, most people had worked on shrimp boats, in the pulp and paper mills, in the seafood packing industry, or at the acclaimed Cloister Hotel and Sea Island Club. Over the decades, though, it has grown dramatically and is now a bustling beach town full of tourists, retirees, many young families, and growing businesses.

Jenny and I first met in Memphis when she worked for Southern Airways after attending Millsaps College in Mississippi. I'd come to Memphis to study at the Southern College of Optometry. I'm from the small town of Perry in central Georgia, which is famous for growing peaches. I attended Mercer University in the nearby city of Macon, where the Allman Brothers lived and recorded many of their albums. Like me, Gregg and Duane were very early supporters of Jimmy Carter even before he was first elected governor. Of course, they were rock 'n' roll stars, and I was just a small-town eye doctor.

...

In 1966, my optometry practice was still slow enough that I frequently answered the office telephone myself. This ultimately proved a good thing because I casually answered a call in the spring of that year that spawned one of the most enduring friendships of my life. The call was from Bob Short, a friend I'd known through the "Jaycees," a civic organization for young business leaders under forty years old. Bob greeted me heartily and told me that he'd recently moved to Atlanta to work on the gubernatorial campaign of an unknown state senator from Sumter County by the name of Jimmy Carter. Bob said they were looking for someone to be Carter's campaign chairman in Glynn County. He said he thought I'd be a good person for the job.

I couldn't have disagreed with him more and told him so, explaining that I'd only been in Glynn County for two years and that I knew very few people, none of whom were in the political world. I tried to tell him that I was far from a political operative—that I was just a small-town optometrist whose patient load was so low that I answered my own telephone. Surely, they could find someone better. Rather than argue with me, though, Bob asked that I stay on the line for a minute, that someone else would like to speak with me.

The voice that came back on the line belonged to Jimmy Carter.

It was the first time I ever heard the man speak. His voice was affable yet determined—a voice I would come to know well over the years. By the time Jimmy finished talking, he was so persuasive that I was not only convinced that this peanut farmer was the person Georgia needed to improve our state government but—somehow, implausibly—I was the person he needed to help get him into the state's highest office.

PREFACE

Two weeks after that fateful phone call, I met Jimmy Carter in person for the first time when he stepped onto the tarmac at our local airstrip where I was waiting to pick him up and help with his grassroots campaign by introducing him to the few people I knew in Glynn County. Jimmy Carter lost that election but went on to be elected Governor of Georgia in 1970 and President of the United States in 1976. I was heavily involved in all three campaigns, and my family and I have enjoyed a close personal relationship with Rosalynn and Jimmy Carter and their family ever since.

Over the ensuing decades, I built a respectable solo optometry practice while Jenny and I enjoyed a happy marriage, raising two lovely, headstrong daughters, Molly and Holly. But I have always been thankful that I wasn't too busy in those early years to answer the phone. Had I not taken that call, I probably would not have met my dear friends, Rosalynn and Jimmy Carter, would not have spent multiple nights in the White House with them, would not have flown on *Marine One* and *Air Force One* with them, would not have played tennis and jogged at the White House, would not have celebrated Jenny's 40th birthday with the Carters at Camp David and—perhaps most importantly of all—I very likely would never have been introduced to fly fishing, one of the great joys of my life.

I am honored to have learned most of what I know about fly fishing from President and Mrs. Carter, who are both devoted practitioners of the art. Together, we have traveled around the globe for going on fifty years, collecting experiences and memories along the way that I will never forget.

. . .

In the spring of 2020, I'd hoped to go with the Carters at least one last time to our first and most frequent fly-fishing destination, Spruce Creek, in central Pennsylvania. We had gone there nearly every year without fail since the Carters' last year in the White House. But their advanced age and the threat of the COVID-19 pandemic made the trip inadvisable for them. So, instead, I invited my friends Tom Sayer and Jim Barger Sr. together with his son, Jim Barger Jr. Before the trip, I drove up to Plains to visit President Carter at his home. He'd called to ask me to help him sort through his fishing tackle. We reminisced about our many fly-fishing trips together as we organized his fly boxes, reels and fly lines, and his many fishing rods. He showed me his most productive flies, including his favored black ant patterns. I could almost have convinced myself we were simply planning another fly-fishing trip. But by the time he pointed to one of his treasured bamboo rods and asked me if I'd like to have it, I'd ascertained the true purpose of the visit.

The president's fly-fishing days were over.

Sadly and proudly, I packed the president's fly rod and fly box and took them back home with me to St. Simons. A few weeks later, as I packed for my first trip to Spruce Creek without the Carters, I put the president's fly rod and his well-worn box of flies in with the rest of our gear. It may sound silly or sentimental, but for me, taking his gear with us was a way of staying connected to my dear fishing buddy—to sort of bring him along on the trip with us.

That spring, we started a tradition that I have endeavored to replicate on each trip back to Spruce Creek. Over the course of the trip, each of us took turns fishing Spruce Creek with President Carter's bamboo fly rod, using one of the flies he'd tied himself on his vise at home in Plains. We each caught and released a trout in the president's favorite fishing hole just in front of the old cabin on Wayne Harpster's dairy farm. As I felt the delicate bamboo rod load the line on the back cast and cast the line forward in a tight loop out over Spruce Creek, it was like he was there fishing with me. I watched the fly drift downstream, saw the little trout circle underneath it, and watched with glee as the unsuspecting fish snatched the offering from the water's surface. I set the hook and fought the angry fish to the bank, knelt beside the stream carefully to net it and remove the hook. Then, I gently released the fish back into Spruce Creek, watching it disappear beneath the cool, clear water.

PREFACE

It was on that trip that Jim Barger Jr. and I conceived this book. He and I have returned to Spruce Creek many times since then to fish and work on the book together. Jim's wife, Burch, and their two sons have come with us, and so have my daughters and two of my grandsons. Jim's dad—an old friend of mine—has come more than once, and I hope to get my third grandson to join us up there one day.

It is my sincere hope that reading this book will give you some insight into this more private aspect of the Carters' lives. Sitting on the porch of the cottage at Spruce Creek with Jim and recounting all the conversations and adventures I've had with the Carters over the past fifty years to help write this book has been an exercise in pure joy.

—Dr. Carlton Hicks
St. Simons Island, Georgia

AUTHOR'S NOTE

My life as a writer is a series of casts with a fly rod, looping backward and forward, again and again, searching, probing, hoping, willing the line finally to travel over the water under the power of its own weight to land imperceptibly enough that the carefully tied fly drifts in front of a fish that, in turn, is propelled by primordial instinct violently to devour the imitation of thread, fur, and feathers only to awaken to an ironic truth as simple and sharp as cold hard steel. When everything goes right, the fish is eventually brought to hand, observed, and released, so much the wiser, and the momentary connection between child of the earth and child of the water sinks to the depths of subconsciousness and disappears like a dream. But more often than not—after one too many false casts—the line ends up in a tangled mess at my feet or stuck in a tree limb or caught in a snag on the river bottom.

Writing this book with my friend Carlton about his fly-fishing adventures with Rosalynn and Jimmy Carter has been a privilege; having it published by *The Bitter Southerner* is an honor. Many have written books about the Carters' lives and their impact on the world—historians, political scientists, social commentators, and even the Carters themselves. Although this book covers a lot of history, it's not a history book. And while it frequently discusses politics, it's not a political book. It's a fishing book. Plain and simple. And, as such, it's made up of the rambling, rolling, scattered memories of anglers told and retold streamside.

Dr. Hicks told me most of the anecdotes in this book over a period of seasons on the porch of Wayne Harpster's cottage on the banks of Spruce Creek—the favored trout fishing retreat of the Carters and the place where they first began to conceive how they might spend the rest of their lives after losing the 1980 election. Other observations were cobbled together based upon my personal experiences fly fishing around the world for nearly all of the species described in this book and by visiting with the Carters at their home in Plains, Georgia. This book covers all the destinations the Carters and Carlton fished together for over half a century. I have visited all of the same or similar waters and places except two—Russia and Mongolia—although I hope to travel to both someday.

Each chapter of the book begins with a description of Carlton's candid memories with the Carters as he related them to me. The chapters also share Carlton's various memories of campaigning for the Carters, the Carter presidency, and the post-presidency. I have done my best to capture Carlton's voice, hoping to share my experience of sitting on the porch with him, listening to his stories about fly fishing and his enduring friendship with the Carters. I have organized, edited, and combined our many discussions over a period of years into these opening first-person vignettes with Carlton's close input and review. The remainder of each chapter contains my personal sketches and observations written about the Carters' impact on the world, the species of fish they sought, and the environments where those species live or other contextual information both from my personal experiences and my additional discussions with Rosalynn and Jimmy Carter, their fishing buddy Wayne Harpster, and others.

Sometimes the vignettes in this book are very short; other times they run quite long and meander through a variety of subjects like a serpentine mountain stream. That's how it is when you get fishing buddies together and get them talking. But, I have found this can also be where some of the most interesting discoveries are made. Be forewarned: while writing this book, we followed the course of the river wherever it led us.

AUTHOR'S NOTE

This book covers the specific destinations where Jimmy and Rosalynn Carter and Carlton and Jenny Hicks went fly fishing together, as well as other places that were important to the Carters, like Sapelo Island, Yellowstone National Park, and Camp David. It also highlights issues that were of interest and immense concern to the Carters, including human rights, climate change, regenerative farming, philanthropy, social justice, history, and environmental conservation.

The book offers glimpses into the Carters' private moments during some of their biggest challenges and how they used their connections with nature and friends to see them through. You'll meet some colorful personalities who have been part of the Carters' inner circle at different times, including George Harvey, Ted Turner, E.O. Wilson, and Jane Yarn. And you'll get to know the three couples rounding out their intimate fly-fishing group: Wayne and Marjorie Harpster, John and Dianne Moores, and Bob and Ineke Wilson. As you make your way through each chapter, I hope you'll indulge Carlton and me the same way you would a fishing buddy who is swapping stories around a campfire or sitting next to you in a boat, hoping for a fish to strike.

As part of my research during the writing of this book, I spent much time poring over Jimmy Carter's speeches, diary, and the exhaustive list of books he wrote over the years—all thirty-three of them. I drew most heavily from *A Full Life*, *An Outdoor Journal*, *An Hour Before Daylight*, *White House Diary*, and *Faith: A Journey For All*. Rosalynn's lovely autobiography, *First Lady From Plains*, provided notable insight into her life, perspective, and experiences. I also reviewed more than a handful of books about the Carters written by other authors, particularly the exceptionally well-researched and engaging *His Very Best: Jimmy Carter, A Life* by Jonathan Alter, which I highly recommend if this book whets your appetite to learn more about the Carters.

—Jim Barger Jr.
St. Simons Island, Georgia

CHAPTER ONE

SPRUCE CREEK

SPRUCE CREEK

CARLTON HICKS

My first fly-fishing experience was a quick lesson from President Carter casting into the swimming pool at Camp David. The Carters had invited us to join them there for my wife Jenny's fortieth birthday. After a few practice casts in the swimming pool, I tried casting in the small stream that runs down from the mountain at Camp David. It was a favorite spot for the president and first lady during their weekends there. Unfortunately, I stayed with my line hung up in the trees most of the time. So, it really wasn't much of a fishing trip for me. It was, however, one of my first tastes of fly fishing, and I became determined from that moment on to learn the fly caster's art, which I have dedicated much of my life to ever since.

Later, in July of 1980 when we had the Democratic National Convention in New York, I received my first real invitation from the Carters to go fly fishing with them. It was my first trip to a place that would prove to be one of my favorite places in all the world: Spruce Creek. President Carter accepted the Democratic Party's nomination after a particularly embattled presidential primary contest against Ted Kennedy. On the last night of the convention after he'd been nominated, we gathered in the president's hotel suite with the family, and he asked if I would like to go fly fishing with him at his friend

Wayne Harpster's dairy farm in Spruce Creek, Pennsylvania, the next day. I'd never been to Spruce Creek before and had only heard a few scattered stories about it up to that point, because it had been a top-secret retreat of the Carters where they could get away from the White House and recharge. They didn't tell too many people about it at that time.

"Well, Mr. President," I said. "I don't have any gear with me."

And he said, "Well, I guess that means you don't want to go."

And I said, "No, sir, it does not mean that. I do want to go, and we'll make arrangements to get the gear we need."

"Well," he said. "I think you can get what you need to wear at Camp David, waders and things, but you may need to shop here in New York for your other fly-fishing gear."

The next morning, my wife, Jenny, flew home with our children along with a good friend of ours from St. Simons, Mary Bishop, who'd also been with us at the convention. Mary and her husband, Jim, had moved to St. Simons about the same time Jenny and I did. Jim grew up in the nearby farming town of Alma, Georgia. He'd come to the coast right out of law school to work for US District Judge Anthony Alamo, a prestigious jurist well known nationwide. As an aside: Judge Alamo was a World War II hero who helped dig the tunnels for the Allied POWs who escaped from Nazi Stalag Luft II prison camp, which was the subject of the movie *The Great Escape*. Anyway, Jim Bishop worked with me on the Carter presidential campaigns; so, the Bishop family had also been with us for the convention, and Jim decided to join us at Spruce Creek, instead of returning straight home with the others.

Bishop and I and the Carters' eldest son, Jack, jumped in a taxi and rode down to a shop called Angler's Roost, which was at that time a world-renowned fly-fishing shop in Manhattan in the basement of the Chrysler Building. The owner, Jim Deren, used to take you up on the roof of the famous skyscraper to practice casting rods before you bought them. People like President

Eisenhower and Ted Williams bought their fishing gear there. Jim Deren used to sit there all day in his little shop at his vise tying flies, telling stories, and chain-smoking unfiltered Camel cigarettes. Jim Deren designed some of the most beautiful and effective fly patterns there at Angler's Roost, like the delicate dry fly called the "Fifty Degrees" or the bold red, green, and black streamer called the "Black Beauty." These were hand-tied flies made from silk threads and the downy feathers collected from molting birds. They were true works of art. On a piece of paper taped to one of the cabinets full of fishing gear in the Angler's Roost, Deren had scribbled his personal fishing philosophy, which I still remember: "There don't have to be a thousand fish in a river; let me locate a good one and I'll get a thousand dreams out of him before I catch him." Angler's Roost closed sometime in the mid-1980s when Deren passed away. They don't make shops like Angler's Roost or anglers like Deren anymore.

While we were perusing the gear there and trying to figure out what we needed to get (none of us knew much at all about fly fishing at that point), a gentleman pulled us aside and started telling us an impassioned story about catching a trout. He was intent on engaging us with his story, almost to the point of madness. Tears came to his eyes as he recalled fighting this particular trout for a long time before lovingly releasing it and watching it swim away. He described every detail of the encounter as if it had happened just that morning, and he was so enthralled with the thought of it that he wanted to stop and share the memory with total strangers. Then, the man slowly extended his hand and opened it to reveal a tiny fly in his palm. "This is an original Quill Gordon," he said in reverent tones as if he were showing us a piece of the true cross. To me, it looked like nothing more than a few feathers tied around a hook. Only later did I realize that the "Quill Gordon" is perhaps the most important fly in all of trout fishing—the fly pattern upon which almost all other American dry flies are based. It was invented in the 1800s to imitate a particular type of mayfly that hatches on the streams in the Catskill mountains. The tiny fly in the man's hand had been tied by the fly's inventor Theodore Gordon himself and was at least one hundered year's old. As it turned out, the storyteller was Hoagy Carmichael Jr., son of the legendary composer of timeless American tunes "Georgia on My Mind," "Heart and Soul," and "In the Cool, Cool, Cool of the Evening," the lyrics to which were penned by Georgia native Johnny Mercer. Not surprisingly, "Georgia on My Mind" is one of President Carter's favorite songs, and one of the best versions of it is by his close friend, Willie Nelson, whose company I have enjoyed on several occasions with the Carters. Jenny, Willie, and I and several other friends traveled with the Carters to Oslo, Norway, in 2002 for President Carter's Nobel Prize ceremony, and Willie performed the song there.

I didn't know it back then, but Hoagy Carmichael Jr. was one of the country's best fly anglers and a world-renowned bamboo fly rod maker. He wrote several books about fly fishing and rod making, including the seminal *A Master's Guide to Building a Fly Rod*. That encounter at Angler's Roost has always stuck with me because it first made me understand just how passionate fly anglers are. Here was this man whose father had composed many of the most enduring musical pieces in the American canon, and he had decided to dedicate his life to fly fishing. All he cared about was catching fish and releasing them back into the wild, and he had studied and mastered the ancient, dying art of crafting fly rods by hand from split bamboo. Here was a man who surely had caught and released more fish than he could ever count, and yet he was reduced to tears by the memory of one particular encounter with one particular fish. To the uninitiated, it seemed a bit fanatical. Of course, I had no idea that fly fishing would seize my imagination, too, and that I would eventually travel to all points of the globe just to catch and release various fish back into the wild—which, I admit, also sounds a bit compulsive.

After we'd gotten our gear and met back up with the president, we made a quick stop at Camp David before flying by helicopter to the Harpsters' farm, where we landed in a cow pasture not far from Spruce Creek. As soon as we arrived, President Carter immediately decided that he wanted to jump in the water. Because Spruce Creek is spring-fed, it's freezing cold at all times of the year, but he didn't care. Without hesitation, the president stripped down to his undershorts, threw his clothes on the bank, and jumped into the freezing cold water! Well, there was nothing to do but to follow him in. I wasn't about to just stand there and let him think I was too wimpy to get in; so, I quickly stripped down and jumped in, too. It took Jim Bishop quite a while—he hemmed and hawed a bit and didn't want to do it—but after the president and I kept teasing him about it, he finally acquiesced and jumped in as well.

The next morning, I rose early to go for a run, which has been part of my daily routine for much of my life. Jogging down by the stream, I went around a bend where the meadow sort of widened out, just as the sun was coming up. All along the stream, wildflowers and wild mint were growing there, just as they do to this day. You can smell the mint as you step on it. A mist was coming off the stream. I've rarely breathed air as clean and fresh as the air at Spruce Creek. It was so calm, so pastoral. But then, as I jogged around a bend in the creek, I came upon two Marine helicopters sitting in the upper pasture with uniformed soldiers patrolling the hillside with firearms among the grazing cattle. It was an eerie sight. I realized then that even in this utterly peaceful setting, the world remained a strange and dangerous place and that much of the weight of the rest of the world at that time fell on the shoulders of my friend and fishing companion. He carried it with him wherever he went.

Spruce Creek was a balm to the Carters during their years in the White House. A secret haven. A temporary escape from the rest of the world. Even so, the rest of the world was always lurking just around the bend. We stayed there fishing with the Carters for three days. Those three days changed my life forever.

JIM BARGER JR.

The corner bedroom is roughly ten feet by ten feet, just big enough to fit the old wooden double bed, a small dresser, and a reading lamp. Draped neatly across the bed is a well-worn quilt with slightly uneven stitching that conjures images of the wrinkled hands and the well-worn sewing needle that crafted it. The bedroom walls are built from hand-hewn black oak logs, and the windows cut into them are open to invite the breeze and the constant sound of the gurgling, rolling, tumbling water of the limestone spring creek that makes a double-bend a short stone's throw from the porch of the little whitewashed cottage. This little corner bedroom on the western bank of Spruce Creek, deep in the heart of dairy-farming country in central Pennsylvania, is arguably one of the most impactful places Rosalynn and Jimmy Carter have laid their heads, second only to their beloved hometown of Plains, Georgia.

It is well known that the Carters spent four years of their lives in the White House in Washington, DC, from 1976 to 1980, and that during that time they also spent many nights at the presidential retreat, Camp David, most notably while President Carter tirelessly negotiated the longest-running peace accord the Middle East has ever known. Signed by Egyptian President Anwar Sadat and Israeli Prime Minister Menachem Begin in 1978, the Camp David Peace Accords effectively ended the longstanding history of war between the two countries. Carter's peace talks at Camp David also became the blueprint used by future negotiators around the world and is taught in law schools to students studying the process of mediation.

Before that, the Carters spent four years in the governor's mansion in Atlanta, Georgia, where Jimmy Carter became the first state executive office holder in the South to publicly denounce the evils of segregation, forcefully proclaiming during his inaugural address that "the time for racial discrimination is over!" Jimmy Carter's proclamation contrasted starkly with the policies of nearly every Southern governor of that time and all his Georgia predecessors who promised in some form or other to subjugate Black people and uphold a disproportionate system of justice—or in the simple, hateful words of then-governor of Alabama George Wallace, to preserve "segregation forever."

When the Reverend Martin Luther King Jr. was assassinated by a white supremacist in the spring of 1968, Carter's gubernatorial predecessor, Lester Maddox, dishonored the slain civil rights leader by boycotting his funeral and refusing to acknowledge Dr. King's death or legacy in any way other than to order a squad of state troopers to surround the Capitol, where he vowed that business "would go on as usual." Three years later, a newly-elected Governor Carter responded by installing a portrait of Dr. King in the Georgia Capitol. It was Jimmy Carter's first official act as the new leader of the Southern state. Every Georgia legislator, businessperson, and lobbyist thereafter would see that portrait and be forced to wrestle with the duality of a Southern legacy that includes the cruelty of white supremacists like Maddox who rose to popularity by threatening Black people with an ax handle but also the transformative power of peace and love exemplified by non-violent leaders such as King.

Notwithstanding having lived under such prominent roofs as the White House and the governor's mansion, the only true home the Carters have known is the humble Sumter County, Georgia, of their birth. The tiny hamlet of Archery and the little town of Plains unquestionably have been the most dominant forces in their lives—both as individuals and as a couple—shaping them from their formative years in the Jim Crow South to their later years as Sunday School leaders at the Maranatha Baptist Church.

Even so, the secret place where they returned again and again to live outside their public personas and responsibilities and to transcend the expectations and responsibilities that they put on themselves and that others put on them—the place where they could concentrate solely on the simple art of catching fish—was their friend Wayne Harpster's cottage on Spruce Creek. It was here in this tucked-away spot that Rosalynn and Jimmy Carter could wake in the corner bedroom to the sounds of a spring-fed stream and put all the world behind them. It was here that they could rise from their beds with the only thought being whether to tie on a dry fly or a nymph.

. . .

When you wake at Spruce Creek, your first thought is whether the fish will be feeding on the surface or somewhere down below. So, you take a cup of coffee out to the porch, sit in one of the rockers, and watch the creek for a while to see if any fish are rising to the surface. If you see fish rising, then you can try a floating dry fly, letting it drift along with the current until a trout comes up to take it from the surface. Maybe a terrestrial pattern, like those little black ant flies that President Carter was fond of tying that look as if the poor insect has fallen into the water and is struggling to survive or maybe a hopper fly that mimics a cricket or grasshopper desperately kicking its legs as it hopelessly washes downstream. Even the wariest of trout can't resist a struggling insect like that—they're just so packed with protein and such easy prey.

Maybe if flies are hatching from the surface of the water, you could try to mimic them with some small pattern like a caddis, cahill, sulfur, or maybe a blue-winged olive or mayfly. It's fun to gently cast the tiny flies, so airy that they float on the slow-moving water, and to watch them drift along in the current downstream to an unsuspecting trout. But it can be difficult to keep the fly from dragging on the line in the current, especially where the water quickens into riffles and eddies and tumbles fast over the rocks and away.

If it looks like the fly is moving faster or slower or at all differently than everything else that is drifting downstream, even the most careless of trout will ignore the offering completely. You have to properly "mend" the line to keep the fly from dragging in the water, gently lifting the floating fly line from the surface without disturbing the fly at the end of the monofilament leader and gently laying the floating fly line back down again upstream to keep it from pulling the fly faster than the flow of the stream or sinking it below the surface.

You could try a nymph, a hare's ear, pheasant tail, prince nymph, or one of those ugly little midge-looking things. In the sub-aquatic stage of their lifecycle, nymphs are baby flies that have hatched from their eggs on the streambed but haven't yet emerged to the surface with unfurled wings to take to the air. They can be a trout's most reliable food source, always tumbling and drifting along somewhere in the water column between the bottom and the top as they slowly emerge to ride in the surface film before flying away. If you don't see any fish rising to the surface, maybe they are feeding on nymphs underwater. You can tie on a nymph imitation, maybe one with a small metal bead head for weight and let it drift deep below the surface. Just like the dry-flies, you'll have to make them drift perfectly along with the current or the trout will detect the fraud and reject the offering. It's not the easiest way to fish, but it can be the most reliably effective and rewarding.

Across the meadow, you can see the black and white dairy cows drifting through the mist, and you can just hear the murmur of them mooing in unison, calling out to be milked. In the pool beneath the cabin just upstream from the short waterfall, the glasslike surface of the water breaks and concentric circles expand from the spot and then dissipate, leaving a smooth surface again as if nothing had happened at all. And you wonder if it was a trout rising that you saw or if you just imagined it. You open your old metal fly box, rusting at its edges, and start picking through the hand-tied dry flies.

∙ ∙ ∙

Fishing is a completely anonymous pursuit. Maybe that's one of the things that makes it so attractive to those of us who become anglers. In the final estimation, it is always just you and the fish, and the fish has no preconceived notion of you. The fish neither knows nor cares anything about you. If you fail to catch the fish, it is always because you failed to make an offering enticing enough to persuade it. If you succeed in catching a fish, it is for the most part through no particular merit of your own. Knowledge, skill, study, determination, humility, and experience all play key roles in determining whether a fish will strike and whether you can thereafter land the fish before it throws the hook or breaks the line, but just as often, success is a fluke caused by mistake or miscalculation by a creature not far evolved from the time before time, when the earth was formless and desolate, and the raging ocean that covered everything was engulfed in total darkness, and the Spirit of God moved over the water.

To catch a fish is to experience grace in its most indiscriminate form. A fish doesn't know or care who you are or who you know or what you believe in or don't believe in or what you look like or where you come from or what you are going through or what you have done or what you have left undone. A fish doesn't know or care if you are rich or poor or sinner or saint or even if you once were the President of the United States of America.

∙ ∙ ∙

From their White House days until they were in their late nineties and the threat of a global pandemic made it too dangerous for them to take the journey, the Carters returned to Spruce Creek annually, gathering with family and friends whose only agenda was to catch fish, tell fishing tales, and listen to the sounds of the water gurgling in the creek. It was here that they fled the rigors of the presidency and here that they came quietly to mourn losing the 1980 election. In May of 1981, less than four months after vacating the White House, Jimmy, Rosalynn, and their 13-year-old daughter, Amy, packed up a camper van and set out on a 900-mile road trip up from their home in southwest Georgia to their friend Wayne Harpster's farm in western Pennsylvania.

No longer the president and first family, they were private citizens setting out on an otherwise fairly typical American vacation with their teenage daughter. It was Wayne's birthday, and he invited the whole Carter family to celebrate with him and spend a week trout fishing. The Carters' three adult sons—Jack, Chip, and Jeff—all planned to bring their families and meet there. Rosalynn and Jimmy looked forward to having their whole family together again in one place and to letting their minds focus on nothing but reading the river for trout and casting a fly line. The biggest worry they faced while there was what to cook for dinner and whose turn it was to clean up after.

The preceding months had been among the darkest in their lives, watching from the sidelines as their political opponents promised to roll back many of the Carters' hard-won achievements. The American people had soundly rejected President Carter, and the reelection loss stung him hard. At home in Plains, he grew despondent and spent most of his time in his woodworking shed, trying to distract himself by making furniture for the family home. Woodworking had become one of the few things that brought him any joy. But as the camper van wound its way up the Blue Ridge Parkway and down through the Shenandoah Valley, Jimmy Carter marveled at the natural beauty of the American countryside.

Once they got to Spruce Creek, the pastoral setting and cool waters renewed him, especially the time he finally got to spend alone with Rosalynn. "She'd smile, and birds would feel that they no longer had to sing," he once wrote in a poem about her. "I loved to watch Rosalynn fishing," Carter later recalled about that week in

1981 on Spruce Creek. "She had a knack for the sport and liked it, especially the solitude and beauty of the woodlands." When they weren't fishing, Rosalynn and Jimmy went on hikes together, holding hands, wandering up across the cattle pasture and back into the woods across the creek from the Harpsters' fishing cottage. Instead of lamenting the things they'd been forced to leave unfinished, they began to discuss all the things they might accomplish outside the confines of the White House.

The presidency had given them great power but was also highly restrictive. Whether it was Congress, the press, foreign leaders, agitators, political opponents, or even his own party, cabinet, aides, and supporters who respected and supported him—everything the Carters did over the prior four years had been subject to some form of scrutiny or compromise. They had accomplished much while in the White House—more, in fact, than any other president before or since on certain issues like land conservation and peace accords—and yet everything Jimmy Carter achieved while in office for his country and the world had required great political self-sacrifice and would only be fully appreciated by future generations.

But now the Carters were free to chart their own path. As they wandered up the hillside into dense woods, the seed of an idea slowly began to germinate. Maybe there was a way they could use their positions as former president and first lady of the United States to promote human rights and democracy around the world, helping America fulfill her promise of liberty and justice for all people everywhere.

Emerging from the shadows of the forest, Rosalynn and Jimmy climbed a steep slope to an outcrop high above Spruce Creek. A bluebird called from somewhere back in the twisted laurels. When they reached the top, the wooded canopy opened in front of them, and they could see out over the entire valley. Exhausted from the climb, they sat on the ground to rest. Rosalynn reached over and took Jimmy's hand. Mountain laurel and rhododendrons bloomed pink and white all around. The sweet scent of flowers hung heavy in the air. A fresh wind swept over them. The bluebird flitted out of the forest onto a nearby branch. Holding hands, the Carters looked across the green pastures as far as their eyes could carry them.

CHAPTER TWO
GOLDEN ISLES

CARLTON HICKS

B efore becoming a fly fisherman, I enjoyed fishing using live bait and tackle in our home state of Georgia, mainly in the vast saltwater streams and rivers that run through the salt marshes along the coastal barrier islands, known colloquially as the Golden Isles. Our local inshore waters around the barrier islands of Sapelo, St. Simons, Little St. Simons, Jekyll, Little Cumberland, and Cumberland are excellent fisheries for a wide variety of species, including redfish, tarpon, flounder, black sea bass, whiting, and spotted sea trout—which we call "speckled trout" or "specs." Redfish and tarpon are famed fly-fishing targets for many anglers around the world, and they are plentiful here in the Golden Isles. But we were hardly aware of such fabled fish at the time.

Speckled trout were always our quarry of choice. I'm sure we probably caught the occasional bycatch of whiting or flounder and maybe the odd shark or saltwater catfish, but in those days, I don't remember going after anything but speckled trout, a prized table fish. Few things are as delicious as fresh speckled trout, dredged in cornmeal and fried to a golden brown in hot peanut oil, with hushpuppies, creamy, vinegary slaw, and a slice of Vidalia onion on the side. Speckled trout is best eaten when it's still hot from the fryer and washed down with an ice-cold beer or iced tea, so sugary it makes your teeth hurt.

Back then, we kept and ate nearly every fish we caught. The Carters love fresh fried fish, and so do I.

When we fished for speckled trout, we went out in small skiffs or johnboats on the outgoing and incoming tides, and we used spinning gear or baitcasting rods. We used live shrimp for bait, which we drifted under big orange and black striped corks on the outgoing and incoming tides. We would cast our lines and let the tide take the cork out, usually near an oyster bed. Then, we'd just sit and watch our cork drift with the current, waiting for it to disappear below the surface. During these times, I listened to my friend talk about all the things he planned to do once he was elected governor and then all the things he hoped to accomplish as President of the United States. When the tides are right and the speckled trout are schooling, you can sometimes catch them as soon as you cast the line and your cork hits the water. The line goes tight, the rod bends, and you reel as fast as you can to bring that fish to the boat before it saws the line in half on a bed of oyster shells. Then, you put another shrimp on the hook, get the line right back out, and repeat until the bait runs out or the fish stop biting. If you hit it just right, you can catch dozens of fish in a short amount of time before the tide turns.

But there is a lot of downtime in a johnboat watching a cork bob up and down when the fish aren't biting and the tide turns slack. During those times, President Carter and I talked about all manner of things—from politics to literature to history, his experiences on nuclear submarines, or the family peanut farm. Other times, we would just sit in comfortable silence. I've learned that silence can be one of the hallmarks of a true friendship. If you can sit in silence with someone, contentedly, thinking your own thoughts and allowing them to think theirs, then you most likely have a friendship that will stand the test of time.

The Carters came down to the Golden Isles two or three times a year. They often stayed on the northeast side of St. Simons Island near Village Creek at Musgrove, a wilderness retreat owned by the Bagley family. Smith Bagley, one of tobacco magnate R. J. Reynolds' heirs, was an influential philanthropist and major Democratic fundraiser.

On other visits to the coast, they stayed on Sapelo Island, which is just north of St. Simons. The State of Georgia owns and operates most of Sapelo, but it's also home to the historic community of Hog Hammock (also spelled Hogg Hummuck), the last remaining Gullah Geechee community on a ferry-accessed barrier island. After the Civil War, formerly enslaved people purchased their homesteads on Sapelo, and succeeding generations of farmers and fishermen have continued to live on these ancestral lands, preserving their cultural heritage and Creole language derived from West Africa. Jenny and I always joined the Carters when they visited Sapelo, and we especially enjoyed the friendships we made there, learning about sweetgrass basket making, cast net weaving, and traditional Gullah Geechee foodways like smoked mullet, red peas, and purple-ribbon sugar cane.

Whenever the Carters visited the coast, inevitably we'd go fishing together. Those times out in the vast marshes and meandering creeks, rivers, and inlets together, anchored in a small boat at the point of an oyster bed, meditatively watching corks bob up and down in the current in the blinding reflection of the Georgia sunshine rippling on the flowing water, listening to the chatter of marsh hens hiding in the spartina cordgrass and the sharp popping of oysters along the mud banks—those times formed the early foundation of my friendship with President Carter.

...

After Governor Carter announced his bid for the presidency in December of 1974, we didn't have much time to go fishing for a while. We were way too busy campaigning. Even though Jim Bishop had a busy local law firm to keep up with and I had my optometrist practice, we both spent much of our time during 1975 and 1976 on the road—campaigning first for the primary and afterward for the general election.

The first and only time that Governor Carter and I were at the same campaign stop was in nearby Jacksonville, Florida. Mostly, though, he sent us on our own or with groups of other supporters to other destinations as surrogate campaigners. We spread out around the country to talk about the pressing issues of the time, advocate for policy positions, and explain why Jimmy Carter was the best candidate for the White House. It really was a grassroots campaign. I campaigned in fourteen different states leading up to the 1976 general election. The most memorable state for me turned out to be the most significant for the campaign as well—Mississippi.

Jim Bishop and I traveled from Brunswick, Georgia, to Memphis, Tennessee, (where I'd been an optometry student) to join a group of grassroots Jimmy Carter supporters the press had dubbed the "Peanut Brigade." I don't know if they meant the nickname to be pejorative, but we took it as a badge of pride. Our group eagerly supported Jimmy Carter for president, and we weren't ashamed of our state's rural farming heritage.

Most of the people in our brigade were students from Morehouse College, a prominent historically Black college in Atlanta. I think I probably was one of the oldest people in our group! We took a rented bus from Memphis down through Mississippi, one of the most regressive states on civil rights at the time.

The Ku Klux Klan was active then, and it was well known that they had murdered James Chaney, Andrew Goodman, and Michael Schwerner, three young voting rights activists who'd traveled through the state just ten years before. One of the murderers was a preacher, and another was a sheriff's deputy. An all-white jury unjustly acquitted most of the accused domestic terrorists, and the few that were convicted served paltry prison sentences, so they were free to roam the streets when our bus rolled into the state. During the decade before we went to Mississippi as part of the Peanut Brigade,

Klansmen had also murdered civil rights leader Medgar Evers and had rioted on the University of Mississippi campus to try to prevent James Meredith from enrolling there.

When we stopped in Jackson, Mississippi, we met with the lieutenant governor, Brad Dye. I knew Brad because his wife, Donna, had been my wife Jenny's maid-of-honor in our wedding in Coffeeville, Mississippi. I asked Brad if he would please meet with and listen to our group and consider supporting Jimmy Carter for president, which he did.

After Jackson, we went to the Mississippi Delta town of Philadelphia. None of us were interested in spending much time where the murderers of Chaney, Goodman, and Schwerner were still running free and might be emboldened to commit further violence against anyone trying to rally citizens to vote for a progressive candidate like Jimmy Carter. So, we just made a quick stop at the radio station in Philadelphia, and that was it, before continuing to stump throughout the rest of the state. Because most of the power structure in Mississippi was committed to segregation and white supremacy, I thought we would have a hard time there, considering Jimmy Carter's vocal support for civil rights and the way he had worked to upend the white power structure in Georgia as governor by appointing unprecedented numbers of Black leaders to positions of power within the state. For the most part, it seemed to be a successful campaign tour, and we all safely made it back to our respective homes.

On the night of the general election, we were packed into a conference room at the Omni Hotel in Atlanta, waiting late into the evening for the results to come in when Governor Carter got a phone call from Bill Waller, the outgoing governor of Mississippi. The two men spoke privately for a few minutes as we waited with bated breath. Governor Carter hung up the phone. He looked at us for a second without saying anything. Then, with a broad smile he proclaimed that we had carried the state of Mississippi—which gave us the electoral votes we needed to win the presidency.

Everyone stared at one another, stunned, and then erupted into cheers of joy.

• • •

A couple of weeks later, President-Elect Carter started putting together his potential cabinet and decided to come down to St. Simons and use the Musgrove compound there as a kind of basecamp to meet with potential cabinet members and to get his staff organized before his inauguration and eventual move into the White House the following January. The Secret Service had informed Jim Bishop and me what time the Carters' plane was coming in, and we prepared to meet the aircraft like we always did. Every other time that the Carters had come down to the coast, they had always called Jim Bishop or me to let us know they were coming and to see if we wanted to go fishing, We sort of anticipated getting a call from him. But we never did. I thought to myself, "Well, things have changed, you know. He's now President-Elect of the United States. Things are going to be quite different from now on."

Jim and I decided to just go over to Glynco Jetport on the mainland in Brunswick to meet the plane, anyway, like we always had. If the Carters didn't have time for us, then that would be all right—we'd understand. When we got there, however, the Secret Service agents meeting the plane ran over to tell us that the president-elect wanted us to board *Air Force One* before anyone deplaned. It hadn't even dawned on us that he'd be coming on *Air Force One*! As it turned out, President Ford had graciously offered the Carters use of the famed aircraft normally designated only for the presiding commander-in-chief. When the plane landed, we were escorted by the Secret Service aboard *Air Force One* to greet the Carters before they exited onto the tarmac. I think it was one of the more emotional moments in my life to step on board *Air Force One* for the first time, realizing that our friend was actually going to be the next President of the United States. It seemed like it was inspiring not only to Jim and me but also to the Carters. We all got a bit teary-eyed as soon as we saw one another.

We found out later that the reason that he had not called ahead of time was that he wanted to wait until they got in the air to call us so that he could put the call through the White House switchboard so we would be the recipients of one of his first calls from the White House. Unfortunately, we had already left and were on our way to the airport when he called, and there were no cell phones back then—so we missed the call. From the airport we went straight to Musgrove, where amid all of his organizational bustle and meetings with future cabinet members, President-Elect Carter managed to sneak away with us in a few stolen moments to go fishing.

. . .

From the 1960s through the mid-1980s, any coastal Georgia speckled trout fisherman worth his salt south of the Altamaha River and north of the Satilla was running in and out of the creeks and through the vast marshlands in a Willy Harris boat. Willy was a boatbuilder on the mainland in Brunswick. After many years of wanting one of his boats, Jim Bishop and I finally commissioned him to build a trout fishing boat for us. Willy had completed it just a few weeks before the preinaugural cabinet meeting at Musgrove, and we planned to take the president-elect with us on the maiden voyage. Willy Harris boats were traditional bateau-style boats designed and built by Willy himself. They were small skiffs 14- or 16-feet long constructed from fiberglass over plywood. Every Willy Harris boat was outfitted with a 40- or 60-horsepower tiller-operated two-stroke engine that you steered by sitting in the back and holding the tiller connected directly to the engine.

We were pretty proud of our little Willy Harris boat. We'd gotten Willy to make it with a live bait well that you could fill by opening a plug in the bottom of the boat and letting in just enough water to keep your bait oxygenated and fresh before replacing the plug. We filled that live well with fresh shrimp and took our new Willy Harris boat for the very first time with the president on one of the days when he and his staff and future cabinet were staying out at Musgrove. Jim Bishop and I got in the little boat with President-Elect Carter and one of the Secret Service agents, and we took off from the floating dock at Musgrove down Village Creek on our way to the Hampton River to Mosquito Creek to fish near Little St. Simons Island. It was a beautiful day for fishing. The tide was going out, and everything was perfect as we cruised out into the inlet . . . until we looked down and all of a sudden noticed that water was bubbling up and filling the bottom of the boat. We had forgotten to replug the live bait well! And so, we got off to a questionable start with our new boat by almost drowning the 39th President of the United States before he got the chance to take the Oath of Office. We did end up catching a mess of trout that day, though, but only after we spent a good bit of time bailing water.

Later that evening, I'll never forget standing on the deck at Musgrove as the sun was setting way out behind the ocean past the inlet between the north end of Sea Island and the south end of Little St. Simons. Jody Powell and I were just visiting with President-Elect Carter after the two of them had been meeting with various potential cabinet members all day. Jody was a brilliant young strategist from Cordele, Georgia, working on a doctorate in political science at Emory University when he first met Jimmy Carter. He dropped his studies to volunteer on Jimmy Carter's gubernatorial campaign and had been a trusted advisor of the Carters ever since. As the three of us looked out over the marsh, President-Elect Carter turned to Jody and asked him to serve as White House Press Secretary. It shocked me a bit to be so casually included in such an important and private moment. And it was then that I realized that although so many things had changed, the things that mattered were going to remain the same. While my close friend had become the president, the president was nevertheless going to continue to be my close friend. And I never again doubted our friendship after that.

JIM BARGER JR.

≈

The Boat House at Musgrove sits on a modest bluff with a wooden deck and floating dock overlooking a small tidal creek that merges into the wide Hampton River, a tributary of the mighty Altamaha that separates the islands of St. Simons and Little St. Simons before washing into the unbroken horizon of the Atlantic Ocean. From the water, the Boat House looks like the profile of a ship, designed to safely weather the daily barrage of rising tides and windswept salt spray. If you walk out onto the dock there at night where a small fishing skiff is tied up bobbing in the water and stand on the bulkhead, looking at the moonlight gently rippling over the surface of the waves, you'll hear the prehistoric sounds of oysters and shrimp popping incessantly and the startling whoosh of dolphins breaching the surface as they prowl the creek for mullet, redfish, flounder, croaker, whiting, sheepshead, and speckled trout.

Behind the Boat House are smaller cottages, a pool house, a barn, and a large open floor plan structure known as the Grove House where President-Elect Carter held his preinaugural cabinet meetings at a large round table in front of a towering bay window overlooking a formal garden. Among those gathered at the Grove House as President Carter convened the people who would serve in his cabinet were Andrew Young, the first Black Ambassador to the United Nations, and Patrica Roberts Harris, the first Black woman to serve in direct line of succession to the presidency.

The buildings and grounds at Musgrove are shaded by ancient live oaks, dripping with Spanish moss and matted with resurrection fern that clings to the wrinkled bark like algae growing thick on a rusty crab trap. The retreat is hidden deep within a vast maritime forest populated by whitetail deer, raccoons, possums, armadillos, diamondback rattlesnakes, alligators, and a wide variety of resident and migratory birds like the secretive, black-crowned night heron and the little rainbow-colored painted bunting.

Musgrove was purchased and built with tobacco money as a rustic retreat for R. J. Reynolds' daughter, Nancy Susan Reynolds, during the late 1930s at a time when much of the world was preparing for war. Nancy Reynolds chose the name, Musgrove, to honor Mary Musgrove, the daughter of a Muscogee Creek Indian mother and a British father in colonial Georgia. Mary Musgrove lived from 1700 to 1765 and was one of the most influential people in both the Georgia colony and the Creek nation during her lifetime. She served as an interpreter and mediator between the British leader, James Oglethorpe, and the Yamacraw chief, Tomocheechee. Mary Musgrove had full rights of Creek citizenship, owned and oversaw a large conglomerate of businesses and landholdings, and was considered by her peers as one of the most impactful leaders of her time.

Local artisans built the structures at Musgrove out of brick, cypress, and tabby, a traditional Lowcountry masonry technique of making concrete by burning oyster shells to make lime that is then mixed with water, sand, and an aggregate of broken and whole oyster shells. Tabby was a common building material in coastal Georgia from the 1600s until well into the 1800s, and tabby ruins that dapple the coastal landscape are in their own way as mysterious and enthralling as the stone ruins of Ireland or the pagodas of Myanmar. Most of the oyster shells used to build the early tabby structures on Georgia's barrier islands were reclaimed from middens, large mounds of oyster shells stacked hundreds of years before by the indigenous human inhabitants of the coast—the Guale (WAL-ee) and the Mocama

(MO-comma)—whose populations were so decimated after early European contact through colonization, warfare, infighting, slavery, and smallpox that there was little trace left of them by the time James Oglethorpe established the British colony on St. Simons in 1732. Oyster middens are now recognized as sacred spaces and important archaeological sites not to be disturbed.

After the introduction of cheaper and stronger cement methods in the late 1800s, tabby began to wane as a building material. Over the next half century, the few remaining craftsmen who knew how to employ the technique began to die out, and the craft slowly died with them. Modern coastal structures sometimes are made with concrete or stucco mixed with oyster and other shells to approximate the look of tabby, but few traditional tabby structures are constructed anymore. The Boat House and Grove House at Musgrove quite likely are among the last true tabby structures ever built.

By the time the Carters began to frequent Musgrove, the retreat had passed from Nancy Susan Reynolds to her son, Smith Bagley, a noted philanthropist and influential Democratic donor who offered it to the Carters as a place to fish and find respite. Over the years, Jimmy Carter visited Musgrove to hide away, staying in a little clapboard house that the Bagleys call the "Marsh Cottage." Fishing and birdwatching were primary pursuits for President Carter at Musgrove, and he was often known to stretch out on the ground or the wood deck behind the Boat House and take a nap in the afternoon sunshine. Today, Musgrove is owned and operated by a family foundation led by my friend Nicole Bagley. As a nod to Jimmy Carter's time spent there, writers and artists are invited to use the cottage as a retreat just as Jimmy Carter did, and progressive nonprofit organizations are invited to use the Grove House—where Carter first gathered with his incoming cabinet members—as a place to hold round table discussions on issues such as racial justice and environmental protection. Hanging on a high wall inside the Grove House at Musgrove is Andy Warhol's portrait of Jimmy Carter.

In 2016, 256 acres of wilderness originally accumulated as part of Musgrove was purchased by a joint effort of the Georgia Department of Natural Resources and the St. Simons Land Trust, a community-supported nonprofit supported by grassroots donations. The wilderness area is now available to the public as a nature preserve with interpretive biking and hiking trails, a public kayak and small boat launch, and a recreational fishing pier. The Bagley family helped set aside a stewardship fund that became available in 2023 to assist the St. Simons Land Trust maintain the preserve in perpetuity. Protected by a perpetual conservation easement held by the State of Georgia, the wilderness area was renamed Guale Preserve, in honor of the indigenous people who once lived there.

...

Although Georgia comprises less than five percent of North America's Atlantic coastline, it contains over one-third of the North American Atlantic salt marshes and is one of the most nutrient-rich, bio-productive ecosystems on earth. Georgia's coastline is fronted by two bands of ever-evolving barrier islands. The outer band began to form approximately 11,000 years ago through sustained accumulation of sand and sediments during the Holocene geological epoch, the period when humans began their eventual impactful reign over the earth. The names of many of these younger islands—Little Cumberland, Little St. Simons, Little Tybee—describe their size and age relative to the larger, 35 million-year-old string of barrier islands behind them. These islands are known as the Silver Bluff, the ancient dune ridge that runs through the middle of the state's nearly half a million acres of salt marsh.

The world here is governed by the moon.

As the moon orbits Earth, the Earth spins in the same direction, chasing her. The oceans rise to greet her. On opposite ends of the world, the oceans swell their banks, resulting in our twice-daily high tides, traveling around the globe like two giant waves following the orbiting moon. And in the spaces in between, the waters of the ocean are drawn away as low tides, giving us our two complete tide cycles over the course of each lunar day. As the rising tides swell from the ocean into the estuaries on the Georgia coast, rushing through inlets, meandering into rivers, pulsing into ever-diminishing serpentine creeks, twisting through cordgrass and glasswort, flooding the marsh, the water rises steadily higher. Hordes of fiddler crabs retreat from the creek banks to the low marsh, from the low marsh to the high marsh, from the high marsh to the salt pan, from the salt pan to the marsh hammocks, and from the marsh hammocks up to the high ground, where they scurry into mud burrows until the tide retreats again. Tiny periwinkle snails slowly climb the spartina grass stalks, keeping just above the rising water line.

Bald eagles, ospreys, peregrine falcons, and harrier hawks prowl the air, circling and soaring on invisible currents. Great egrets, snowy egrets, tri-colored herons, roseate spoonbills, and armies of ibis wade the shallows. Families of raccoons swim out of the flooded marsh and waddle out onto high ground, shaking the water from their oily fur like wet bird dogs. Mink and otters scurry about in the open water, searching for places to hide. Clapper rails, known colloquially as "marsh hens," call out pleadingly to one another with a staccato sound more akin to nervous human laughter than birdsong. The incoming tides bring detritus and phytoplankton, mud minnows, menhaden, mullet, white shrimp, brown shrimp, blue crabs, stone crabs, and untold schools of baitfish. Oysters and clams gently open their shells to strain the nutrient-dense water, gorging themselves, filtering the murky water until it runs clear. Schools of speckled trout ease into position behind the oyster beds, ready to ambush shrimp and baitfish that drift by with the incoming current.

Live shrimp and soft plastic jigs, drifted over an oyster bed on the incoming tide for speckled sea trout, will usually provoke a strike. But so will a well-placed fly. Any medium-sized streamer with some weight and action to it, like the tried-and-true Clouser Minnow, will draw an aggressive strike from a speckled trout. You can experiment with any number of newer generation flies designed to mimic the ubiquitous movements of fleeing prey—baitfish, shrimp, and crab all at once. These wild, alien-looking flies have zany made-up names like the "Wildlife Bug," "Crystal Shrimp," "Buggy Bunny," or "St. Simons Scampi." Let the fly drift with the current, sinking. Give it a quick, sharp strip. Pause. Let it drift. Strip it again. When it gets to the end of the oyster bed, pick it up and go again. Let it drift. Strip it once. Strip it twice. Let it drift. Strip it again. When the fly stops hard, you feel the unmistakable tug of the predator.

When the fish strikes, you hold your breath and strip three times quickly, setting the hook into the fish's jaw. Then, it turns and runs with the line. Few things are as satisfying as feeling the hypnotic pulse of a weighted fly drifting with a fast-flowing current, then feeling the sudden stop as its natural movement turns into a hard knock, knock, knock on the line in your hand. You feel the immediate resistance as a speckled trout turns and hooks itself, shaking its head, arching the tip of the rod, drawing out line, spooling from the reel, turning with the tide, and searching for the safety of deep water. A brown pelican bobs on the water in the glistening sun before awkwardly flapping its great wings and taking flight.

As soon as the tide washes in, it begins washing out again, leaving behind exposed oyster beds, large mud flats, and isolated pools of water in deeper depressions that remain cut off from the creeks and river systems until the tide turns again. If you search out these temporary ponds—these ebb tide holes in the marsh—and if you're lucky, then sometimes you can find schools of speckled trout and large redfish that have become trapped there, waiting for the tide to return and free them. These are the hungry fish, the greedy fish, the reckless fish. These are the fish that ventured too far back into the creeks, that lingered too long to gorge on the easy prey of hemmed-in mud minnows, crabs, and snails. And when you find these fish, if you're careful and quiet and don't spook them in your approach, they will readily eat a live bait shrimp, a plastic jig, or a well-tied fly.

CHAPTER THREE
ROCKY MOUNTAINS

ROCKY MOUNTAINS

CARLTON HICKS

After we lost the reelection bid for the presidency, everybody was pretty down. Of course, the Carters were. I was. It seemed the thing to do was come back home, regroup, and get my optometry practice going again. Spend more time with my family. The Carters moved back to their home in Plains, Georgia, and began rebuilding their farming business. Ultimately, they had to sell their peanut warehouse to pay for debt the farm incurred during the Carter presidency. Eschewing the high-paying speaking gigs of corporate America and the big city estate homes of many other former White House residents, the Carters chose to live in the relatively modest ranch-style house they built for their family in 1961 before entering politics, and they've lived there ever since.

Together with their youngest child, Amy, they also went back to Spruce Creek to get away and brainstorm what their post-presidential life would be like. As we were all regrouping, several years went by when we didn't fish together at all. President Carter and Rosalynn came back down to the Georgia coast and visited Sapelo Island in 1982 to formalize the design and purpose of their Presidential Library and The Carter Center. I got to spend some time with them then, but I don't remember any fishing that we did together on that visit. We took beach walks, went jogging, and swam in the ocean.

It was during that period that the Carters began their volunteer work with Habitat for Humanity, which became one of the most enduring partnerships and projects of their lives. Habitat was initially conceived at Koinonia Farm, a Christian community where people of all races and backgrounds lived and worked together and shared resources. Founded in 1942 in Americus, Georgia, Koinonia is about ten miles or so from the Carters' home in Plains. Koinonia's pioneering views on racial equity, social justice, and environmental stewardship had a tremendous impact on the Carters. Few white people in the South entertained the idea of racial integration in the 1940s, much less lived in communion with and worshiped with people of color; however, the people of Koinonia pooled and shared resources as equal partners. They worked together to develop and implement sustainable farming practices, which as farmers themselves, the Carters admired.

Ironically, Koinonia's white leaders were excommunicated from the Southern Baptist Church because of their actions to implement racial equality and live out the tenets of their faith. Likewise, in the 1970s, the Carters left their home church, Plains Baptist, when the congregation refused to accept a Black member. They joined nearby Maranatha Baptist, which welcomed people of all races, and they remained loyal and regular attendees there for the remainder of their lives. For decades, President Carter's weekly Sunday School classes drew people of all colors, creeds, and religions, including agnostics and atheists, who came to the tiny Georgia farming town from all over the world to hear him expound on his faith and how his relationship with God impacted his life and life's work.

I am somewhat conflicted about my religious beliefs, and I've often thought about how religion is used to justify much of the evil and cruelty that plagues our world, even as it serves as a source of great comfort, love, and compassion for many people like the Carters. Most of the people I grew up with practiced some form of Christianity, and I have seen over my lifetime many self-described Christians not only fail to love their neighbors but also choose to treat others with contempt and hatred. As for the Christian ideal of loving one's enemies? Well, that seems to me to be a completely foreign concept to so many who claim to follow the teachings of Jesus. It never ceases to amaze me how the very same religion can prompt some people to act out of fear and hatred and conversely prompt other people, like the Carters, to act out of courage and love. Over the years, I discussed my misgivings about religion with President Carter, and he listened patiently to my concerns. Although his faith remained unwavering, I believe he understood all too well my concern that religion can often be wielded as a force for evil, rather than for good.

Knowing the positive influence that Koinonia had on the Carters, I wasn't at all surprised to learn in those first few years after they left the White House that they had begun volunteering with members of the farm's community in a unique approach to addressing homelessness. Of course, many worthy causes were courting the attention and interest of the Carters in those first few years, but Habitat for Humanity seemed to be the most natural fit. Birthed at Koinonia, the initial idea behind Habitat was simple: people around the world lacking adequate shelter could partner with volunteers to build solid, safe, comfortable homes at zero profit, and the materials and other costs could be financed by no-interest loans repaid over time by the new homeowners. President Carter often described Habitat's concept as removing "the stigma of charity by substituting it with a sense of partnership."

The impact was and continues to be enormous: Habitat for Humanity has partnered with volunteers and homeowners to build homes in all fifty states and in dozens of countries, resulting in affordable housing for tens of millions of people, and the list of new homeowners continues to grow exponentially. Beginning in 1984, the Carters became enthusiastic and committed volunteers with Habitat, personally helping build over 4,000 homes over nearly four decades until they were well into their nineties. One of the most enduring partnerships in their Habitat builds has been with country music singers Trisha Yearwood and Garth Brooks. Brooks often noted that the president was among the hardest-working people he'd ever known, which has also been my experience with the president in a number of different contexts. Once when President Carter found Garth Brooks taking a much-needed break on a particularly hot day on a Habitat build in Haiti, the president quipped, "You need something to do, Garth?" A bit chastened, the country music star quickly responded, "No, sir!" and jumped right back to work. I can just hear President Carter saying that even though Garth Brooks is one of the most beloved, bestselling musicians in the world.

When President Carter was ninety-five years old, he sustained a fall and got a nasty cut on his head the day before a Habitat build in Nashville, but he still showed up. Even with a bandage and fourteen stitches in his head, he was quickly nailing and drilling wood again to get the houses built. Both the president and Rosalynn described to me many of their firsthand experiences on home-building projects and their observations of the effect of Habitat on the individual families who partnered with them. One of my great regrets in life is that among the many adventures I've had with them, it never worked out for me to join the Carters on any of their annual building projects with Habitat.

• • •

Around 1985, we finally decided that we needed to make it a priority to set aside time at least once a year to fish together. So that year, I went back to Spruce Creek with the Carters for the first time since we'd been there during the general election as we were fighting what proved to be a failed battle to win Jimmy Carter a second term. In the early mornings, I would rise and fish alone. President Carter and Rosalynn usually fished together. If they chose to fish upstream, then I hiked downstream and fished my way back up to meet them for a late breakfast or early lunch. Most of the time, we cooked our own meals and did our own washing up. It was a simple, no-frills fish camp. In the afternoons and evenings, if they decided to fish downstream, I would pull on my waders and tie on a dry fly—usually a midge or a caddis—and work my way upstream from the cabin, carefully stalking along the creek bank, looking for rising fish. I almost always fish with dry flies in the evenings at Spruce Creek, even if there are no flies hatching and the fish aren't rising. For me, even the hope of seeing a fish rise to the surface in the dimming light to slurp down a dry fly can eclipse the thrill of actually catching and releasing a fish. Even when I know somewhere in the back of my mind that I will have a better chance switching to a nymph or a streamer, I will defiantly fish a dry fly so that I can experience the hope of watching a fish dramatically rise to the surface.

During those evenings, I would usually fish right up until it was too dark to see the fly on the water or too dark to tie a new fly onto my leader after losing one in a miscalculated cast to an overhanging branch. Then, I would hike back downstream under a canopy of stars to find President Carter still fishing in the pool in front of the cottage. Unable to see his fly drifting in the creek current, he would listen for the sound of a fish as it splashed to the surface and set the hook by ear. Sometimes he would be successful. More often than not he would miss, and the fish would get away. But that didn't stop him from trying. After watching his fruitless efforts for a while, I'd usually take my waders off on the steps, hang them on the porch rail, and go up to sit in a rocker beside Rosalynn. We'd talk and watch the president's seemingly futile efforts until eventually out of sheer determination or luck he'd finally land one last fish for the day and release it and come walking up to the porch with a proud broad smile, knowing he'd not only outlasted the fish but that he'd outlasted Rosalynn and me as well.

Since then, I've caught and missed more than my share of trout by listening for the fish to rise and break the water's surface after darkness has fallen. It's just one of the many things I've learned by observing President Carter throughout our friendship. When we weren't fishing, we sat in the rockers on the porch of the cottage, listening to the gentle sounds of the water tumbling over the rocks in the creek. We talked about the fish we'd caught that day and the fish that had snubbed our offerings. We talked about the fish that we hooked but that somehow broke free and got away. We talked about all the fishing adventures around the world chronicled in books and magazines that we'd read about and longed to experience.

President Carter was always a voracious reader. He loved to read about fly fishing, fly tying, and anything to do with the natural world. We mused about the possibilities of fly fishing for peacock bass in Central America, for permit in the Yucatan, and Atlantic salmon in Russia. I don't think I ever fully let myself realize that we might eventually visit all those places in search of all those glorious fish.

We were like kids in that way—hoping and dreaming of far-flung adventures. It's hard to imagine the President of the United States ever considering anything to be beyond his grasp. But after all, he was just a country boy from rural Georgia like me. That is the way with anglers, part of our nature, to believe that something is just out of our grasp and reach for it anyway, hoping against hope. To catch a peacock bass deep in the rainforest, to trick the finicky and elusive permit on the equatorial saltwater flats, to get an Atlantic salmon to eat after a thousand casts refused. These are improbable dreams anglers hope to will into reality. Sometimes we succeed, and sometimes we don't. My friend, the president, was no stranger to failure. He understood it well, grappling with it like few people have. His faith always promised that in the face of utter failure, something even greater awaited. Failure is the stock-in-trade of any honest angler—reaching and hoping against hope for that thing that remains just beyond your grasp. That's what fly fishing is all about.

Most evenings, our dear friend and host Wayne Harpster, the dairy farmer who owns Spruce Creek, would come by. He'd sit with us on the porch and enthrall us with stories about fly-fishing trips he'd taken to crystal clear rivers in Patagonian Argentina, life-threatening bear hunts in North America, or stalking plains game in Africa. President Carter regaled us with stories about his experiences fly fishing for bonefish in the British Virgin Islands. Hesitantly but excitedly, I shared stories about my many trips down the Gunnison River through the Black Canyon in Colorado.

We went back to Spruce Creek together every year after that for nearly forty years. We might have missed a year in there somewhere, but if so, I can't remember it. During those first few annual trips, President Carter, Rosalynn, Wayne Harpster, and I continued to ponder the other great fly-fishing spots we might visit together. We eventually vowed not only to fish every year together at Spruce Creek but also to plan trips to other adventurous fly-fishing destinations around the world.

After I told the Carters and Wayne about my float trips down the Gunnison River through the Black Canyon, we all agreed that the Rocky Mountains of Colorado should be the first trip that we'd take together outside of Spruce Creek. At that point, I'd probably floated through the Black Canyon about eight times myself. It didn't take much arm-twisting to convince them that it was something we all should do together. It's an experience that every fly angler should have if they get the chance. It's almost indescribable, but I'll try.

You hike straight down into the Canyon, which is an adventure in itself. It's one of the steepest hikes in the world. The Canyon walls are nearly vertical—so steep that it's difficult for sunlight to get down to the bottom. That's why it's called the "Black Canyon." Not far into the hike, you can hear the river's roar. When you finally get down to the bottom of the Canyon, guides who are experts at navigating the unique white water and fly fishing the river await. They lead you down the Gunnison River in rafts, as you fish and camp riverside for the next three days. To this day, our trips into the Black Canyon remain among my favorite fly-fishing experiences. The one exception may be pursuing golden dorado in the marshlands of Argentina. But my time in the Black Canyon with the Carters is certainly right up there among my very favorite experiences I ever had with them. It is the place we went more than any other besides Spruce Creek.

The first trip we took together through the Black Canyon of the Gunnison began with the Carters coming out to stay at my vacation home in Crested Butte in August of 1988. By that time, Jenny and I had bought a little place out there, and we spent as much time in Colorado as we could, skiing in the winter and fly fishing in the summer. After the Carters arrived, we had a couple of days to kill before we'd planned to float the Gunnison through the Black Canyon. The first morning we spent some time up at the ski resort there in Crested Butte, which was owned at the time by Howard H. "Bo" Callaway and his family. The Callaways are an old Georgia family who have been involved in politics and the resort business for a long time, owning and operating Callaway Gardens in Pine Mountain, Georgia, not far from the second home of President Franklin Delano Roosevelt in Warm Springs.

Warm Springs is still known today as the "Little White House" because FDR went there often to soak in the mineral waters as a therapy for his polio. Some of FDR's experiences in rural Georgia were influential in helping him craft his policies for rural communities under the New Deal. Warm Springs is less than two hours west of my childhood home in Perry, Georgia, so I have little trouble imagining what he would have encountered. The harsh realities of rural poverty at the time would have been on full display, particularly the cruel brand of poverty that permeated the South during the first half of the twentieth century. Bo Callaway's father, Cason Callaway, and FDR were actually close friends although they were nearly diametrically opposed politically. Similarly, Bo Callaway and Jimmy Carter were political rivals who eventually became friends. They both ran for Governor of Georgia in 1966. Carter ran as an FDR-styled Democrat, and Callaway ran as a Republican backed by big business. Neither of them won. Violently racist firebrand Lester Maddox narrowly claimed the election, running on a platform of opposing school desegregation and upholding Jim Crow white supremacy. It was the worst of all options for Georgia.

Fast-forward to the late 1980s: The Callaways were very hospitable to our guests, the former president and first lady. Bo Callaway co-owned the resort with his brother-in-law, Ralph Walton, who ran the day-to-day operations. I asked Ralph if there was a good place to take the Carters fishing the next day before our trip down the Gunnison. "Let me make a phone call," Ralph said. He got back to me a little later and said, "I've arranged for you to go up and fish the Taylor River on about four miles of stream just below the reservoir. It's wonderful fishing. Your hosts will be Perkins and Ann Sams, and they are expecting you in the morning."

Well, the president always had to be doing something. With nothing planned that afternoon, he said, "I'm going to go up and look at everything." He wanted to scout out the fishing we would be doing the next day and see the river. We didn't announce it to the Sams or let them know we were coming by; we just rode up to see the river without telling anyone. I thought we would simply ride around and scout good places to fish, but President Carter suddenly said, "I'm going to go up and knock on the door."

He told the Secret Service to pull over right there in their driveway. People we had never met. I have to admit it made me a little uncomfortable. But President Carter just got out of the car, walked up, and knocked on the door unannounced. Ann Sams unknowingly came to the door in her bathrobe! There she was in her bathrobe meeting the former President of the United States for the first time. Of course, Ann handled it with grace, but she forever remembered the surprise visit and never let us forget it either.

The next morning, we fished the Taylor River with Ann and Perkins, the first of many annual trips to their place over the next decade. In addition to being excellent hosts and fishing guides, the Sams were well-known environmental stewards in that part of Colorado. Their shared interest in environmental preservation endeared them to the Carters and my family. Over the years, we got to fish the Taylor River with some luminaries of the fly-fishing world, including Leigh Perkins, president of the legendary outfitting company Orvis, and Johnny Morris, founder of the giant outdoor retail company Bass Pro Shops. Texas Governor Mark White fished with us one year on the Taylor River with the Sams. Then in 1998, the Carters invited Bob Wilson, a North Carolina building contractor whom the president and Rosalynn had met through their work with Habitat for Humanity. Bob eventually joined us on a couple of our last camping trips on the Gunnison River through the Black Canyon and became a regular on many of our global fly-fishing trips.

...

The trip through the Black Canyon takes three days in a whitewater raft, and you camp along the river at night. Before you start down the river, you have about a two-mile hike down a National Park Service hiking path called the Chukar Trail. Even though it's just a couple of miles, it is an extremely tough little hike because it's almost completely straight down along a trail of loose rock that shifts underfoot. Guides bring the gear down on horseback or pack mules a different way the night before your arrival and are waiting there when you arrive at the bottom of the canyon to the river where you float for three days and camp out on sandbars in pre-arranged places each evening.

While the fishing was pretty good on that first trip, the president was struggling with the knowledge that his brother Billy was suffering from pancreatic cancer and likely to die. While we were on the river the Secret Service received word that Billy had taken a turn for the worse. Unfortunately, there was no way for the president to receive or make a telephone call in that remote area. The Secret Service landed a helicopter on one of the sandbars along the river ahead of us and were waiting there to deliver the bad news. Agents took President Carter to a place where he could talk with his little brother Billy on the telephone. It was getting close to the end, and I think the president knew it.

Billy Carter was the complete opposite of his older brother. A chain-smoker and heavy drinker, he adopted the character of a sort of country bumpkin when he frequently appeared on television talk shows when Jimmy Carter was in office. Billy's Secret Service codename was "Headache," if that tells you anything. But in reality, Billy was much more complicated and interesting than his hokey public persona.

He was incredibly intelligent, witty, informed, and very well-read, but he leaned into that redneck personality that the media and the public had come to love and expect. It was more an act than anything, but he willingly profited from it even if it didn't give a fair and accurate portrait of who he really was and even if it caused some difficulty and frustration for the president. Once while the Carters were still in the White House and Billy had been in the news for one thing or another, President Carter turned to me and said, "One day the press is going to turn on Billy." And eventually they did. Throughout President Carter's last two years in office, the press relentlessly denigrated Billy, which the president's opponents used to their advantage in the 1980 presidential campaign.

Despite their many differences and the strains some of Billy's activities put on their relationship while the Carters were in the White House, President Carter and his brother Billy were very close and deeply loved and respected one another. President Carter often called Billy the hardest worker he ever knew—high praise from Jimmy Carter—and affirmed Billy for eventually confronting and defeating his alcoholism and becoming a mentor who helped many others do the same through Alcoholics Anonymous. I remember how devastated the president was when Billy was diagnosed with pancreatic cancer. President Carter's two sisters and his father all died of pancreatic cancer. So, it was a serious concern for him in the middle of our trip down the Gunnison that Billy had taken a turn for the worse. It was a tense time for all of us, sitting on the sandbar outside our tents, listening to the sounds of the river, waiting for the president to return. When the helicopter finally brought him back to the river beach, President Carter reported that he'd had a good conversation with Billy, who had encouraged him to finish the trip and catch a bunch of fish. A few weeks after the Carters returned to Plains from our trip, Billy died.

...

On at least two of the five trips we took through the Black Canyon, we managed to hit the stonefly hatch, which meant fantastic fishing for big trout. On the stonefly hatch, those big trout will come up and run the little trout off. On the steep walls of the canyon, you'll see splash marks where fish jumped at a stonefly. We found that if we cast up, let the fly hit the canyon wall, and drop down into the water along the wall, our casts would invariably get strikes. Those June trips with the stoneflies were really, really good trips.

My youngest daughter, Holly, is a pretty decent angler, and she joined us on those trips. She and I fishing together in the same boat is a memory I cherish. Holly always saw the Carters as extended family members rather than national figures. Her fondest memories from those times are sitting around the campfire after dinner or in the early mornings after emerging from her tent. As the sunlight tried to sneak its way down into the canyon and the mist burned off the stream, she watched Rosalynn silently meditating and performing Tai Chi on the sandy riverside. She said it felt like she was in another world down there in the canyon and that we were the only people in it.

In that setting, camping along the Gunnison River deep down in the canyon, we were able to live a very simple life together, at least for a few days. Holly saw the Carters wash up their plates after dinner with sand from the beach and water from the river like everyone else. After saying goodnight, she watched them crawl into their tents where they nestled into sleeping bags on the hard ground like the rest of us.

On one trip, Wayne Harpster, Bob Wilson, and their guide pinned their raft on some rocks. Holly was on that trip, too. She and I were in front of Wayne and Bob, further downstream, and hadn't seen them in a while. The Carters were in a raft even further in front of us. Wayne and Bob and their guide were pulling up the rear. All of a sudden, I looked down in the river and noticed life vests, Coca-Cola cartons, fishing and camping gear, and other debris floating by. I thought, "What in the world is going on?" Then another boat came down and told us that Wayne and Bob's raft was pinned on some rocks. Thankfully, with a little help from the Secret Service who were following in another raft, they finally got free. They were a little wet and frustrated, maybe, but mostly unharmed.

The Black Canyon has dangerous rapids up to Class 5 in several places. The whitewater scale goes from Class 1 up to Class 6, which is life-threateningly extreme. The Class 5 rapids in the Gunnison have deep holes and drops that should only be maneuvered by experienced experts. A few times, we had to get out and portage around, just because the guides didn't want us staying in the raft, especially in low water where it can get pretty rough and dangerous. Holly is experienced with white water, so she often went down the rapids in the raft, rather than portaging. President Carter is also a very experienced whitewater paddler, having paddled many of the more dangerous rapids in north Georgia, including the harrowing sections of the Chattooga River featured in the film *Deliverance* based on the book written by his friend James Dickey. But most of the president's whitewater experience is in a canoe, not a bulky river raft. So, he usually elected to hike with the rest of us and let the guides take the rafts and gear down the more dangerous rapids while we hiked downriver to meet them.

RIVERS & DREAMS

...

Once, years ago, when I was on a trip through the Black Canyon without the Carters, the guide got thrown out of the raft. I'd just tied on to another trip that was going one week with some other anglers whom I didn't really know. I can't even remember now where the fella that was in the raft with me was from, but when we were going down some pretty tricky rapids, the guide hollered for the two of us anglers to get up on the high side to balance the raft. I did, but the other fellow didn't. Just like that, the boat tipped up, and the guide fell out. Fortunately, he was floating at the same pace the raft was and eventually was able to clamber back in. I learned a valuable lesson that day, though: always listen to your guide. A lot of anglers try to rely only on their personal skills and experience, and they refuse to hire guides or—much worse—they hire guides but don't listen to them. The way of a fool is right in his own eyes, but a wise man listens to counsel, as the old folks used to say. If you have the time to get to know a place, to fish an area repeatedly and learn by trial and error, that is one of the most rewarding ways to learn, particularly if you are exploring waters near your home. But learning from others is also just as valuable and extremely advisable if you are traveling to a new place.

I have found that wherever you go, you can learn more about a place if you'll take the time to seek and listen to local knowledge. Ultimately, that is much of what fly fishing is about for me: getting to know a place, getting to know the people of that place, allowing them to share the stories of that place and what it means to them, listening and learning and appreciating. A good fishing guide will have spent years—often decades—getting to know the place that you may only have days to learn. A good guide will have a vast experience reading the water and the weather conditions and all of the unique idiosyncrasies of that particular place. If asked to give one piece of advice to beginning anglers, I recommend finding a good guide, either a local friend who is willing to mentor you or a paid guide service. One of the positive economic effects of the recreational fly-fishing industry is that it provides unique jobs for local guides who are paid to closely observe their ecosystem and ultimately to become environmental stewards as well as ambassadors advocating to others around the world why a particular place should be valued and protected. Finding a good guide is far more important than choosing the best tackle or deciding what clothes to wear or even learning how to cast a fly proficiently.

It's actually pretty good advice for all of life: Find a good guide, someone you can trust who always strives to do the right thing. Someone who will inspire you to try your best, who will show you new things and new ways of doing things, who will admit their own mistakes and help you through yours, and who has an ever-growing wealth of knowledge that they are willing to share. Find someone who will learn from their successes and their failures and inspire you to do the same. Find yourself a good guide. That's the best advice I can give. For me, that person has been Jimmy Carter.

...

On that first trip, when it was just the Carters and me, we floated out at the end of the trip in a little area called Pleasure Park, and the press was there waiting for us. They wanted to take pictures and interview the Carters about the trip. A representative of Ross Reels was also there. Ross Reels was founded back in 1973 by an aerospace engineer named Ross Hauck, who was an avid fly angler. Up until that point, fly reels had mostly been die-cast out of brass or a mixture of brass and aluminum. Ross figured he could make a better reel out of anodized aircraft-grade aluminum, which is the industry standard today. Ross also made stronger, more attractive reels by hand machining them from solid pieces of aluminum, rather than melting the alloy and pouring it into a die.

A good fly reel is a thing of beauty, a unique combination of strict utilitarianism and art. It must function flawlessly, not only holding line and retrieving line but also reliably and smoothly applying tension that anglers call "drag" to slow the progress of a fish as it fights the line, gently applying steady pressure to wear down the fish so that it can be safely brought to hand. It must function well while constantly being assaulted by the corrosive effects of water, sand, mud, gravel, rocks, shells, and sometimes salt. The operation of a good fly reel is akin to that of the world's finest timepieces. In fact, the earliest designers of fly reels were watchmakers, gunsmiths, and jewelers. A fine fly reel can and should be an heirloom, something to be enjoyed, admired, and passed down to others who will recognize its true worth. And the true worth of a fine fly reel is not just that it holds the fly line, but that it holds the memory of every fish that was ever caught with it and every fish that ever got away.

Ross Reels are made in Montrose, Colorado, only about ten miles from the Black Canyon. Their most celebrated reel is called the "Gunnison." Ross' Gunnison reel was introduced in 1988, the same year that the Carters first joined me in the Black Canyon. It's now considered to be among the most iconic fly reels ever made. While other fly reel designs and even companies routinely come and go, the Ross Gunnison is still hand-crafted by artisans near the river from which it takes its name. It was very special for the folks from Ross to be able to present the president and Mrs. Carter each with a Ross Gunnison reel as they stepped out of the river. Of course, I was standing right there with them, too, when they accepted the reels. We've always joked about how I was standing there with my hands out, but there were only two reels.

They each got one, and I didn't get one. It's just been sort of a standing joke, but the truth is that I really did covet those beautiful reels. I'm sure the folks from Ross were wondering, "Who is this guy?" I was just the president's anonymous fishing buddy, so of course I didn't merit one. But that didn't stop me from wanting it. All those years later when President Carter asked me to help him sort through his tackle and he gave me his personalized bamboo fly rod, the reel he gave me to go with it was that first-generation Ross Gunnison. It's engraved to President Carter on the inside and is now one of my most treasured possessions. Someday, I'll pass it along to the next generation just as the president passed it along to me.

JIM BARGER JR.

Seventy-two million years ago, the tectonic plates beneath present-day Colorado began to shift. Those shifts forced a great uplift along ancient fault lines, resulting in the major subranges of the southern Rocky Mountains, including the mighty Sawatch Range and the Gunnison Uplift. The steady flow of the Gunnison River has continuously cut the Black Canyon for more than two million years at a rate of roughly one foot per millennium. The patience of rivers astounds me. At that rate, the Black Canyon has increased in depth no more than two feet since the time of Jesus. Yet, the canyon drops nearly vertically 2,000 feet to the river below, meandering around smooth-stoned beaches, crashing over boulders, and sometimes washing right up against the towering canyon walls. The river both creates and is guided by the canyon through which it flows. And, like all rivers, it is a miracle.

The Gunnison cuts through a broader geographic region of high desert, studded with pygmy forests of cedar-scented junipers and pinyon pines. Colonies of yellow-bellied marmots sit on high rock perches on squat little legs with plump bellies hanging out. Covered in mottled gray and golden fur, squinting snub-nosed white-whiskered faces, they defiantly chirp choruses of high-pitched barks at a golden eagle soaring lazily overhead, and at a skinny coyote loping carelessly below. Both would happily snack on one or more of the pugnacious little rock chucks if they strayed too far from their burrows.

In the sage scrublands, a male Gunnison grouse dances his bizarre courtship ritual, ponytail feathers flung wildly back into the air, billowing white air sacs bulging from his lusty throat, half-moon spiked tail feathers pluming in speckled black and white silhouette behind him as the rising sun cuts across the open prairie. A female sage grouse watches discriminatingly, eyeing his every move, carefully determining whether the genetic code of this male will be selected to pass along to the next generation. These birds are among the last of their kind, and this is one of the last places on earth where they continue to survive. A mule deer swishes its black-tipped tail, dips its antlers to feed on golden flowers of arrowleaf balsamroot before disappearing into the thick scrub brush. Far in the distance, a herd of elk drifts across the open meadowlands painted purple by lupine blossoms.

The canyon rim is scattered with wildflowers: trumpet-shaped scarlet gilla, delicate white alpine pennycress, purple penstemons, blue and white columbine, yellow blossomed red-stem cinquefoil, fire-red paintbrush, and periwinkle milkvetch. Bees, butterflies, and broad-tailed hummingbirds hover among the flowers, greedy for nectar. Descending into the canyon, the north-facing wall is stenciled with fir trees, while the steeper south-facing wall is barren and shrouded in shadows. A family of Rocky Mountain sheep hops cavalierly from one outcrop edge to another. A cougar eyes them from her high-shadowed perch but chooses not to pounce. Far below, the river rushes across the canyon floor. Cottonwoods edge the riverbank. Their billowy seeds float on the breeze following the river downstream. Below the rushing water, unusually large rainbow and brown trout hide in eddies, waiting for the stonefly hatch to begin.

. . .

Stoneflies predate the dinosaurs. Their annual mating ritual celebrates the moment when sea creatures first evolved to crawl onto dry land. It's an orgy of sex, death, and birth. Stoneflies are among the oldest living creatures on Earth, endemic to every continent except Antarctica, and their survival depends on clean, cold, highly oxygenated water. They are an indicator species for the health of cold water rivers. Where stoneflies are abundant, a river likely is flourishing. A river is likely threatened or in peril when stoneflies are in decline or non-existent. Gently turn over a rock or two in a healthy cold water river anywhere in the world, and you will inevitably find the nymph of one of these ancient creatures or the exoskeleton from which it emerged as it cycled through its stages of life. Trout fishing is the study of the life cycle of insects.

Each stonefly nymph hatches from one of as many as a thousand eggs scattered by a single female across the river's surface. The eggs are dispersed according to the whims of water, eventually sinking to the bottom and sticking to the surface of stones. Thus, the name "stonefly." It can take as little as a day and as long as a year for a stonefly egg to hatch into a nymph, looking like a wingless version of its future self: a swallow-tailed insect up to two inches long with an oversized segmented abdomen, six alternating hinged legs, and two long, dangling antennae. Clumsy swimmers, stonefly nymphs initially seek the shallower rock bottoms at the edge of streams, feeding on detritus, minuscule organic matter, and sometimes other smaller insects for most of their lives.

Unlike butterflies, which undergo a complete three-stage metamorphosis, elegantly transforming from caterpillar to chrysalis to winged insect bearing almost no resemblance to their former self, stoneflies undergo incomplete metamorphosis. They crudely claw through their exoskeletons as bigger, larger versions of their former selves, again and again and again. The nymphs may undergo this process for as many as two or three years as they finally grow to adulthood, crawling out one last time with two low-functioning wings stacked one on top of the other.

Once their lumbering wings have dried, adult stoneflies call out to one another by grinding their abdomens against rocks, creating a low-drumming sound. They couple briefly, mate awkwardly, and die within a matter of minutes, hours, or days. The only objective of an adult stonefly is reproduction. Immature stonefly nymphs cycling through their various growth stages for months or years provide trout with a steady, reliable, subsurface food source. In contrast, the newly hatched, suicidal, sex-crazed adult stoneflies that intrepidly hover over a rushing river or struggle and tumble along in the murmuring current offer a gluttony of protein for trout—and a legendary opportunity for anglers in the right place at the right time to witness the wild spectacle unfold.

. . .

The rafts bump along downstream in a path preordained by the current. Rivers choose where they take you, and they won't be redirected. Rivers are sovereign. They never obey. At their wildest, rivers deliver you white-knuckled and paddling deep into a vortex carved by time itself. In those first exhilarating seconds when you launch a canoe, kayak, drift boat, or raft into a river and row or paddle into the flow, you immediately cede control to a force oblivious to the many mundane urges of the human will. "Here we go, out of the sleep of mild people, into the wild, rippling water," proclaimed James Dickey in his novel *Deliverance*.

The book is often unfortunately reduced to its harrowing depiction of sexual violence, inequitable stereotypes, and nightmarish caricatures of southern Appalachia as depicted in the Oscar-nominated 1972 film adaptation, starring Jon Voight, Burt Reynolds, Ronnie Cox, and Ned Beatty. But *Deliverance* is not just some crudely drawn horror story. It's a portrait of a particular river from Dickey's imagination and experience, a river well-known to his friend Jimmy Carter. But it also somehow depicts something bigger and more universal than just one particular river. In *Deliverance*, Dickey describes all rivers everywhere drawn by the imagination and experience of every person who reads the story. It is the river in the green rhododendron Smoky Mountains of the American South. It's a river in the recesses of the Black Canyon in the southern Rocky Mountains of Colorado. It is a river as a metaphor for humans awakening to the natural world and the context of humanity within it. "I had not really been aware of the water, but now I was," Dickey wrote. "It felt profound, its motion built into it by the composition of the earth for hundreds of miles upstream and down and by thousands of years."

President Carter and James Dickey were unlikely friends: the hard-living poet and the earnest Sunday School teacher. Carter admired Dickey's poetry, and Dickey called Carter "the man destiny has cast in the role of deliverer." Both were Georgia-born and bred, and both saw in their native southland something immediately beautiful and horrifying. When President-Elect Carter asked Dickey to deliver a poem for his inauguration, he wrote "The Strength of Fields" for the occasion. In the poem, Dickey imagines Jimmy Carter walking the streets of his hometown one evening, hoping against hope that the horrors of his native land and the collective sins of the present and the past might be transformed into something beautiful:

> Lord, let me shake
> With purpose.   Wild hope can always spring
> From tended strength.   Everything is in that.
>   That and nothing but kindness.   More kindness, dear
> Lord
> Of the renewing green. That is where it all has to start:
>   With the simplest things. More kindness will do nothing less
>   Than save every sleeping one
>   And night-walking one
>
> Of us.
>   My life belongs to the world. I will do what I can.

RIVERS & DREAMS

...

The rafts quicken with the pulse of the river, and the water deepens. The river narrows and concentrates, and the sound narrows and concentrates with it. It gets louder. This is not a place for fishing. The fishing upriver earlier in the day was good, but this is not a place for fishing. The water moves too quickly here and drops too steadily, too dangerously. This type of water doesn't hold fish. Fish need eddies and pools where they can wait to ambush insects washed down by the river. Along the shallow streamside, the anglers step out of the rafts awkwardly, clambering in their chest waders, chattering excitedly about the fish they caught further upstream. The sound of the approaching white water pounds like blood in their ears.

They hike single-file downstream, tipping their outstretched fly rods in front of them. The guides row back out into the flow and let the river tumble the rafts up, over, around, and down the swiftly moving white water. They row among the rocks and smooth stones and boulders, almost weightlessly over the rapids, water splashing over the bows of the rafts and into the rubber bottoms of the boats around their well-worn wading boots. When the anglers meet back up with the guides, three rafts are beached on the sand where the river widens and flattens out. Everyone works together to pitch camp. Wood is gathered and stacked for the fire. Dinner is cooked over the open flames. Smoke rises through the canyon. Darkness falls. A river of stars stretches above at the top of the canyon walls. The sound of the river has softened and become peaceful again. Nestled in his sleeping bag, the Sunday School teacher turned president turned Sunday School teacher again listens to the sound of the river like an old hymn:

When peace like a river, attendeth my way
When sorrows like sea billows roll,
Whatever my lot, thou has taught me to say
It is well, it is well with my soul.

ROCKY MOUNTAINS

He reaches over to hold Rosalynn's hand. No longer a president or even a Sunday school teacher, he's just one of a group of anglers following a river through the high western landscape of his childhood daydreams. His buddy Carlton and Carlton's daughter, Holly. His buddies Wayne and Bob. His wife. Inside their tents on the beach at the base of the canyon with the river gurgling nearby, the anglers drift to sleep, dreaming of fish.

CHAPTER FOUR
ARGENTINA

ARGENTINA

CARLTON HICKS

Argentina has loomed large for our fishing buddy Wayne Harpster for decades. Wayne goes there almost yearly to fish or hunt, sometimes for a month or more. He may have gone more than once some years. Just as I talked up the Black Canyon in Colorado to our group for years, Wayne regaled us with stories of his many adventures in Argentina. Fishing for golden dorado in the sprawling marshes of the Esteros del Iberá Reserve off the northeastern province of Corrientes. Wading for trout in the shadows of the Patagonian Andes. Throwing streamers for giant sea-run browns at the end of the South American continent in the wind-swept rivers of Tierra Del Fuego. For years, we dreamed about exploring Argentina together. Around the campfire in the Black Canyon or on the front porch of the cottage at Spruce Creek, the Carters and I listened to Wayne describe his experiences in the southern cone of South America.

...

But before talking about our times together in Argentina, I'd be remiss if I didn't first give some background on how we got to know Wayne and about the Harpsters' farm, which the Carters and

I visited nearly every year for almost fifty years. In 1936, Wayne's parents acquired the house along Spruce Creek, where Wayne and Marjorie live. Mr. and Mrs. Harpster started the farm with just a few hundred acres for grazing dairy cows. Then, in 1957, they acquired the cottage where the Carters have always stayed and another mile or so of Spruce Creek—some of our favorite fishing water. In 1965, Mr. and Mrs. Harpster retired from the farming business. They sold 17 Holstein cows, 18 heifers, 100 Guernsey milkers, and the dairy and farming equipment at cost to Wayne, who'd just gotten back home after serving in the navy. Wayne and Marjorie rented the pastureland from Wayne's parents to raise feed for the cows.

They began renting and acquiring additional land after that, expanding the farm as the business prospered. In the 1960s, Wayne became an early adopter of no-till farming, which naturally increases organic matter in the soil and reduces the need for fertilizers and their associated monetary and ecological costs. While the eco-friendly practice decreases erosion, it increases the ultimate yield farmers can expect from the land. Wayne's no-till farming methods also helped preserve the trout habitat in Spruce Creek, alleviating the runoff from fertilizers and pesticides that can be deadly to freshwater aquatic ecosystems. This runoff has ruined many native trout streams in the US and worldwide.

A farmer himself, President Carter always admired Wayne's forward-thinking farming methods and his accomplishments in growing and expanding a profitable farming business. When we were all together at Spruce Creek or abroad, the talk between the Carters and the Harpsters often turned to farming. Over time, Wayne and Marjorie grew Evergreen Farm to over 6,000 acres. Some of the finest stretches of fabled Spruce Creek trout water run right through the middle of the farm, with thousands of dairy cattle peacefully grazing the gently rolling hills on either side. Eventually, Wayne and Marjorie followed Wayne's parents' example and passed the farm on to their three sons. Abraham, Aaron, and Andrew have grown the family farm into a large agribusiness. They are leaders in their own right in the sustainable farming movement.

Wayne and Marjorie first came into our lives after a mutual fly-fishing friend from Yellowstone introduced the Carters to the Harpsters in 1979. Yellowstone National Park was a special place for the Carters. Through the years, President Carter, Rosalynn, and their daughter Amy made many trips there and befriended the park rangers, guides, and other employees. In fact, on an old wooden wall inside the park service's employee pub on Yellowstone Lake, you can still see where Jimmy Carter signed his name in bold, cursive letters after buying a few rounds of beers for the park rangers. Above his name, he wrote the simple message: "Great Pizza – Beautiful Park – Fine Rangers."

The Carters loved all of America's national parks and visited many of them often, just as so many American families do each year. Unlike other Americans, though, Jimmy Carter was uniquely positioned as president to protect and expand the national park system. He created almost forty new national parks during his presidency and signed the Endangered American Wilderness Act, designating ten new wilderness areas. One of his most underappreciated pieces of environmental legislation was his Surface Mining Control and Reclamation Act of 1977, which prohibits mining inside national parks and tightly regulates mining within a buffer zone of their boundaries to protect against the potential adverse effects of nearby mining. There is no telling what the state of our national parks would be today without that preventative measure established by President Carter nearly half a century ago.

During his visits to Yellowstone, Jimmy Carter formed a close friendship with a fly-fishing guide named Bud Lilly. While Bud's name might not be well-known today, his influence on conservation and fishing is huge. Bud was one of the pioneers of the "catch-and-release" practice, which is now a common approach among outdoor enthusiasts. Before he began advocating for returning fish unharmed to their natural habitat, most people kept every fish they caught. By the 1970s, a growing human population with more leisure time was endangering fish populations, especially trout.

Although ethically catching and eating fish within set limits is a tradition that connects us to nature and our ancestors, if every angler today kept more than just a few fish, trout populations would be depleted beyond recovery. Thanks to Bud's advocacy, catch-and-release has become the standard. This shift has not only helped preserve fish populations but also increased the number of anglers who now enjoy fishing and support conservation efforts.

During their first days fishing together in Yellowstone, Bud introduced the president to another fishing guide, Don Daughenbaugh, who happened to be a teacher and football coach at South Williamsport High School near Spruce Creek, Pennsylvania. Don taught during the school year and guided out west during his summer breaks. While fly fishing with President Carter, Don told stories about the incomparable trout fishing on Spruce Creek. After the Carters' 1978 Yellowstone vacation, the president remembered Don's stories and asked him to arrange a trip to Spruce Creek.

Don contacted a member of the Gray's Run Rod and Gun Club, who arranged for President Carter to spend a day on the club's section of the river. They also allowed the presidential helicopter, *Marine One*, to land on Wayne Harpster's nearby cornfield. Wayne says the corn was about eighteen inches high at the time. He lost a good bit of it when the helicopter landed, but he didn't mind.

Even though Wayne was and is a fiercely loyal lifelong Republican, he and Jimmy Carter quickly realized they had a whole lot in common outside of politics. They grew up in rural communities in the first half of the twentieth century, served in the navy, and became farmers. They both told a good story, loved woodworking and hunting, were highly competitive, and were obsessed with fly fishing. The bond they forged over all the years we fished together was more like brothers than friends.

Wayne recalls the water being pretty high and murky on President Carter's first visit. Although they fished all day, they didn't do as well as he'd hoped. He figured the president shared his disappointment, but it turns out President Carter was enthralled. Even if the fishing wasn't up to the typical Spruce Creek standards, they caught quality rainbows and browns in the double digits, and the president was overjoyed to discover a fishing destination close to the White House. He thanked Wayne and told him he'd like to return sometime.

I don't think Wayne believed the president would ever call. But a couple of weeks later, he was cleaning fish in the cabin's kitchen when a buddy said the White House was on the phone. Hands slimy with fish, Wayne put down the fillet knife and took the call.

When President Carter returned to Spruce Creek, the water was clear and the fishing was better than he'd enjoyed the first time. There was just one slight mishap. President Carter and Wayne were wearing these old-fashioned, heavy, rubber hip waders that came all the way up around the thighs and attached to their hips with belt straps. At one point in the day, President Carter leaned over to net a fish, stepped in a hole, and filled up his waders! But the fishing was so good that he didn't mind getting soaking wet.

Wayne presented the president with some special gifts on that second visit to the Harpsters' farm. He had the legendary fly-fishing instructor and fly tier George Harvey make some flies for the president and Rosalynn. Harvey tied a simple black ant fly pattern that he'd designed for fishing Spruce Creek and the trout streams of western Pennsylvania. After that the black ant became President Carter's favorite fly. Wayne also asked his friend and noted fly angler Lloyd Riss of Fenwick Fishing Rods—a legendary fly rod making company—to make a custom, personalized fly rod for Jimmy Carter. In May 2020, when the president gave me his bamboo fly rod, he also entrusted me with that custom Fenwick rod to take back to Spruce Creek with instructions to return it to Wayne.

• • •

It's funny to me how a simple day or two shared on the water can have ripple effects that alter the course of one's life. President Carter wrote that his first day with Wayne on Spruce Creek had "opened a new era of pleasure and friendship" with the Harpsters that carried our little group of anglers all around the world. So, it was only natural that Argentina—the place Wayne loved almost as much as his beloved Pennsylvania farm—was our first destination abroad and a country that we'd return to more than any other over the years.

All total, our group visited Argentina six times: three times to the Iberá marshes, twice to Patagonia, and once to Tierra Del Fuego. The Tierra Del Fuego trip was the only one I ever missed. The dates conflicted with a trip I'd been promising to take with my grandchildren, and I wasn't about to back out on that! Of course, President Carter and Rosalynn were the first ones to understand that time with the grandchildren takes precedence over everything else. He'd taken his first grandchild, Jason, to Alaska once—just the two of them. I probably heard more stories from President Carter about that trip than any other he ever took.

My first trip with the Carters to Argentina was to fish for golden dorado in the Esteros del Iberá Reserve. Fishing for golden dorado turned out to be not only my favorite Argentine experience but also my favorite of all our trips abroad. We went back several times, giving me the chance to know and understand the fish and the place better and better. The president and Rosalynn were captivated by the marshlands in northern Argentina and the ferocious golden dorado almost as much as I was.

• • •

The Iberá Wetlands comprise a unique environment—a living, floating freshwater marsh that changes with the force and direction of the wind and flow of the water from day to day. It encompasses nearly three million acres and is among the most extensive freshwater wetlands in the world. It's six times the size of Georgia's Okefenokee Swamp, which President Carter used to fish with his father. The Okefenokee is the largest blackwater wetland ecosystem in North America, but the Iberá marshlands dwarf it. With the Iberá Reserve's dizzying patchwork of waterways and lagoons, I was always amazed at the skill and knowledge of our native Argentine guides. They ran the small boats wide open, navigating the various canals and river systems flowing in and out of the seemingly endless series of lakes and swamps where we fished. I don't know how the guides always got us back to the lodge at the end of the day without getting lost. No matter how you enter the marsh, you never come back the same way. It's a maze.

The marshes teem with wildlife, including caimen, wolves, monkeys, swamp deer, capybaras, and giant anacondas. Many of the hundreds of bird species found in the wetlands were familiar because they also make their home in the vast marshlands where I live in coastal Georgia: wood storks, kingfishers, anhinga, ibis, and night herons. But many other species were there that I couldn't begin to name or identify.

President Carter and Rosalynn were avid birdwatchers who always pointed out and identified different birds we saw. On many of our trips, the Carters substituted their fly rods for binoculars for at least one day, during which they did nothing but birdwatch. They would always come back to the lodge excited to have found some new species to add to their life lists that they'd never seen before. My competitive streak would often come out to tease them about what they'd missed on the water while the rest of us had been fishing and how many or how big the fish we'd caught.

...

Golden dorado are large, toothy fish, close relatives of the piranha, but much larger and more yellow in color, with thin black stripes running horizontally along the length of their bodies like striped bass. They have large, thick heads and can grow to weigh as much as 60 pounds, though the typical catch is around 10 to 12 pounds. They are highly acrobatic, and when you get a strike on one, they often come straight out of the water several times and do flips in the air to try to throw the hook. They are quick to strike any fly pattern that even reasonably resembles a minnow, a mouse, or other prey species found in the marsh, including rodents and small birds. Nothing is beyond their appetite. While golden dorado may eat anything and aren't picky about fly patterns, getting the fly out in front of them can be challenging, especially when the wind gets up on the open water across the marshlands.

One of the tricks I learned while fly fishing for golden dorado was how to cast effectively in a heavy wind. I had to learn to be proficient with back casting. To get the fly the way we wanted, we often positioned the skiff so the forward cast was directly into the wind and the fish were behind us. In those times, we released the line on our back cast to get out pretty far with the fly in front of the fish, working with the wind instead of against it. Our back cast ended up being our forward cast. It's just another one of those little lessons that you learn with fly fishing. You have to adjust, which can be true with life, too. Sometimes, the only thing that works is doing the opposite of what you might typically do. When the wind is up, and you're having trouble casting into it, you may need to learn to turn your back to your target and lay down the line on your back cast instead of your forward cast if you want to achieve your goal.

...

In addition to fishing for golden dorado in the Iberá Reserve, we took two trips to northern Patagonia to fish for trout. Our first trip there was in March 2011 to Estancia Alicura, a 250,000-acre ranch known for its excellent rainbow trout fishing on the Caleufu River and for red stag and quail hunting. We all had good fishing there and caught many fish, even if they weren't that big. President Carter caught many more fish and bigger fish than the rest of us did, which didn't go without being noticed. He caught way more fish than all of us combined on that trip and didn't mind pointing that fact out. He was very methodical about his fishing. He would cast across the stream. Let the fly drift. Then, he'd cast two feet further and let it drift. Two feet further, and let it drift. With that method, he covered every inch of water and caught a lot of fish. The rest of us caught plenty of fish, but not like the president did. Even though we were all pretty experienced anglers at that point, President Carter joked that we were fishing like novices, enjoying his moment where he'd put us all to shame. On the flight home, as we were talking about it, he took out a piece of paper and drew a diagram to show us how he did it, actually making fun of us.

Four years later, we took our second trip to Patagonia, staying on a 50,000-acre estancia in the shadows of Tipiliuke Mountain, which has operated as a working cattle ranch for almost 120 years. The Quilquihue and Chimehuin Rivers run for miles through the estancia and are world-famous for eager rainbow trout in the fast sections of water and monster brown trout that lurk in the slow-moving shadows. We were all very excited to fish in these cold, clear Patagonian rivers, hoping to make up for the prior trip when the president outfished us. We were looking forward to spending our days casting dry flies and nymphs at the rainbows and swinging big streamers for the browns in the evenings as the sun set over the snow-capped mountains of Patagonia. We dreamed of catching so many rainbows each day that our arms would be sore and throbbing from fighting them.

As all anglers tend to do, at least secretly, most of us hoped to catch the fish of a lifetime—maybe our best stream-run brown trout. I know I did. Brown trout have been known to live for as long as twenty years and can grow as large as 30 pounds or more. Sea-run trout that spend much of their lives in the ocean and return to the rivers of their birth to spawn like salmon can grow abnormally large, just like steelhead, which are essentially sea-run rainbow trout. The waters of Tierra Del Fuego are famous for such sea-run monsters.

It's an extraordinary thing when a land-locked brown has spent its entire life in the river and lives long enough to outsize its environment, reaching double digits in weight and stretching to 25 inches or more. I realized it wasn't likely, but I had visions of hooking such a legendary beast and knew my chances were better in a storied place like Patagonia. But not every trip turns out as you imagine it.

We caught trout, but it definitely wasn't easy. I've never been on a river bottom that was that slick. For every one of us, the guides had to hold onto our arms just for us to wade through the water without falling in. I don't know what it was about the river, but it was very slick. The guides actually referred to it as "river dancing!" And the fish weren't nearly as eager to take the fly as we'd dreamed they'd be. They eluded us, although we tried every trick we knew. We did catch some trout, but it was difficult. No one caught any seriously big trout. There weren't any standout days, either. It was tough going every day, and as the trip wore on, we became increasingly frustrated. Our arms didn't get sore from fighting fish, that's for sure. Our legs and bodies got sore from trying to balance and navigate those slick river bottoms. Our egos got a bit sore from not catching as many fish as we'd hoped.

Fly fishing teaches you that all days cannot be banner days. Some days you come up empty. When things are difficult, the fish aren't biting, and you're barely able to stay on your feet because the river bottom is so slick, you have to look for other things to bring you joy and for which to be thankful. The shared experience. The scenery. The food. All of which were fantastic on that trip, even if the fishing was a letdown.

Fly fishing is a mental, physical, and emotional discipline. It's easy to enjoy the emotional highs of catching big or numerous fish.

It's much harder to suffer the emotional lows and frustrations that accompany lousy fishing days when nothing seems to go right on the water. And we had more than our share of bad fishing days during our time there in Tipiliuke. Despite a few rocky points and slippery moments, it was a testament to our little group that we hung together and stuck it out.

Originally, we'd planned to leave the estancia and stay a few days in the mountain city of San Carlos de Bariloche, which is a fairytale setting on a giant crystal-clear alpine lake surrounded by the fabled Patagonian Andes. Despite the gorgeous setting, though, everyone was sort of bummed out about how difficult and trying the fishing had been. We were tired, grouchy, and even in that beautiful place, so ready to be home. The Carters and I considered cutting the trip short by a day. A few others in the group felt the same way, but one couple insisted we stay and see it through. Not without misgivings, we relented.

Our dinner that night in Bariloche turned out to be the highlight of the trip. Al Parker, the head Secret Service agent of our detail, found a steakhouse where filets were about two dollars apiece and were as big as could be! We all piled into the SUVs and took off for that steakhouse, where we had one of the best meals we'd had on any of our trips.

JIM BARGER JR.

A fact not lost on Jimmy Carter but often given short shrift by historians is the quiet role Argentina inadvertently played in his 1980 reelection loss. The episode involved one of the most personal crises of conscience he faced as president: his fraught decision to leverage American farmers to affect US foreign policy goals, ultimately flipping a vocal sector of his base and a previously reliable bloc of the Democratic Party.

On Christmas Day, 1979, the Soviet Union launched a surprise invasion of Afghanistan, seeking to bolster its influence in the Middle East. For months, a civil war had been simmering in Afghanistan between Islamic fundamentalists and Marxist communists loyal to Moscow. The country's communist president, Nur Muhammad Taraki, had been killed in his sleep the previous summer, smothered with his own pillows. Following Taraki's death, KGB operatives attempted to assassinate his successor, Hafizullah Amin, an Islamist nationalist leader. They laced his Coca-Cola with poison, but the carbonation in the iconic American soft drink apparently neutralized the poison, saving Amin's life—at least for a few weeks. He was ultimately shot dead inside the presidential palace on Christmas Day.

The Soviets' Christmas invasion of Afghanistan, which was expected to last only a few weeks, ultimately led to a nearly decade-long war, vastly draining Russian resources and geopolitical influence and leading in part to the ultimate dismantling of the Soviet Union. At the invasion's onset, President Carter had to decide how to respond to the Soviets' unilateral aggression. The primary non-military tool at his disposal was a US grain embargo against the USSR, which depended at the time on the United States as a trade partner for the fundamental commodity in its food supply. But the president's two top advisors, Rosalynn and Vice President Walter Mondale, adamantly opposed the idea. They recognized that a prolonged grain embargo would drastically affect US export markets, potentially harming American farmers in an election year.

Although Jimmy Carter was the son of a farmer, and himself a lifelong farmer with relatives and a son in the farming business, owning and operating a grain elevator, no one could persuade him to put his personal and family interests and short-term political ambitions above what he believed to be the best long-term national security policy for the United States. He also recognized that his decision to levy a grain embargo might be incorrect and almost certainly hurt the sector of people he loved and identified with most:

farmers. He also knew full well that the grain embargo would hurt him politically. The day the embargo was announced, he noted in his diary: "We expect serious adverse reaction from Midwest farmers, particularly in Iowa."

Nevertheless, he opted to gamble his political future on the bet that as the Russians lost the ability to feed themselves and their livestock, they would pressure the Soviet Union into withdrawing from Afghanistan, foreclosing a brutal war and deterring future invasions of vulnerable nations. But that didn't happen. Almost immediately after the embargo was enacted, Argentina stepped in to replace the United States as the Soviet Union's largest grain supplier. Because of Argentina's willingness and capacity to supply the USSR with the grain it needed, the embargo barely affected the Soviet Union. Instead, the American heartland felt the harshest effects of the president's policy.

As the embargo wore on throughout the summer, US grain supplies skyrocketed, grain prices plunged, and angry farmers from Georgia to Nebraska turned against Carter. Despite being one of their own, Jimmy Carter already had a rocky relationship with American farmers, who had become disillusioned with his administration as early as 1978 because of the inflationary costs of fertilizer, fuel, and farming equipment. They wrote what the press called "John Deere Letters" to the White House, begging for action. Frustrated farmers staged tractor protests, surrounding government buildings with farming equipment and threatening to strike. Carter's beloved sister, Gloria, even rode in one tractor rally to support American farmers and draw attention to their plight.

As the protests popped up across farming country, the president and Rosalynn visited their family farm back in Georgia for the weekend. Carter amiably strolled the streets of Plains in blue jeans, visiting with neighbors. He hunted quail with a farming friend, Frank Chappell, who was tending the president's bird dogs while he was away in the White House. He met with local and regional leaders of the farm protests and listened to their complaints. Afterward, Rosalynn and he walked the fields of a neighbor's farm where Rosalynn found six arrowheads and Jimmy found three—remnants of an ancient civilization of indigenous people, fellow farmers, who had been swept from their land almost two centuries earlier by the brutal policy decisions of two past presidents.

President Carter was keenly aware of our nation's history, the good and the evil. He carefully considered every decision in the context of the decisions made by the presidents who came before him. Thomas Jefferson's unjust Georgia Compact of 1802, which unilaterally extinguished the land titles of indigenous people, and Andrew Jackson's brutal Indian Removal Act of 1830 were of particular interest and personal relevance to Jimmy Carter, who had an abiding respect for Native Americans. Jabbed and prodded with bayonets by federal troops, families were herded west from Georgia and other eastern states. As many as 100,000 indigenous people were forced to abandon their homes and farms, marching west as refugees. More than 20,000 died along the way. Almost certainly among them were people who once inhabited President Carter's beloved family farm.

That evening, as Rosalynn and he walked hand-in-hand over freshly plowed fields back in Georgia, reflecting, seeking solace, and searching for answers, Jimmy Carter felt a deep connection to the land and people who lived there, past and present. History and his role in it weighed heavily on him. In his childhood memoir, *An Hour Before Daylight*, Jimmy Carter confessed his deep lament for the US government's treatment of indigenous people, recognizing "that our family's farmland had once been theirs and that our ancestors had confronted and replaced them." As he considered how to address the problems American farmers faced during his presidency, he reflected on the plight of the many generations of farmers, including Native Americans, who had come before them. Jimmy Carter's commitment to people who till the soil was more than politics; it was deeply personal.

By the summer of 1980, US farmers' plight had worsened. President Carter not only failed to rectify their complaints about inflation, but his foreign policy was now artificially deflating prices, delivering a one-two punch to the already fragile farming economy. Aggrieved farmers accused him of handing vital American farm exports over to Argentina and other foreign nations, crippling US farms with no discernible effect on the Soviet war in Afghanistan. In November, farmers whose voices had helped propel Carter to the White House expressed their frustration by voting against him four years later.

Rosalynn, it appeared, had been right. No matter how well-intentioned, in hindsight, the grain embargo was an utter failure by any measure. After the Carters lost the 1980 election, Ronald Reagan lifted the grain embargo, enticing many farm belt Democrats to defect to the Republican Party for good. But by then, the Soviet Union had begun developing its own domestic grain production in Ukraine, and Argentina had completely assumed America's role as the Soviet Union's principal grain exporter. The unpopular grain embargo was just one of many factors that led to Carter's failed reelection bid. Still, it serves as an example of Rosalynn's sage political instincts and her husband's ethical stubbornness—sacrificing his own political and personal well-being for what he believed to be the greater good. It was almost certainly one of the many things he reflected on when visiting Argentina years later.

• • •

Even as Argentina's opportunism thwarted Jimmy Carter's grain embargo during his last year as president, the South American nation presented him with a multi-layered human rights crisis beginning with his first day in office. In 1976, while Carter and Gerald Ford battled for the hearts of US voters, Argentina's right-wing military government waged war against dissenting citizens, particularly the intelligentsia: scientists, students, teachers, reporters, artists, and clergy. At the same time, Communist guerrilla groups aligned with the Soviet Union attempted to violently overthrow the government with ongoing terrorist attacks. While both sides of the conflict expressed open disdain for democracy and the rule of law, ordinary people in Argentina were dangerously caught in the middle. In May, three US citizens were kidnapped and tortured, including a member of the Fulbright Commission, the United States' prestigious international cultural and academic exchange program.

While Congress and the United Nations fretted about Argentina's human rights violations in the summer of 1976, US Secretary of State Henry Kissinger—a Nixon holdover in the Ford administration—secretly encouraged the Argentine generals to do the "things that have to be done" but "do them quickly." After receiving the apparent go-ahead from Kissinger, more than 10,000 people were "disappeared" by the far-right government and presumably assassinated before year-end. When President Carter took office in January of 1977, he immediately inherited this foreign policy nightmare spawned in part by his predecessors' furtive support for Argentina's far-right military regime and tacit approval of its human rights abuses.

From Day One, the Carter Administration committed to a new approach to unraveling the chaos in Argentina and to managing foreign policy worldwide, prioritizing human rights and eschewing political intrigue. While not yielding immediate results, President Carter's policies eventually led to Argentina's return to democracy and the election of self-described "Carterite" and relative moderate, President Raul Alfonsin, who credited Jimmy Carter with preventing the additional slaughter of thousands of Argentinians during the so-called "dirty war." President Carter's human rights-focused foreign policy posed such a threat to the right-wing Argentine military junta that regime members reportedly toasted one another with champagne when they received the news that Ronald Reagan had defeated Carter in 1980.

ARGENTINA

...

When you travel to a foreign country as an angler, your thoughts inevitably turn to the new wilderness environment and the species of fish you are trying to catch, your tackle, the weather, the water flows or the tides, your selection of flies, and the birds and other wildlife you hope to encounter. My wife and I traveled to Argentina the year before our first child was born. My memories of that time are of the sprawling San Telmo Market in Buenos Aires where tango dancers spill out into the streets, the rolling hills of Malbec grapes hanging thick on the vines in Mendoza, the crystal-clear streams flowing beneath the Patagonian Andes and spilling into blue glacial lakes, the shimmering rainbow trout rising to take our dry flies, and the streamside lunches of fire-grilled bife de chorizo washed down with cold red wine.

What I can't imagine, though, is experiencing a place of such immense beauty set against a backdrop of painful memories. Negotiating with a former dictator of that country for the release of tortured political prisoners. Or the stinging reminder of being lambasted for allowing that same foreign country to usurp my nation's exports as I struggled in vain to prevent a war half a world away. Responding to the criticisms not only from a frustrated political constituency but also from my neighbors, family, and friends. Jimmy Carter's humility humbles me. His resilience outpaces me. Undoubtedly, he is a skilled and studied fly fisherman. But one of his greatest skills, both as an angler and a human, may well be his unbending will to confront his most difficult public moments introspectively and to learn what he can from them without repeating them or allowing them to define him.

CHAPTER FIVE
VENEZUELA

VENEZUELA

CARLTON HICKS
~

Over the decades, through their work with The Carter Center, the president and first lady developed a lasting interest in and connection to the country of Venezuela, its people, its culture, its stunningly diverse wilderness environments, and its struggles with democracy. The Carter Center began working in Venezuela in 1996 as part of the organization's global effort to eradicate river blindness. Black flies spread this disease that infects people's eyes and skin with parasitic larvae that spread through the body and even to others, causing painful rashes, unbearable itching, and eventually blindness. As an optometrist, I have always been interested in the disease and spent much time discussing it with the Carters, following their efforts with The Carter Center to eradicate it.

When the Carters began their program of distributing antiparasitic drugs to combat the debilitating disease in the late 1980s, hundreds of millions of people were at risk from river blindness, primarily in the Southern Hemisphere. Much of The Carter Center's efforts have concentrated on fighting the disease on the African continent coordinated with their ongoing battle against guinea worm there. In South America, The Carter Center's almost thirty years of effort have completely eradicated river blindness in countries where it once was a scourge: Colombia, Ecuador, Mexico, and Guatemala. The last remaining infections on the continent are in a remote corner of the Amazonian rainforest along the border of Colombia and Venezuela, where the nomadic indigenous Yanomami people live. The lack of roads and infrastructure and the nearly impenetrable rainforest make it challenging to deliver and administer antiparasitic drugs to the Yanomami. Still, The Carter Center continues to work to eradicate the disease by flying into remote airstrips and even forging through the forest on foot with machetes and backpacks full of medicine to locate and treat people who need their help.

In 1998, the Carters expanded their work in Venezuela beyond health care to include conflict resolution, free press initiatives, and monitoring and helping ensure fair elections. That same year, the Venezuelan government invited The Carter Center to monitor the presidential election. During that visit, Jimmy and Rosalynn first met the fiery leader of the socialist Bolivarian Revolution and soon-to-be President of Venezuela, Hugo Chávez. A few years later, when Venezuela spiraled into a political crisis in the early 2000s, President Carter was invited by both sides of the conflict to mediate a solution that avoided bloodshed. Apparently, the only thing supporters of embattled President Hugo Chávez and the opposition groups seeking his ouster could agree on was that Jimmy Carter was someone they all could trust to help peacefully preserve their democracy.

Between spring 2002 and fall 2006, President Carter traveled many times to Venezuela to negotiate a peaceful accord among the fractious groups. The Carter Center's efforts resulted in the signing by all parties of a "Declaration Against Violence and For Peace and Democracy" followed by a formal agreement in May of 2003, brokered and witnessed by The Carter Center. Unbeknownst to many outside of Venezuela, our group of motley fly fishermen tagged along on two of Jimmy Carter's peace missions. While he was there to help preserve the South American nation's democracy during a tumultuous time, we were there to explore the country's unique freshwater and saltwater wilderness habitats.

This wasn't the first time President Carter tried to use fly fishing to informally pursue peace-brokering and achieve his foreign policy. In April of 1977, not long after he'd been in office, the president called me and said that he was sending King Hussein of Jordan down to St. Simons and that he wanted me to take the king fishing, which I did. President Carter was hoping to build a relationship with King Hussein to help him with his Middle East peace talks. Unfortunately, I'm not sure King Hussein turned out to be the best peace partner, but he was a pretty good fisherman. We enjoyed one another's company, caught plenty of fish, and I got to be probably the only eye doctor on St. Simons who has ever fished with a president and a king!

At the Camp David Peace Accords in 1978, President Carter again tried to use fishing to bring people together by arranging to take Egyptian President Anwar Sadat and Israeli Prime Minister Menachem Begin fly fishing. They'd been through the difficult first week of negotiations, which seemed like they were getting nowhere. President Carter was actually pretty despondent and frustrated about it at that point and didn't think they'd reach an accord. He thought a morning of fly fishing might focus the leaders' minds on nature, calm them, and build trust among the parties. But tempers got so hot between Sadat and Begin that the negotiations almost broke down completely. President Carter had to separate the two men and cancel the fishing trip. Carter was so worked up that he didn't even go fishing himself, opting instead to take out his frustrations on the tennis court in a match against Secretary of State Cy Vance.

As an aside, President Carter and I both were avid tennis players for most of our lives and often played together. Apart from our time fly fishing and taking long jogs together, we enjoyed many singles and doubles matches. Those matches are some of my fondest memories with the Carters. The Carter family had a dirt tennis court on their farm, and they played regularly. Jimmy said his daddy put a racket in his hand almost as soon as he could walk. The president often shared stories with me of Sunday afternoons during his childhood when people would drive over from Plains to the Carter farm to play and watch tennis matches after church—playing "beat the winner." Jimmy's daddy usually commanded the court the longest, terrorizing challengers with a wicked slice. Ground strokes were President Carter's strength, as was his tenacity. He never gave up a shot and demanded the same from you if you were his partner.

In fly fishing, you focus on the cadence of your casting. You aim to place the fly precisely in front of the fish to entice a strike. You become completely immersed in your thoughts and everything else melts away. You and all your troubles cease to exist, and all that is left is the water, the fish, and the sound of the fly line cutting through the air. Similarly, the world melts away with the back and forth of the tennis ball as you focus on the stroke of your racket. The movements become second nature as you anticipate the moment when you take the shot that you hope will best your opponent. It's not surprising to me that President Carter chose tennis as his next best option after fly fishing to temporarily vent his frustrations in the heat of the Middle East peace talks.

Whatever reprieve he got from the tennis match didn't last long, though. The pressures of brokering peace and knowing that bloodshed would ensue if these leaders left Camp David without an accord definitely got to him. Failure seemed inevitable, he told me. President Carter was so frustrated one day that when he broke for lunch with Cy and Rosalynn, the three beleaguered peacemakers ordered drinks. For me, that's proof of how rough things must have gotten. The Carters rarely drank at lunch. We usually had a beer or two at the end of a fishing day and maybe wine at dinner. President Carter and Rosalynn were also known to drink the occasional martini. The only time I ever knew them to drink at lunch, though, was on Saturdays in Plains, where they had a quirky tradition of eating hot dogs for lunch and drinking Bloody Marys—which, as it turns out, is an oddly delicious combination. Unlike many of their White House predecessors, however, the Carters were fairly temperate in their alcohol consumption. But at that critical moment in time, I have no doubt everyone needed a drink.

The following day they had a moving and encouraging breakthrough. The Carters took both entourages on a trip to the nearby Civil War site of the Battle of Gettysburg. Before leaving Camp David on the outing, Carter laid ground rules that there would be no discussion of the Middle East peace issues. He even sat directly between Sadat and Begin on the drive. When they arrived at the battlefield, the icy feelings between the factions seemed to melt somewhat as they shared their knowledge and familiarity with the Civil War battle. As former generals who had studied military history, the respective cabinet members chatted somewhat amiably as they walked the battlefield discussing what they had only read about in books. Sadat engaged eagerly in the discussion, but Begin still seemed detached. The Israeli Prime Minister didn't say much until they arrived at the spot where Lincoln delivered the Gettysburg Address.

President Carter later described that moment on the battlefield as the point when he began to believe again they might eventually find a path to peace. Prime Minister Begin spoke in hushed tones, and everyone gathered in to listen. Standing on that once blood-soaked ground, they realized that Begin was extemporaneously reciting the Gettysburg Address—word for word. The Gettysburg battlefield served as a stark reminder of the inhumanity that occurs when humans aren't treated equally and when peacemakers fail. I always thought it was pretty clever of President Carter to take them there.

President Carter said that Sadat and Begin immediately retreated to their respective cabins when they returned to Camp David. They didn't see each other again until the peace accord was done. Putting aside their emotions, they allowed President Carter to go back and forth between the parties, focusing on the difficult details of the treaty until finally achieving an accord. Of course, even rougher days lay ahead, including one point when President Carter worked for 36 hours straight without any sleep. Rosalynn and he completely lost their appetites and rarely finished meals. On multiple occasions, just as it seemed peace was within reach, the talks would sour and both Jimmy and Rosalynn would lose faith in the process. Rosalynn said the president confided to her that the seemingly impossible negotiations at Camp David were the worst thing they'd ever endured.

Although the fly-fishing trip with Sadat and Begin fell apart, the Carters' tenaciousness ensured that the precarious peace talks somehow never did. An unlikely treaty was eventually signed after thirteen straight days of often angry and bitter negotiations with the parties holed up at Camp David refusing to come down from the mountain without an agreement. When Rosalynn heard the news, she cried. When Begin shared the news with his wife, he cried. They all hugged one another. Sadat and Begin jointly received the Nobel Prize for the Camp David Accords, and the resulting treaty brokered by Carter has proven to be the world's most resilient peace agreement since the end of the Second World War.

• • •

President Carter knew that bonds forged among anglers out on the water were incredibly strong. When he planned our fly-fishing trips to Venezuela, he believed spending time with powerful Venezuelans on the water would prove beneficial to him in his role as a mediator. Perhaps more importantly, I think he also knew that it would be invaluable to his credibility with the Venezuelan leaders and people if he became intimately acquainted with their beloved country. He was able to demonstrate a bona fide interest in Venezuela's natural environment and the people who lived there based on his firsthand experiences in the jungle.

VENEZUELA

Carter demonstrated his commitment to Venezuela by traveling into the wilderness, leaving behind the hotel rooms and government buildings where peace agreements were ostensibly formed and political disagreements were more often fomented. And we were lucky to be able to go along for the ride. Of course, he also wanted to catch fish! We all did. On numerous occasions, I witnessed firsthand his equal passions for promoting global peace and exploring the wild, often with a fly rod in hand.

The two fly-fishing trips we took as a group to Venezuela were very different. In 2005, we visited Madrisqui Island in the Archipiélago de los Roques in the north coastal region of the country among the blue waters of the southern Caribbean approximately 450 miles due south of Puerto Rico, roughly midway between Curaçao to the west and Grenada to the east. That trip, where we stalked white sand flats and sight casted to elusive bonefish was a stark contrast to our first trip in January 2003 when we traveled to the dark jungle waters of the southeastern Venezuelan state of Amazonas—home to crocodiles, giant anacondas, piranhas, jaguars, and several different species of peacock bass.

The trip was arranged by Venezuelan media mogul Gustavo Cisneros. Cisneros was born in Cuba and was a resident of Venezuela where he held dual citizenship with the United States. He was one of the wealthiest people in South America—if not the wealthiest. Cisneros was a proponent of free-market capitalism and an owner of multiple large businesses inside and outside of Venezuela. One of the things that President Carter was trying to do was to intervene a little bit with Cisneros and President Chávez, as the two individuals perfectly represented the sparring factions of government-led socialism on the one hand and wealthy private-owned business interests on the other.

President Chávez was looking at nationalizing a lot of companies in Venezuela, and Cisneros owned many of those companies that were potential targets for nationalization. He owned the national beer company. He owned newspapers, television stations, and the Coca-Cola enterprise there. One of the interesting stories we heard on the trip was how Coca-Cola came to dominate the country's soft drink market. Apparently, Cisneros originally was the owner of the Pepsi distributorship in Venezuela, which he built up over decades into having almost a 50-percent share of the market—one of the largest Pepsi markets in the world. But sometime in the mid-1990s, Cisneros became frustrated with Pepsi's refusal to allocate capital into further expanding the business in Venezuela, so he turned to a friend he knew from his childhood in Cuba, Roberto Goizueta, who was CEO of Coca-Cola at the time. Overnight and without warning, Cisneros had tens of thousands of blue Pepsi trucks painted red with a swooping white stripe and the iconic cursive words Coca-Cola. He flipped his entire distribution from Pepsi to Coke overnight. All of the country's Pepsi machines were removed in a single day, and Coca-Cola machines were put in their place. That was the kind of power that Gustavo Cisneros had over commerce in the country at the time.

Additionally, Cisneros butted heads quite a bit at times with Hugo Chávez over the power of the press. Cisneros' television network, Venevisión, was highly critical of Chávez and his government. Conversely, Cisneros had drawn unwelcome attention and ire from Chávez, who sought to silence the free press and nationalize the private businesses owned by Cisneros and other wealthy Venezuelan business leaders. Things became so bad between the two men that Chávez's government once raided the very jungle fishing camp where our fly-fishing group stayed! Of course, everything was quite peaceful during our stay at the camp in the jungle, although we eventually would have a different experience witnessing riots in the city of Caracas.

Through his work fighting river blindness in Venezuela, Jimmy Carter had garnered the respect and admiration of both men, who agreed to let him mediate their differences. The hope was that President Carter could strike some sort of balance and middle ground between too much economic and media power being held in the hands of a few elite families and too much economic and media power being appropriated and potentially manipulated and mismanaged by the socialist government. Warming relations between Chávez and Cisneros would be vital to resolving the Venezuelan conflict, Carter believed.

So, he planned to discuss the issues with Cisneros at his fishing camp and then to discuss the issues with President Chávez at the national hotel in the capital city of Caracas. The plan of meeting with the two men separately on their own turf and going back and forth was basically the same strategy President Carter employed decades earlier with Sadat and Begin at Camp David. By keeping the two factions separated, he could listen and concentrate on the concerns of each without interruption and flaring tempers. Meanwhile, our group would lend some informality and a spirit of camaraderie to the trip. We would fish with Cisneros in Amazonas and later dine with President Chávez in Caracas with no agenda other than to catch fish and enjoy the company of both men.

Chávez and Cisneros clearly were polar opposites. While Cisneros was from the prerevolutionary Cuban elite and had grown his family fortune to a level of international prominence, Hugo Chávez was a solidly middle-class kid from a sugar production town in northern Venezuela who had worked his way up the ranks of the Venezuelan military. He'd gone on to start the Revolutionary Bolivarian Movement and attempted a failed coup on the Venezuelan government. After two years in prison for trying to overthrow the government, Chávez emerged even stronger and more popular than before and eventually became the leader of the United Socialist Party of Venezuela and ultimately president of the country.

Chávez did much early in his presidency to provide health care, food resources, housing, and education for the Venezuelan people, leveraging the nation's vast oil resources, and prioritizing the poor and the marginalized, including the indigenous population who previously had been neglected and exploited. But he also suppressed the freedom of the press, nationalized much of Venezuela's formerly free market industries, ruthlessly persecuted and imprisoned his critics, tried to manipulate the democratic electoral process, and ultimately threw the Venezuelan economy into turmoil. He was a fierce critic of the United States and a staunch ally of socialist dictators in the region such as Fidel Castro, Evo Morales, and Daniel Ortega.

After Chávez died in 2013, President Carter issued a statement mourning his death and giving his honest, firsthand appraisal of Chávez's positive and negative attributes and acknowledging the deep divisions and national problems created by Chávez and the need for Venezuela to heal in the wake of his passing. Jimmy Carter drew criticism over the years for refusing to follow the easy narrative to simply denounce complicated national leaders like Hugo Chávez. But that was one of the things I've always admired most about my friend: he never took the easy path. He refused to compromise the truth even if it caused people to become upset with him and even if his viewpoint was unpopular. President Carter spent a lot of time one-on-one with Hugo Chávez and witnessed the good and the bad results of Chávez's leadership, personality, ideology, and methodology, developing a nuanced view that few others were privy to. Ultimately, President Carter and Rosalynn disagreed with much of the controversial leader's methods, but they never doubted his commitment to improving the lives of the Venezuelan people.

. . .

Cisneros' fishing camp was deep in the rainforest of Amazonas in Manaka, where the Orinoco and the Ventuari Rivers meet in southwest Venezuela about 150 miles west of the Colombian border. Until mining interests began exploiting the area in the 1980s, there had never been a permanent human settlement in the region. The area was part of the wider distribution area of the nomadic Huottüja De'aruhua (also called Piaroa) people—a peaceful, pre-Columbian ethnic group that has seasonally migrated through that part of the rainforest since before recorded time. The name, Huottüja, in the native language loosely translates in English to "Knowledgeable People of the Forest." And that is exactly how we found them to be. They welcomed us into their territory, cooked wonderful meals for us—primarily freshwater fish—and guided us on our fishing excursions in the myriad waterways of the Orinoco River system. The Orinoco is the third largest river in South America, connected to the Rio Negro through the Casiquiare distributary and ultimately from there to the Amazon. Our quarry on that trip was perhaps the wildest, most exotic, and most ferocious species of freshwater fish known to the fly angler: the colorful peacock bass.

Our group on that trip consisted of Bob Wilson, Wayne Harpster, President Carter, and myself. It was a pretty eventful trip. Every morning, I'd wake up to the sound of macaws and parrots outside my window. That was my wake-up call. Then, we'd have breakfast and immediately go up the river fishing. Cisneros sent us out in helicopters. We'd land on these huge rocks in the middle of the jungle that would emerge from the river when it was not the rainy season, and we'd fish all day. At lunchtime, Cisneros would have a longboat sent up the river to meet us with a chef on board, and we'd have lunch out on the river. We set up hammocks on these huge rocks—some of the rocks were as big as houses—and we would have food, drink, and siestas before going back out fishing. Even though it was one of the wildest, most remote places we'd ever been, it was still much more fancy than we were accustomed to. We were treated to an amazingly first-class experience out in the middle of this vast wilderness on the Orinoco River in the heart of the Venezuelan state of Amazonas.

We caught a lot of peacock bass, too. They come in two or three different varieties with varied and beautiful striped and spotted color patterns. Peacock bass fight like crazy. They are among the hardest-fighting fish for their size known to the fly-fishing world. And when they strike, they really strike hard. They'll scare you when they strike if you're not paying attention. At one point, I had a fly that I was casting back, and it was a really large, heavy fly. I guess I didn't have my casting loop high enough on my backcast, because that heavy fly hit the water behind the boat as the line stretched out behind me. And as soon as it did, a peacock bass hit the fly the moment it touched the water.

When we left the camp at Manaka, we flew back to Caracas and the plan was for us to spend the night in the international hotel there. President Carter had planned to go straight from spending time with Cisneros to meet with President Chávez. There were protests going on in the streets outside our window. It definitely was a genuine state of civil unrest, and we were warned by the Secret Service not to leave our hotel. In addition to the Secret Service, who were always along on all of our trips, we had State Department security on that trip as well as Venezuelan national security.

President Carter left us to meet with Chávez but said that he wanted us to be ready to have dinner with them once the talks were over. They even sent someone out to get traditional Latin American dress shirts for all of us for dinner. But as time wore on that evening and we waited for the call to come join them for dinner, the call never came. Instead, Chávez and Carter talked straight through dinner, working late into the night to forge a peaceful resolution to the Venezuelan crisis. Shortly after our visit, the parties signed the agreement vowing to pursue a peaceful democratic solution, which they ultimately did. Venezuela's democracy has continued to struggle through the years, though, and The Carter Center is involved in election monitoring and mediating disputes there to this day.

• • •

In March of 2005, our group again went to Venezuela but this time to the blue waters of the Caribbean, to Los Roques, Venezuela, to pursue bonefish. We were the guests of Gustavo Cisneros once again. The group consisted of President and Mrs. Carter, John, Wayne, Bob, and myself.

And just as the last trip to Venezuela had been my first opportunity to seek out the exotic peacock bass, this trip was my first time trying to catch bonefish, the iconic saltwater fly-fishing species. Los Roques stands for "The Big Rock," a beautiful place off of the coast north of Caracas, Venezuela. It was a great trip. Cisneros had some friends who had a large catamaran sailboat, and we would meet up there every day for lunch.

We caught a lot of bonefish, but it took me a little while to get the feel for it. It wasn't just my first bonefishing experience but one of my first experiences with any kind of saltwater fly fishing, which is very different from trout fishing in freshwater streams. My Venezuelan guide was very patient, though. He let me practice casting quite a few times to get a feel for casting into the wind. Somehow when you're bonefishing it seems like you're always casting into the wind. And he was very careful to tell me that if I got a strike, he would let me know exactly when to set the hook and that I should leave the tip of the rod down in the water until I felt the fish turn with the hook in its mouth. You do not raise the rod to set the hook on a bonefish or on most saltwater species like you would on a trout. Instead, he taught me to set the hook with my left hand by jerking very forcefully on the fly line while pointing the rod tip with my right hand down at the fish in the water.

After making a few casts, we did spot some bones, and my guide pointed me in the direction I should make the cast. Fortunately, I made a good cast, and the bonefish went for it. My guide quickly hollered, "Strike!" And I lifted the rod instinctively like I would with a dry fly on a trout in a mountain stream, and I pulled on the line. Obviously, I missed the fish because I didn't follow the guide's instructions to set the hook properly, and instead simply yanked the fly right out of the fish's mouth. It was just a habit after decades of primarily chasing trout with dry flies and nymphs. My guide turned to me and said, "Nice trout strike, sir." That stuck with me, and after that bit of gentle sarcastic scolding I don't think I had any more trouble properly strike-setting the hook on a bonefish.

The trip was nice, but there was one thing that put a damper on it. We all got the flu. I don't know where it came from, but we all got really sick with the flu toward the end of the trip. When we reminisced about that trip to Los Roques, President Carter remembered it differently. He said that everyone got sick except for him. Rosalynn and I don't remember it that way, but we ultimately decided not to argue with him about it. I was never really sure if he was just teasing us about how tough he was and how weak we were or if he really thinks he didn't get sick at all. Of course, he'd never let on either way. Whether the flu got him down at Los Roques or not, it obviously didn't suppress his energy to continue quietly negotiating between Chávez and Cisneros. Over time, the two men eventually came to a point of mutual respect and a pragmatic determination to compromise and coexist and to strive jointly to remove the heavy bias that plagued their country's media and threatened its democracy.

In the years that followed, The Carter Center—with the support and participation of both Chávez and Cisneros—developed a project to depolarize the Venezuelan news media, reduce partisanship in reporting, and establish and institute ethical and balanced journalistic standards. I'm not sure how well they achieved their goal, but they certainly tried and learned a lot about it in the process. Afterwards, The Carter Center took that model and used it to set up workshops around the world to attempt to tamp down partisanship in the media in other countries, encouraging polarized media outlets to join in a respectful dialogue with the goal of prioritizing accurate reporting of facts, rather than simply pushing a political agenda. I often think that no country's media needs such depolarizing training more than our own right here in the United States. I've come to understand, particularly in recent years, that bias in the media is one of the greatest threats to democracy, particularly related to topics such as opinion polling and election processes and standards. That is why President Carter's efforts to mediate the dispute between the state media controlled by Chávez and the privately-owned media controlled by Cisneros was so important.

JIM BARGER JR.

Rain pelted softly onto the canvas tent. Outside my small sleeping quarters, the world was pitch black. The night sky was black. The dense forest was black. The water in the river was black. A thick, low cloud hovered over everything, enveloping our campsite, shielding even the light from the night stars and the moon that shone somewhere in the hidden sky above.

Everything was black and wet. As I tried to sleep, each breath was thick and damp. The bedsheets were damp. They clung to my skin as I tossed and turned on the military-style cot, eager for the morning to come and for my first chance to explore the rainforest and cast a fly into the black waters of the Rio Negro. The deep, guttural roar of a jaguar echoed through the night.

About a decade prior, I'd run into Dr. Hicks at the beach while home on St. Simons from law school spring break. Always a man of healthy habits, Dr. Hicks had been out on his daily jog, and when we saw each other he ran up to me and said, "You'll never guess where I've just been." It was a statement I'd become accustomed to from him. After I'd first left the island for college, whenever I'd return for a holiday, I'd invariably run into Dr. Hicks at the beach or at a cocktail or dinner party. He'd inevitably have an exciting anecdote about fly fishing with the Carters. I looked forward to this tradition when visiting home—hearing about his adventures and comparing notes about the various fly fishing we'd done since we'd last seen one another. On that particular day, it had been just a month or two since he'd returned from his peacock bass fishing trip; standing there on the beach he regaled me with the stories of this ferocious jungle fish that previously I'd only dreamed about.

"You've got to do it, Jim," he'd said. "It's an incredible adventure."

I'd heard stories about this strange insatiable species endemic to Central and South America that would devour a fly, ripping away the feathers and sometimes even bending the hook. The most intriguing thing about fishing for it was that it particularly thrived in the most remote parts of the 55 million-year-old Amazonian rainforest, where no fly had ever been cast—where, in some places, perhaps no human had ever been. Underneath a canopy of nearly 400 billion trees, dark waters swirled in my imagination, thick with piranhas and giant catfish with electric-red tails, a place where the elusive payara prowled—the so-called "vampire fish" with fangs growing out of its lower jaw so long and sharp that they poke right into the top jaw—slashing its prey in the water to bleed it to death before returning later to feed.

The place seemed almost mythical to me then. I don't think I'd ever actually met anyone who'd traveled into the South American jungle to fly fish for peacock bass before. Unlike other iconic species like trout, steelhead, salmon, bonefish, and tarpon where whole libraries could be filled with the books anglers have written about them, very few words had been written about peacock bass at that time. To this day, the literature on them remains slim compared to other prized game fish. An outdoor writer I admired named Larry Larsen had self-published an incredibly informative and well-researched book called *Peacock Bass Explosions* back in the mid-1990s, and I'd also read an article or two about peacock bass fishing in outdoor magazines. Other than that, the idea of fly fishing for peacock bass in the jungles of South America with Jimmy Carter was about as far-fetched an idea as joining Teddy and Kermit Roosevelt on their 1914 expedition down the River of Doubt.

VENEZUELA

Around about the same time that Dr. Hicks told me about his jungle adventure with President Carter, writer Candice Millard was finishing her engrossing book about the Roosevelts' harrowing adventure to map the uncharted Amazonian tributary known at the time only as the Rio da Dúvida. I read her book, *The River of Doubt: Theodore Roosevelt's Darkest Journey*, cover to cover and then read it again. It tells the almost forgotten tale of a dejected Teddy Roosevelt who—despite all he'd accomplished in his life including two terms as US President—was so morose over losing a third presidential bid that he fled with his son, Kermit, to one of the most remote and treacherous places on the planet just to prove to himself and to the world that he could accomplish something most people believed couldn't be done. The expedition stretched on for months, and for much of the time the entire world presumed the former president and his expedition party were lost forever.

The truth wasn't so far off. Starving and delirious from fever and still suffering with a bullet lodged in his back from an assassination attempt two years prior, President Roosevelt lay in the jungle for days, at one point incoherently repeating the first stanza of "Kubla Khan," the epic poem by Samuel Taylor Coleridge set near the mythical river Alph. In her book, Millard eerily quotes Roosevelt's demented recitation: "'In Xanadu did Kubla Khan a stately pleasure-dome decree. In Xanadu did Kubla Khan a stately pleasure-dome decree. In Xanadu...'" Kermit knelt nearby, expecting his famous father to die at any moment and wondering what to do next. In the end, it was the devoted son's singular determination that finally pulled them through, even as the elder Roosevelt contemplated suicide and at least two, most likely three, other members of their party died. One drowned in the river, and another was murdered by a third whom he'd caught stealing food. The murderer-thief fled into the jungle, never to be heard from again. The expedition left its mark on President Roosevelt, who died four years later, still suffering from lingering malaria.

For the rest of his life, Kermit said that his most vivid memory was sitting with his fever-rattled father, expecting him to die beside the "'black rushing river with the great trees towering high above along the bank; the sodden earth under foot; for a few moments the stars would be shining, and then the sky would cloud over and the rain would fall in torrents, shutting out the sky and trees and river.'" I remember reading that quotation in Millard's *River of Doubt* and realizing that Roosevelt and Carter were, and likely forever will be, the only US Presidents ever to brave Amazonia. And at that moment, I promised myself that one day I'd go there as well.

My journey into the jungle wasn't nearly as harrowing as the Roosevelts'—but it was far less luxurious than what Dr. Hicks describes. I didn't ride on a billionaire's helicopter. Instead, my fishing buddies Thomas Fleetwood, Norman Donati, and I took a dubious-looking float plane out of the Brazilian city of Manaus, flying roughly west by northwest through zero visibility skies for several hours toward the Colombian and Venezuelan borders. Twice, we descended from the clouds to emerge just over the tree canopy and touch down on isolated waterways, only for our pilot to open a paper chart and study it wordlessly for a few minutes before taking off and flying back into the thick clouds again. The third time we landed, an indigenous Baré Indian in a small boat came out to meet us in the river. He introduced himself as Gabriel, and we quickly unloaded our gear from the plane to his boat and rode through myriad twisting waters deep into the jungle. Flocks of roseate spoonbills scattered before us. "Boto!" exclaimed Gabriel just as pink river dolphins breached the tannin-black water.

Our camp was a cluster of canvas wall-tents erected on aluminum pontoons, anchored alongside an isolated sandbar. The Baré guides who hosted us towed the floating fish camp to a new site each week during the season so that anglers who visited would have the opportunity to explore and fish nearby waters that had never been fished before. In the evenings, we dined by firelight on fresh fried peacock bass we'd caught earlier in the day. As in many places I've visited over the years, the adventure fishing industry offered the local people an income in harmony with their traditional and preferred way of life. Their operation stood in stark contrast to the illegal deforestation by outside business interests that continues to threaten the entire Amazon River basin, an area that accounts for some 40 percent of the entire continent.

Roughly the size of Australia, the Amazonian rainforest is responsible for producing approximately 20 percent of the earth's oxygen and storing some 120 billion tons of carbon. Life as we know it depends on the preservation of this one ecosystem, and yet it's vanishing at an alarming pace. During 2020 alone, when industry otherwise slowed globally due to the COVID-19 pandemic, Brazil lost an area of Amazonian rainforest roughly the size of the state of Connecticut due to deforestation. Mining, agricultural expansion, and related fires south of the Orinoco River in Venezuela have consumed hundreds of thousands of acres of rainforest in that section of Amazonia since President Carter, Dr. Hicks, and their fishing buddies first visited there.

It's maddening to know that there yet remain people who steadfastly refuse to believe in the problem of climate change, who refuse to believe the earth is warming at an alarmingly dangerous rate, and who refuse to believe that human activity such as deforestation and the burning of fossil fuels is causing the polar ice caps to melt, sea-levels to rise, and the mass extinction of varied and diverse species with whom we share the planet. We all are part of the problem, but unfortunately we are not all part of looking for a solution. According to the most recent scientific estimates, as much as one-fourth of the earth's flora and fauna will likely become extinct by 2050 if climate change continues at the current rate unabated.

In his book, *Half-Earth*, world-renowned scientist E. O. Wilson proposed an answer that is brilliant in its simplicity: set aside half of the planet as a nature reserve. As Wilson pragmatically pointed out, logging and mining in remote areas like the Amazonian rainforest operate on an incredibly thin margin. Accordingly, conservation can be an economically viable alternative to deforestation and development, particularly in the most wild and remote areas of the earth (which also happen to be the most worthy of protection). By purchasing land outright or by purchasing logging, mining, and development rights in wilderness areas, conservation organizations like The Nature Conservancy and Conservation International, together with local and regional land trusts with the buy-in from resident populations, can outbid industrial exploiters and protect natural areas permanently.

I have seen the real-world effects of this conservation strategy espoused by E. O. Wilson firsthand just outside my window in my own backyard. From my writing desk, I can see the Hampton River wash into the Atlantic Ocean as one of several distributaries of the mighty Altamaha River. Long nicknamed "Georgia's Little Amazon," the Altamaha is the largest free-flowing river system on the East Coast and is a watershed of global significance. Over 120 species of rare and endangered plant and animal species rely upon it, including seven species of mussels found nowhere else in the world. Upriver in its freshwater sections, it provides a crucial spawning area for two endangered species of giant sturgeon. Downriver in its saltwater sections, it is a primary calving area for the critically endangered North Atlantic right whale, whose numbers are down to less than 350 individuals and whose annual deaths currently outpace births.

The sandbars, beaches, freshwater wetlands, and saltmarshes found throughout the Altamaha watershed offer vitally important nesting grounds and migratory havens for dozens of species of shorebirds and wading birds. In fact, some of the very same migratory birds the Carters and I saw during our respective trips to Amazonia might very well have spent time in the marshes outside my window during their biannual migration. One of the three largest water basins on the entire Atlantic seaboard, the Altamaha pours over 100,000 gallons of water into the ocean per second, feeding one of the ocean's largest nurseries for numerous species of sharks. It's also home to the oldest stand of trees on the east coast of North America.

The ancient stand of bald cypress growing in the Altamaha River swamps of Lewis Island began growing around the time of the Islamic Prophet Muhammad. But by the early 1970s, over a thousand years later, this last remaining virgin stand of old-growth cypress was set to go to the sawmill—until Jimmy Carter intervened. Together with Georgia environmentalist Jane Yarn, then-Governor Carter established the Georgia Heritage Trust in 1972 to purchase Lewis Island for the state, protecting the trees in perpetuity. Yarn, who later would become the head of President Carter's White House Council on Environmental Quality, set in motion the protection of the entire Altamaha when she and her family donated Egg Island and worked to raise the money to also acquire nearby Little Egg and Wolf islands, which together now form a more than 5,000-acre national wildlife refuge at the mouth of the Altamaha. The most remarkable part of that story is that when Jane Yarn got involved she was just an ordinary citizen, a member of her local garden club, a woman who loved wild spaces and felt compelled to protect them. She wasn't a career environmentalist or a wealthy benefactor or a politician with an agenda. She and her husband mortgaged their home to protect Egg Island. She marshaled an army of garden club women to send letters to the governor to prevent Georgia's barrier islands from becoming exploited by phosphate mining corporations.

But that was just the beginning.

For decades now, a wide variety of interested parties—including family farmers, hunting clubs, fishing clubs, billionaires, environmentalists, timber companies, conservation organizations, land trusts, and various state and federal agencies ranging from the Georgia Department of Natural Resources to the US Department of Transportation, Fish & Wildlife Service, and even the military—have cooperated to protect over a quarter of a million acres of uplands and wetlands along fifty-six contiguous miles of the lower Altamaha forever.

One of my dear friends and personal heroes, Christi Lambert, coast and marine director of conservation for The Nature Conservancy, tirelessly worked with a host of friends and colleagues and interested parties on every transaction. She met with hunters gathered around fires at their camps, with farmers out in their fields, with foresters out in the woods, with soldiers on military bases, and with every stakeholder along the Altamaha River to string together purchases, conservation easements, and natural buffer zones. Christi calls what she does, "landscape quilting"—individually placing covenants on many different patches of land through a variety of conservation tools with the voluntary participation of public, private, and corporate landowners to ultimately blanket an entire geographic area with environmental protections that will benefit everyone in perpetuity. Christi and her colleagues will continue to sew the landscape quilt along the Altamaha, working their way along the upper portions of the river, until someday the entire watershed is protected. They have expanded the quilting concept to begin protecting some of Georgia's other vital river systems, like the Satilla and the Ogeechee, and to serve as a model for protecting other threatened ecosystems across the nation and around the world.

The cooperative effort to save the Altamaha proves the feasibility of E. O. Wilson's wildly ambitious half-earth concept. It's not just a pipe dream; it's actually doable if we just muster the collective will to achieve it, bringing diverse interests together toward a common goal to preserve one wild space at a time. Just as the Carters set out to do the unimaginable in fighting to completely eradicate specific infectious diseases, like river blindness, we also can set out to do the unimaginable and strive to set aside half of the earth's lands and waterways in their natural state if we are willing and committed. Protecting half of the earth as wild spaces not only will slow the progression of global warming and the mass extinction of species but also will protect ancient ways of life for indigenous people and shrink the ever-increasing wealth gap around the world.

Wilderness areas can then be put to use not by industrial exploitation but by the development of noninvasive income production such as low-impact extraction of medicinal products and eco-tourism—hiking, kayaking, canoeing, mountain climbing, birdwatching, swimming, diving, and sustainable hunting, fishing, and foraging. In turn, anglers, hunters, and outdoor enthusiasts, motivated by their experiences in wild spaces, can become vital partners in the conservation effort through a shared desire to interact with nature.

E. O. Wilson and Jimmy Carter had a lot in common: both grew up in the Southern United States during the Great Depression and both shared an insatiable curiosity for the natural world. While Carter spent much of his childhood picking cotton, selling boiled peanuts, and hunting and fishing the woods and waters near his rural home, Wilson was on his hands and knees in the South Alabama dirt with a magnifying glass, obsessively studying ants. Jimmy Carter placed his faith in the religious teachings of a first-century Middle-Eastern Hebrew carpenter and went on to become a US President and warrior for world peace. Wilson placed his faith in observational science and became a beloved college professor and one of our nation's most influential and prophetic evolutionary biologists. In 1977, President Carter awarded E. O. Wilson the National Medal of Science.

In 2001, E. O. Wilson joined Jimmy Carter and civil rights icon Senator John Lewis in headlining Emory University's "Reconciliation Symposium." The three visionaries—all respective products of the twentieth-century Deep South—discussed the growing disparity between the world's richest and poorest people. They called for reconciliation not only among individuals, races, and countries, but also between humanity and the earth. Their shared vision mapped out a course for the twenty-first century that despite increasing urgency remains achievable, but only if we dedicate ourselves to it.

CHAPTER SIX
HONDURAS

HONDURAS

CARLTON HICKS

≈

In 2010, we traveled to the Bay Islands of Honduras to fish for bonefish, permit, and tarpon. Our host was Steve Brown, a fly-fishing acquaintance we'd met the previous year in Colorado, who was launching a new fishing lodge in the area. Steve first visited Guanaja while backpacking in Central America and was excited to tell us all about it. White sands, crystal-clear waters, and giant schools of bonefish had us all captivated. The prospect of catching a permit, the most elusive prize in all of saltwater fly fishing, hooked the president and me.

Rosalynn, President Carter, Wayne, Bob, and I made up the group for this trip. We stayed at a small, rustic lodge situated on the beach of Jones Cay, just off Guanaja Island. Guanaja lies northeast of the larger island of Roatán in the Caribbean Sea, approximately sixty miles north of the Honduran mainland.

When we got to Guanaja, Steve explained that the marine ecosystem in the Bay Islands was still struggling to recover from Hurricane Mitch, which devastated Honduras in 1998. The massive Category 5 storm destroyed nearly all of the mangroves there, and because Honduras' Bay Islands are so remote, no nearby seed trees could help naturally replace them. This piqued the Carters' interest because they had traveled to the Central American nation as part of their humanitarian work with The Carter Center just days after Hurricane Mitch hit Honduras. Twelve years after the hurricane, Steve was bringing anglers to the islands not just to fish but to raise awareness and funding for a mangrove restoration project. Mangroves provide vital habitat for all sorts of aquatic species, including bonefish, tarpon, and permit and all of the fish and shellfish people rely on for food and commerce. As environmentalists and humanitarians, President Carter and Rosalynn asked to meet with project leaders and joined the mangrove restoration efforts by wading out and planting mangrove seedlings in the shallow flats around Guanaja.

. . .

Our trip to the Honduran Bay Islands was among the most enjoyable trips that we took together. We all caught many bonefish and ate fresh fish and ceviche on the veranda of the rustic beach lodge. Before and after meals, we often spotted big schools of bonefish cruising peacefully in the flats right in front of the lodge.

On several mornings, the president rose before the rest of us and fished alone in the surf. While we drank our strong Honduran coffee, he'd tell us about all the bonefish he'd caught while the rest of us were still sleeping. After breakfast, we'd usually split up into groups, with two anglers and a guide in each boat, to explore the wide-open salt flats around Guanaja. Wayne and I usually fished together, and President Carter and Rosalynn fished together.

Often, we'd take lunch and stay out all day. But on some afternoons, we met at the lodge for lunch. On those days, Rosalynn usually stayed behind to rest and read a book. I would take her place in the boat and fish with the president in the afternoon.

We ventured out around the islands where we would get out of the boat and wade the wide open flats in search of bonefish.

Wading in the clear water was extremely peaceful. Bonefish have an uncanny ability to blend in and disappear in the white sand shallows. In that wide open environment, your eyes will try to wander clear out to the horizon. But to catch bonefish, you have to look for what anglers call "nervous water," barely perceptible disturbances on the surface that might indicate the presence of a bonefish. You also have to look down through the water, because bonefish will sometimes make shadows as they move across the white sand and give away their position. If you lose your concentration, bonefish can easily swim right by your feet before you see them. You might see them for a split second before they disappear. That's why they're sometimes called "gray ghosts."

The thing I liked most about fishing in Guanaja was that peacefulness, being alone on those wide open salt flats with just the wind and the water. No one was around except the birds flying overhead and my closest friends and local guides. Guanaja Island is extremely secluded, and I don't remember seeing any other anglers or even any other tourists of any kind the whole time we were there.

...

During our week in Honduras, I had my first and probably best chance to catch a permit, the most elusive and prized fish you can pursue on the fly. My guide and I were walking along the beach looking for bonefish. We stopped when we spotted a couple of really big permit side-by-side in the surf. They were just ahead of us, in the breakers, very close to shore.

I approached without spooking them and made a pretty accurate cast. I was fishing with a Dungeness crab fly pattern and put the fly down right in front of the nose of the largest permit as it faced me. My heart raced. I started stripping the line, and the permit began following the fly. Just about the time I thought the fish was ready to strike, a wave came and spooked both fish away from the crab. My guide and I stood there for a while with the waves lapping at our legs, hoping the permit would come back. They never did.

When we returned to the lodge, I told the group how I'd had a perfect shot at two permit before they disappeared under an incoming wave. President Carter listened intently. For much of the time we'd been there, he'd been poring over an old dog-eared copy of *Permit on the Fly* by famed fishing writer Jack Samson that Steve had loaned to him. While reading it, the president had become a bit obsessed with the idea of catching a permit. He spent just about any down time we had walking the beaches, scanning the surf to see if he could see any permit tailing in the waves. Before and after meals, he glassed the shoreline with binoculars, hoping to see permit fins slicing through the crystal-clear water. At that point in the trip, he'd spotted a number of permit and had even gotten close enough to cast to a few of them, but none had shown any real interest in his offerings. The way he was staring at me as I told my story, I assumed he was thinking that if only he'd been the one to have a shot at those fish, he might have landed one of them. But that wasn't it at all.

When I'd finished telling my story, the president told us that almost the exact same thing had happened to him. Then, he proceeded to tell a nearly identical story of how he, too, had just come up empty after finding two big permit swimming together in the surf. The president and his guide were fishing from the beach on the incoming tide, just as I had been, when two big permit materialized in the surf right near his fly. He could see their big scythe-like tails actually touching as the fish dipped their broad, rounded heads into the sand to feed. He just knew that one of them was about to pick up his fly.

The president had been fishing all week with a small fly that approximates a shrimp or crab, called a "Crazy Charlie." It was actually a slightly modified version of the standard white Crazy Charlie with some gold flash and olive-colored rabbit fur that Steve Brown had tied for him earlier in the day. The president said he stood in the surf for what seemed like an eternity waiting and hoping that the permit would take the fly. The guide whispered for him to continue to be patient and not move the fly at all but to just wait until the permit found it resting in the sand and picked it up.

Permit are extremely finicky and will spook at just about anything, even a tiny crab or shrimp that moves too quickly or aggressively. President Carter obeyed the guide's advice perfectly and continued to wait patiently. Then, just as the permit dipped its head to pick up the fly, a wave crashed behind it. Both permit spooked and swam away, and the president never saw the fish again.

The president and I looked at one another in amazement, realizing that we had had almost the exact same experience. After that trip, we promised each other that we we would fish for permit together again someday. Only the next time, we vowed the fish wouldn't get away!

JIM BARGER JR.

≈

Hurricane Mitch was the single deadliest Atlantic hurricane of the twentieth century, killing more than ten thousand people and nearly destroying the nation of Honduras. Mitch hovered over the entire country for more than two days straight, churning 180 mph winds and dropping over six feet of rain. Whole communities were completely wiped out. Entire ecosystems washed away from the mountains down to the coast.

The hurricane uprooted and washed away mangroves, the dense shrubs that form tangled webs in tidal pools and provide habitat for all manner of fish and seabirds. Almost all of the nation's infrastructure, including roads and highways connecting the towns and cities, were gone. For years afterward, erosion made it nearly impossible for the Honduran agriculture industry to rebound. I remember it all vividly.

As someone who grew up on an island in the annual path of hurricanes, the visual of a Category 5 storm spanning the breadth of a whole nation was horrifying. Throughout my youth, it seemed like we evacuated St. Simons Island at least once annually, and as a child I'd always cavalierly considered it to be nothing more than a welcome opportunity to get out of school. After seeing what happened to Honduras in 1998, as a young adult, however, I was forced to confront the reality of what the unbridled force of nature can do.

In the years immediately after Hurricane Mitch, I volunteered to lead two disaster relief teams in Honduras to help rebuild the tiny village of Germania, one of hundreds of remote villages ravaged by the storm. Together with architects and local Honduran supervisors, we spent weeks each summer rebuilding houses. Doctors and nurses on our team provided on-site health care. In cooperation with Honduran engineers, we explored ways to implement a replacement well and water system in the village.

Because the infrastructure of the country had been so decimated, there were no longer any adequate roads leading in and out of Germania, and the only way we could get building materials and medical supplies into the village was by carrying them by hand or with wheelbarrows. Together with the village residents, we formed human chains to pass cement blocks, rebar, and sacks of concrete up the hillside. One day, an elderly Honduran man showed up with a packhorse to help carry supplies up the rocky slope. The group effort I participated in was only one of hundreds conducted by

Hondurans with support of people from all over the world to try and address the devastation caused by Hurricane Mitch.

...

Out on the Bay Islands, habitats for resident and migrating fish, crab, shrimp, and all manner of birds—storks, frigatebirds, flamingos, spoonbills, cuckoos, parakeets, terns, sparrows, vireos, and countless other species of migratory songbirds—disappeared overnight in the winds and waves of Hurricane Mitch. When the Carters returned to Honduras to fish Guanaja more than a decade later, the effects of the great storm were still being felt there. By taking the time to plant mangrove seedlings with their friend Steve Brown, the Carters participated in an essential effort to aid the survival of aquatic, avian, mammalian, and human life—not just in Honduras but around the globe.

Across tropical and subtropical saltwater ecosystems, mangrove forests provide wetlands between land and sea. They offer safe areas for birds to nest and fish to spawn. The mangroves are nursing grounds for sharks, tarpon, snapper, grouper, and other fish species that humans depend on for both food and ecotourism, a primary industry and economic driver in Caribbean communities and around the world. Mangrove forests also create living shorelines that prevent erosion.

Worldwide, mangrove forests are one of the most important offsets against the effects of global warming. They are capable of sequestering nearly four times as much carbon as land-based forests. Scientists are still learning how global warming and sea level rise affect hurricane formation, but the short answer is that in the early twenty-first century we are seeing stronger storms, longer hurricane seasons, and hurricanes that move more slowly through areas, causing greater destruction—all due at least in part to the ongoing warming of the planet. Hurricanes gain their energy from warm waters, so it stands to reason that as more heat is trapped in the atmosphere and that heat is absorbed by the oceans, increased ocean temperatures lead to stronger storms. Warmer air temperatures also allow for greater absorption of water vapor, leading to more intense rainfall and flooding. Finally, over the past century, sea-levels have risen nearly a foot and continue to rise, causing the danger of storm surge to increase exponentially.

And the problem builds upon itself.

As the storms destroy forests on both the land and in the sea—such as mangroves—the planet loses its ability to absorb and store carbon, further contributing to the warming of the planet, which, in turn, continues to increase the likelihood of stronger hurricanes and longer hurricane seasons. Steve Brown's initiative to restore the mangroves in Honduras ultimately resulted in the planting of almost a million mangrove seedlings and the near-complete restoration of the forest. He credits that success, at least in part, to the Carters' willingness to be among the first people to sign on to his vision and to amplify it with their voices.

...

The year before the Carters and their friends visited Honduras, the Central American democracy endured a political storm from which it has yet to fully recover. On June 28, 2009, Honduran soldiers invaded the home of President Manuel Zelaya in the middle of the night. They kidnapped him at gunpoint and deported him to Costa Rica. The coup d'état was the culmination of a constitutional dispute between Zelaya and the Honduran Supreme Court that had been brewing for more than a year. While President Zelaya had defied a court ruling and attempted to use unconstitutional means to amend the Honduran constitution, the Supreme Court had grossly exceeded their own constitutional authority by secretly ordering the military coup. The result was chaos.

HONDURAS

The United Nations, the Organization of American States, and the international community at large uniformly condemned the takeover. As Secretariat for the Friends of the Inter-American Democratic Charter, which is made up of former Western Hemisphere leaders who affirm the role of democracy in the Americas, The Carter Center formally denounced the military coup and drew up a roadmap for peaceful resolution of the constitutional crisis.

Over the ensuing decade, however, Honduras continued to experience democratic backsliding and erosion of the rule of law. Hondurans streamed out of the country, and many sought asylum in the United States, contributing to a large influx of immigrants along the US–Mexican border. Immigration became a dominant political topic in the United States, dividing the nation between those who hoped to craft humanitarian solutions and others who vilified asylum seekers and sought to wall off the country.

In 2022, Honduran President Juan Orlando Hernández was arrested and extradited on drug trafficking charges. The Carter Center played a key role in supporting Honduras' efforts to restore democracy by deploying delegates from the Friends of the Inter-American Democratic Charter. The delegates monitored elections, designed reforms, and helped implement them. The delegation was led by former Panamanian President Martín Torrijos, who had a notable connection to Jimmy Carter: his father, Omar Torrijos, had negotiated the Panama Canal Treaties with Carter decades earlier.

...

Jimmy Carter's decision to give up control of the Panama Canal has been one of the single greatest stabilizing factors in Central America, a region often defined by conflict. When Carter assumed office, Central America was in grave and dangerous political turmoil. Authoritarian regimes had been variously deposed and replaced again and again by military coups in El Salvador, Guatemala, Honduras, Nicaragua, and Panama. Revolution and civil war were the norm. Migrants fled the unrest from almost every Central American nation.

The Torrijos-Carter treaties marked a milestone in US-Panama relations, as Jimmy Carter transferred control of the Panama Canal to the Panamanian people. This move not only reduced US influence in Central and South America, but also averted decades of potential conflict and bloodshed that would have put US soldiers and civilians at risk. Furthermore, by relinquishing control of the canal, Carter earned valuable goodwill for the United States from nations that had long resented US dominance over the critical waterway.

While the treaties were politically unpopular in the United States at the time, people across the entire political spectrum now agree that relinquishing the Panama Canal was one of the boldest and wisest presidential decisions of the late twentieth century. To accomplish the Panama Canal treaties, President Carter relied heavily on his ability to build coalitions across party lines. Although every politician on Capitol Hill knew giving up the canal was the best long-term strategy for the country, they all also understood that it was short-term political suicide.

Tennessee Republican Senator Howard Baker was one of Carter's primary allies in pushing through the measure. Doing so ultimately cost him the 1980 Republican presidential nomination. In fiery campaign rallies and television ads, Ronald Reagan used the Panama Canal treaties as a political bludgeon, first against Baker and then Carter, even though privately he praised the measures and declined to repeal them during his eight years in the White House. At the time, Carter thanked Howard Baker for "doing the right thing," according to Jonathan Alter in *His Very Best*. The weary senator retorted "that with any more 'right things,' he'd lose his seat in the Senate."

HONDURAS

Decades later, after Senator Baker retired from a distinguished career in public service, my first job as a young lawyer was working with the elder statesman in his law firm. I asked Senator Baker about his experiences with President Carter. I will never forget how sternly he looked at me as he said the word "relentless," chewing on the adjective like it was an overdone piece of meat. He described Jimmy Carter's refusal to surrender the greater good even when it meant possibly sacrificing his own political future and the political futures of those around him. Senator Baker's deep admiration for Jimmy Carter was clear to me in that moment, but so too was his acute frustration—even those many years later—at the thought of what President Carter's principled stand had cost him politically.

...

The sun is high and bright. A tern cruises overhead, casting a shadow on the white sand at your feet. The water is barely twenty inches deep here and clear as you wade slowly, trying not to make a sound or cause a wake, easing along the edge of the open flat. Soon, parts of the flat will become an open sandbar. A small stingray scurries across your path, fleeing ahead of the retreating tide. Sixty feet in front of you, off to your left, the water is nervous. White sand churns beneath the surface like gray smoke in the water. It's a large school of bonefish, gorging on prey in the last moments before being forced to follow the tide off the flat.

Just as you begin to gather your line to make a cast, darkness covers the water, and the fish disappear. You look up straight overhead and see one small cloud eclipsing the sun. There are no other clouds in the sky. Standing in the middle of the only shadow in a thousand-yard radius, you wait for the cloud to pass. You consider blind casting into the area where you last saw them; but if they've moved closer, then your fly line will land on top of them and probably scare the whole school. So, you wait. How long does it take one small cloud to move out of the way of the sun? In the shadows, it is nearly impossible to see anything below the surface. They may be right in front of you, but there is no way to know for sure. You stare intently where you last saw them, hoping, straining to see them in the shadow until the cloud finally passes. The veil lifts, but now they are gone. You scan the water all around and begin to wonder if you saw them at all or if you just imagined it.

Hypnotized by the sunshine on the gently rippling water, you almost don't see the solitary bonefish cruising along the edge of the flat directly toward you until the shadow rippling over the sand beneath it catches your eye. It's much larger than the ones in the school you saw earlier. It's cruising slowly, peacefully, unconcerned, alone. With a quick roll and one false cast, your fly line is up in the air and then looping out in front of you. The Crazy Charlie fly makes a faint splash in the water and settles gently down onto the shallow sandy bottom. The large bonefish continues toward you undisturbed. You pull steadily on the line, making one smooth, two-foot-long strip causing the fly to rise at the end of the leader out of the sand like a shrimp scurrying away, and the big bonefish shoots forward and grabs it.

You tug hard on the line in your hand and feel the hook take hold as the big fish turns and charges back across the edge of the flat, taking every bit of line from your reel. It makes three long runs like that, each a bit shorter than the rest, until the fight is confined to a circle no more than a few dozen feet in diameter and the circles become ever smaller and the fish is finally just hovering in the water, pulsing at your feet. You don't need to take a picture. The mental image is sufficient. Bending down, you take hold of the barbless hook with your pliers and gently turn the hook until it drops freely from the fish's mouth.

Unhooked, the big bonefish rests in the water beside you like a tamed dog. Then, with a casual kick of its tale, it follows the tide off of the flat and is gone.

CHAPTER SEVEN
RED HILLS

RED HILLS

CARLTON HICKS

In March of 2012, President Carter called and said that media mogul Ted Turner had offered us the use of his home, Avalon Plantation, in the southern Red Hills. This fertile region of rolling red clay hills spans roughly from Thomasville, Georgia, to Tallahassee, Florida. The Red Hills region contains some of the nation's last large concentrations of longleaf pine forest and consists of large tracts of public and private land, like Avalon, meticulously managed as wildlife habitat for bobwhite quail, wood ducks, deer, and wild turkey. While there, we planned to fly fish for largemouth bass, something we had never done before as a group. The Carters were also hoping to do some birdwatching for various rare species endemic to the Red Hills region.

Avalon comprises about 30,000 acres of protected wilderness, including thousands of acres of old-growth longleaf pine trees. These trees provide habitat for the endangered red-cockaded woodpecker, the gopher tortoise, and the rare eastern indigo snake. Two freshwater lakes frame a striking 1938 home built in the antebellum style. The lakes are full of largemouth bass, catfish, bluegill bream, and other freshwater sunfish; the trees around the lakes provide perches for a variety of avian predators like osprey, anhingas, and bald eagles. Anxious to experience this beautiful ecosystem and catch up with my fishing buddies, I immediately made plans to meet the Carters a week later. Wayne and Marge Harpster also came, as did Bob Wilson and his wife, Ineke. John Moores' wife couldn't make it, and neither could Jenny, so John and I were the bachelors on that trip.

Ted Turner has been close friends with Jimmy Carter for a very long time. If I'm one of President Carter's oldest living friends, I'd say that Turner would be the second oldest. Maybe Bob Dylan or Willie Nelson have been friends with him as long as Ted has, but I'm not sure. I know that all three met Jimmy Carter *after* he became governor of Georgia, while I helped him through two hard-fought gubernatorial campaigns to get him there.

While I was stumping for Carter for governor, Turner was turning his dad's billboard business into an international media empire. By all accounts, Ted's father was abusive, berating his son and often beating him with a coat hanger, supposedly to toughen him up. Ted's father died by suicide in 1963, leaving the billboard company saddled with debt and his 24-year-old son to pick up the pieces. Ted spent the rest of the decade expanding the advertising business to include radio and television stations. He bought up old, out-of-circulation movies that some people thought worthless and aired them on heavy rotation on his television stations. As it turned out, viewers adored the old films, and Turner earned advertising dollars with no recurring investment in content. When satellite technology emerged, Turner was an early adopter who vastly expanded the reach of his television networks, allowing him to broadcast an expanding catalog of old movies into homes across the country. Eventually, he bought MGM Studios and its entire film library and founded the popular cable network Turner Classic Movies, replaying vintage titles on a 24-hour loop.

The most famous film Ted Turner acquired was the epic Civil War saga *Gone With the Wind*, based on the 1936 novel by Atlanta author Margaret Mitchell. Ted's home at Avalon has several props and set pieces from the film, including a huge portrait of the British actress

Vivien Leigh as the iconic character Scarlett O'Hara—the hauntingly beautiful, spoiled, determined Southern white woman struggling to maintain a family fortune built on the backs of enslaved labor. In the film, the portrait hangs prominently in the fictional plantation house, "Tara." In one scene, the roguish character Rhett Butler, played by Clark Gable, becomes enraged at Scarlett for refusing his sexual advances. After Scarlett threatens to lock her door at night to keep him out, he throws a glass of brandy at her portrait in contempt. You can still see the brandy stain from that scene on the painting as it hangs at Ted's place. The film won eight Academy Awards, including the first Oscar for a Black performer for Hattie McDaniel, who played the character Mammy, an enslaved housekeeper. *Gone With the Wind* is considered a masterpiece in filmmaking and remains among the most successful and popular movies of all time, but it's filled with racist tropes and sexual violence and has long perpetuated a dangerously false history that dishonestly glorifies the Old South.

In 1976, the same year the Carters won the White House, Turner bought the Atlanta Braves and began broadcasting baseball games on his television and radio networks. Communities that had never before received regular Major League Baseball coverage got the games, quickly making the Braves "America's Team" and creating a devoted national fanbase. Four years later, in the summer of 1980, we were in the last leg of Jimmy Carter's failed presidential reelection campaign against Ronald Reagan, and Turner founded his groundbreaking 24-hour news network CNN. People thought Turner's idea of a nonstop news cycle was crazy at the time; surely no one wanted to watch the news all day long. But he transformed the media industry with that one stroke and made a fortune for himself doing so.

In retrospect, I believe that shift in how we disseminate and monetize the news has hurt our society. The tipping point came when Rupert Murdoch, the Australian tabloid mogul, entered the scene. His 24-hour news cycle spawned a proliferation of sensational and divisive stories with questionable credibility. Given Murdoch's background in publishing tabloids like *The Sun* and *News of the World*, which focused on celebrity gossip and outlandish alien abduction stories and such, it's no surprise that journalistic standards suffered when he launched a TV news channel to rival CNN. The result was angry pundits shouting in America's living rooms, fueling division. Murdoch's Fox News appears to operate on the same business model as his tabloids: profiting from both information and disinformation, no matter how sensational or baseless. For better or for worse, though, the 24-hour news cycle made Ted Turner a billionaire.

Jimmy Carter became something of a mentor and sobering influence on the otherwise swaggering Turner. They fly fished together for trophy trout on the Soque River in north Georgia and for bass and bream in the lakes at Avalon in Florida's Red Hills. Through their many quiet talks wading in cold trout waters shaded by towering hemlocks and flowering rhododendrons or huddled together in a small johnboat on a lake ringed with lily pads and cattails, Carter influenced the flamboyant Turner to give away large chunks of his wealth to help the poor and protect the environment. Turner heeded Carter's advice and became one of the world's most impactful philanthropists, and he continued to turn to Carter to guide him in his efforts. At various times, Ted Turner sought Jimmy Carter's input on a wide variety of things from addressing the global threat of nuclear weapons through the Nuclear Threat Initiative—which he co-founded with fellow Georgian and longtime US Senator Sam Nunn—to personal dating advice.

As President Carter tells the story, Turner and he were bass fishing back in the late 1980s when Ted turned to him and said that he'd heard that the actress and activist Jane Fonda might be getting a divorce. He was thinking about asking her out on a date and wanted to know what Jimmy Carter thought of the idea. Well, President Carter obviously approved. Not long afterward, Jane Fonda became a regular in Turner's seats at Atlanta Braves baseball games along with the Carters. After Turner and Fonda married, the two couples bonded over their shared love of baseball. In fact, President Carter threw out the first pitch of the first game of the 1995 World Series. The couples sat together throughout the entire series, which the Braves ultimately won. Long after Jane Fonda and Ted Turner divorced, the four remained close friends.

During a Braves game in 1997, Jimmy Carter advised Turner to make what was then the largest charitable donation by a single person in history—$1 billion to establish the United Nations Foundation. Turner's enormous gift has had an unparalleled impact on global issues such as addressing climate change, eradicating land mines, creating sustainable economic development in poverty-stricken nations, promoting peace and human rights, and protecting and empowering women and children around the world. President Carter advised Turner that the fund should be established to support on-the-ground, action-based, real-world initiatives to help communities and protect the environment, rather than being eaten up by administrative or other operational costs associated with the United Nations. Turner's groundbreaking gift represented about a third of his entire wealth at the time, which was unprecedented. It also followed years of his giving away tens of millions of dollars annually.

Even though Turner was among the wealthiest people in the world, wealthier folks were giving far less of their resources to help others at that time. After making the first ever billion dollar donation, Turner called on other billionaires to do the same, half goading them and half tugging at their egos with his Southern charm. He chided Bill Gates and Warren Buffett for their relatively paltry philanthropy up to that point. Gates was second only to the Sultan of Brunei in his personal accumulation of the world's wealth, and Buffett was just a step or two behind. Both men were among the top five wealthiest humans on the planet, and Turner wasn't even in the top 150. Combined, their wealth was thirty times what Turner commanded; yet, Ted had donated more than ten times the amount Gates had and many multiples more than Buffett.

Turner's outsized donation must have shocked the two men into recognizing a moral obligation to distribute their grossly disproportionate share of the world's resources. Over the next two decades, Buffett donated more than $50 billion to charitable causes and committed to eventually giving his entire fortune away. He and Gates pooled their resources, making them the two largest philanthropists in human history. In the years to come, other like-minded billionaires followed suit to divest themselves of their wealth and voluntarily redistribute it to causes benefitting people and the planet. Yvon Chouinard, founder of the outdoor outfitter Patagonia and a pioneer in rock climbing and fly-fishing equipment, gave his entire company away in 2022, turning all future profits over to environmental causes.

A few years prior, Chouinard and the Carters collaborated with other notable fly anglers on a beautifully illustrated book called *America's Favorite Flies* to benefit native North American fish species. Each collaborator was asked to identify and elaborate on their favorite fly pattern. Not surprisingly, President Carter chose the deer hair black ant, the fly I often watched him tie and which he used more than any other to tempt trout to rise to the surface on Spruce Creek. Similarly, Rosalynn chose a black ant fly tied with foam instead of deer hair. Yvon Chouinard chose a soft hackle pheasant tail dry fly, which he claimed to have used exclusively for almost a year, catching everything on it from trout to bonefish to snapper, steelhead, and salmon. That's pretty hard to believe, but I have no reason to doubt him. Most of us who've fished long enough under various conditions for different species have come to understand that it isn't so much the type of fly used but how it's presented to a fish that will elicit a strike.

Another person whom Jimmy Carter influenced to give large portions of his wealth and resources away is our friend, John Moores. John is without a doubt the most generous person I've ever known. He'd give you the shirt off of his back and then go without one himself. That's just the kind of person he is. I first met John in Oslo,

Norway, when he and I accompanied President Carter to accept the Nobel Peace Prize. John and I first fished together on our trip to Kamchatka, Russia, and after that, he was on pretty much every fishing trip we took together. He actually let us use his jet for both of our trips to Russia. It's funny how different and unlikely our little group of friends who went on all these fishing trips is. We had Jimmy Carter, a Georgia peanut farmer and former US president; Wayne Harpster, a Pennsylvania dairy farmer and diehard Republican; Bob Wilson, a dock builder from North Carolina; myself, an eye doctor in a small coastal Georgia community; and John Moores, a self-made Texas billionaire and member of the San Diego Padres Hall of Fame.

John is the son of a single mother whose birth father abandoned them. He took the name, Moores, from the man who later married his mother and adopted John and his two brothers. He was from a very humble background and put himself through college and law school at the University of Houston. Originally, he went to Texas A&M but dropped out to scrape enough money together to pay for college. He took a job as a programmer at IBM before earning enough to reenroll at the University of Houston. Eventually, he earned his bachelor's and a law degree, but never practiced law. Instead, he was an early entrepreneur in the computer software industry, working out of his garage before eventually selling his first company for a fortune and moving to California to start other, even bigger companies. In 1994, he bought the Padres, which he owned for eighteen years, the longest anyone had ever owned a baseball team at that time. He had a positive effect on the team, too, which isn't always the case with some team owners.

I remember John was extremely preoccupied with getting TV rights for the Padres while we were on our bass fishing trip in the Red Hills at Turner's place. He spent a lot of time on the phone with baseball commissioner Bud Selig and others to put that deal together, and I think he really increased the value of the franchise by doing so. I remember thinking how crazy it was that I was on a fishing trip with one Major League Baseball owner trying to negotiate TV rights for his team while we were staying at the home of another Major League Baseball owner and TV magnate. Meanwhile, President Carter, Rosalynn, and the rest of us were just preoccupied with catching the biggest largemouth bass.

Even though John went on most of our trips with us, he was always more interested in the camaraderie and making sure everyone else was having a good time than he was in catching fish. He took a lot of the pictures on our trips over the years and made scrapbooks for everyone. The rest of us were highly competitive, always trying to catch the most or the biggest fish and outdo one another. President Carter was the most competitive of all. In contrast, John always seemed just happy and thankful to be along for the ride.

John Moores first met the Carters through their shared interest in eradicating river blindness. In the 1980s, he'd read an article about the infectious disease and, like the Carters, realized that hundreds of millions of people were unnecessarily at risk of this horrible disease that actually had a cure. The only problem was getting the medicine to the people who needed it in remote areas of Africa, Latin America, and the Middle East. One of John's brothers was an optometrist who studied at the University of Houston Optometry School, where Dr. William Baldwin was dean. When John learned that Dr. Baldwin was trying to raise money to buy a van to drive from Houston to Central America to help administer the drug, he picked up the phone and called him. But instead of just giving Dr. Baldwin the money to buy the van, Moores donated $25 million and personally jumped headfirst into the cause. Together they established the River Blindness Foundation, which later merged operations with The Carter Center.

John and I have never talked much about money. He is very modest and humble about his extensive philanthropy. Rosalynn once told me, though, about a conversation she had with John on a trip to Africa on one of their healthcare initiatives. She said that John told her, "I've been extremely fortunate and have become wealthy—but

I don't want to die wealthy." Shortly thereafter, he began earnestly divesting his wealth, quietly giving large sums to The Carter Center and other charitable organizations like the Innocence Project, which works to exonerate people who've been wrongly convicted of crimes. In 1991, he gave over $50 million to the University of Houston, which was then the largest donation ever made to a public university. The University made a big announcement about it, but John never mentioned it to any of us. He probably sought President Carter's advice privately about it, though. But with the rest of us, he was just one of the group. John eventually became board chair of The Carter Center and assisted the Carters with many of their healthcare initiatives and peacekeeping and election monitoring projects. For many of those humanitarian trips, he donated the use of his Gulfstream jet. He also lent the plane to our group for more than a few of our fly-fishing trips, even when he couldn't join us.

. . .

I like to think that Jimmy Carter's influence on people like Turner, Gates, Buffett, Chouinard, Moores, and others who spent large portions of their lives accumulating wealth was a key factor in their eventually turning their time, talents, money, and resources to helping the people and places that need it most. And I definitely believe that in asking them to give away their money, Jimmy Carter had a lot of credibility because he never tried to amass wealth for himself after leaving the White House. While he has had close friendships with several of the richest people in the world, President Carter has always remained relatively modest in his personal finances.

More than half of all of the presidents our country has ever had were wealthier than Carter. Of all of the US presidents since 1950, only Harry S. Truman—who was also famously financially modest—had a lower net worth than Jimmy Carter. It's probably no coincidence that Truman was Jimmy Carter's personal hero. President Carter always said that he thought Truman was the greatest president of the twentieth century. He considered Truman to be honest and "down-to-earth," and he tried to follow his favorite predecessor's example in that regard both in the White House and afterward.

In the years since Jimmy Carter left office, other former presidents and several first ladies have taken enormous honorariums for speaking engagements and otherwise leveraged their political fame to vastly increase their personal and future generational family wealth and power. Former President Trump even started for-profit businesses based on his time in the White House. He founded his social media platform, sardonically named "Truth Social," to monetize his political rantings and grievances. After losing reelection in 2020, Trump sold everything he could think of to extract money from his fanbase: signature tennis shoes, digital images of himself dressed like a superhero, even expensive Bibles with his name, face, and slogans stamped right on them.

But Jimmy and Rosalynn Carter always refused to leverage their political fame for personal profit. They never accepted payment for speeches or appearances or for any of their work with The Carter Center. They never lent their name or image to any for-profit venture. Jimmy Carter has always been adamant that politicians should never profit from public office. He believed that because a public official's influence is granted through the electoral process and funded by the taxpayers, it's subject to an implicit trust that such influence never will be used for private gain—even long after the politician's term or career is over. For over forty years, Rosalynn and he have donated their time and lived almost solely from the royalties of their books and his government pension, spending frugally and serving others. They moved from the White House right back into their home in Plains, and they never moved again. President Carter built most of the furnishings in their home in his woodshop. And since the 1980s, he's bought most of his clothes at Walmart—that may be hard to believe, but it's true.

In fact, one of the biggest arguments I ever witnessed between the president and first lady was about Walmart. We were driving together on a fishing trip up to western North Carolina, and Rosalynn criticized the president for habitually shopping at the big box discount store. She said that by shopping there he was endorsing the company's unfair treatment of employees and excessive reliance on cheap Chinese products that exploit child labor and harm the environment. She told him that she also didn't like the way big discount stores pulled customers away from small local businesses in rural communities.

The president was having none of it. He responded that Walmart provided a vital source of goods at a fair price to communities that otherwise would go without. He said that only people of great privilege were in a position to boycott Walmart or look down their noses at others who shop there. Besides, he liked the prices. They had to agree to disagree on that one, but I think Rosalynn got the better part of the argument.

President Carter is by far the thriftiest person I've ever known. As a child of the Depression, he understood the value of a dollar, and his religious faith wouldn't allow him to waste on himself what he could give to others. When Jesus said in the Bible, "Sell your possessions and give to the poor," President Carter and Rosalynn tried to follow that almost literally. They encouraged others to do the same. All of the world's major religions require people to share their wealth and influence with the poor. For instance, the early Hebrew texts say that charity is as important as all of the other rules in the Torah combined, and giving to the poor is one of the five pillars of Islam. In the years I've known the Carters, I witnessed them practice what they preached.

...

We caught a lot of bass and some bluegills on our trip to the Red Hills, fishing primarily with topwater popping bugs. They're fun to fish, because the fly floats on top of the water and as you retrieve it with quick jerks on the fly-line, the fly gurgles and splashes, making a popping sound like a frog swimming across the water. That action is irresistible to largemouth bass and can provoke some pretty violent strikes, especially when cast along the banks of a lake or among a bed of lily pads or back among the shadows of flooded cypress trees. It was a restful trip and we enjoyed our time together with nothing to do but bask in the spring sunshine and visit and enjoy the wonderful food and Southern hospitality. In the evenings, we ate bobwhite quail that had been harvested on hunts there at Avalon earlier in the year, and in the mornings we woke to the sound of quail calling to their mates nesting somewhere hidden in the wiregrass amid the towering longleaf pines.

JIM BARGER JR.

~

Fog hovers over the water of the pond in the cool semidarkness of the early morning. The last lonesome call of a whip-poor-will fades away. The surface of the water is still. The high trill of a northern parula echoes in the tree canopy. red-eyed vireos whistle; mourning doves coo back and forth like whispering owls. Cardinals, towhees, yellow-breasted chats, hooded warblers, great crested flycatchers, Carolina wrens, wood thrushes, chickadees, swamp sparrows, and a host of other spring migrants—you cannot differentiate them all—sing together in perpetual canon, stirring the woods awake with their songs. A red-bellied woodpecker barks.

You squint to see the thin transparent fishing leader between your fingers in the growing light as you thread the leader through the eye of the hook tightly wrapped with dense deer hair, closely cropped to make a buggy-looking fly that approximates a frog or maybe a mouse or a large dragonfly. It plops loudly on the water when you cast it and gurgles and struggles helplessly on the surface as you retrieve it. Somewhere in the muddy depths of the pond a largemouth bass stirs from primitive hypnosis. A small alligator basking in the sun on the bank opens her eyes. Bream and sunfish dart and hover. Minnows scatter. Mosquitoes hum, dancing in the air. You pause your retrieve and leave the awkward-looking fly bobbing in the water. The ripples fade away, and the surface of the water grows still again. You wait and anticipate.

. . .

I've spent the vast majority of my life in Southern wild spaces, much like Avalon, ecosystems of complex beauty supporting myriad interconnections of wondrous flora and fauna. They are also places harboring a human history of great cruelty, pain, and shame. I have come to understand that in the context of the American South, the word "plantation" carries grave connotations. I grew up in the 1970s and 1980s on St. Simons Island, under the shadow of the very same oak trees where white enslavers once forced captive Africans to toil on cotton plantations. My childhood home was very close to sinuous Dunbar Creek, which cuts through vast salt marshes on the east side of the island. In 1803, brave members of the West African Igbo (also Ibo or Ebo) tribe once staged an uprising there after surviving the horrors of the Middle Passage. Defiantly, they fought and drowned in the creek rather than suffer the indignity and horrors of slavery, and they righteously took a few of their kidnappers down to their death in the murky water with them.

Pierce Mease Butler, an enslaver who owned a plantation on the north end of the island in the mid-1800s, was responsible for our nation's notorious "Great Slave Auction." To satisfy his gambling debts, Butler ordered 436 men, women, and children taken from plantations on St. Simons and Butler islands. They were separated, stripped, and corralled into filthy stables at the horse track in Savannah to be sold to the highest bidders and scattered to other work camps on plantations across the South. It rained for days throughout the auction. This ruthless moment in my community's history is known as "The Weeping Time" because of the constant sound of the crying parents and children and the relentless pelting rain. Now, each year many of us gather to place 436 lights on Butler Island, which is now a state-owned nature preserve, to commemorate the Weeping Time and honor the families who were separated and displaced from our community.

Before he separated families and sold them like chattel, Pierce Butler inherited a possessory legal right to do so from the estate of his namesake grandfather, one of the original founders of the United States and a signer of the US Constitution. The younger Butler was a playboy who squandered the wealth that two generations of his family had amassed through exploitation of forced African labor. The elder Butler was the author of the US Constitution's notorious "Fugitive Slave Clause," which mandated that the federal government defend the rights of enslavers and use taxpayer resources to subsidize the capture and return of escaped enslaved people. Article IV, Section 2, Clause 3 of the US Constitution, as authored by enslaver Pierce Butler, remains to this day unedited in our nation's governing document, though its operation was abrogated by the Thirteenth Amendment during the Civil War. The words in that clause offer a chilling reminder of our nation's past.

When I was a teenager, our family and some of our friends bought a neglected old rice plantation called Merrifield, just south of St. Simons in Camden County, Georgia, along the Satilla River. I spent countless happy, carefree hours at Merrifield hunting wood ducks in the swamps that bordered the rice fields. I walked old dikes with a shotgun, kicking up clapper rails and common snipe, one of the most delicate game meats I've ever eaten. Though fallow for more than a hundred years, the fields remained an ingenious patchwork of drainage ditches and dikes, expertly designed and dug for the mass production of long-grain rice. I didn't realize or appreciate then that the impressive irrigation systems and agricultural fields were designed by enslaved African engineers and that the labor required to dig and maintain those fields was performed by enslaved people, some of whom likely lost their lives in the process.

During college, I spent much of my free time on quail-hunting plantations owned by family friends in west Georgia and Florida, places like Avalon, peanut and soybean farms carved from former antebellum cotton plantations. We followed fine pointing dogs in mule-drawn wagons in piney woods and hunted whitetail deer and wild turkeys in swampy bottomlands. My friends and I prowled ponds and oxbow lakes, fishing for largemouth bass, bream, and red-breasted sunfish as the sun set over cypress swamps. Often, we stayed up all night shining headlamps across ponds gigging bullfrogs that we fried the following day in hot peanut oil and washed down with cheap, cold beer. Those nights and the meals that followed were something straight out of the books of Marjorie Kinnan Rawlings. Years later, in a little bistro in Mirepoix, France, my wife Burch and I ate pan-fried frog legs in beurre blanc sauce while sipping Viognier under candlelight as darkness slowly enveloped the snow-capped Pyrenees. In that perfect moment, the memory of those feral nights as a careless college kid with a headlamp and a barbed gig immediately returned to me.

• • •

After college, I spent two years pursuing a master's degree in Southern Studies, and I lived on Sapelo Island, Georgia, the large barrier island north of St. Simons which once was one of the most profitable slave labor camps of the eighteenth and nineteenth centuries. Sapelo is one of the last Southern barrier islands that can only be reached by boat. Descendants of enslaved people on Sapelo are the guardians of an important American cultural heritage there, preserving many of the traditional West African customs and practices passed down through generations in a uniquely American way of life proudly known as "Geechee," a word etymologists believe derives from the Kissi (pronounced Geezee) ethnic group of the region of West Africa that today encompassees coastal Guinea, Sierra Leone, and Liberia.

The Geechee community of "Hog Hammock" (sometimes phonetically spelled "Hogg Hummuck") welcomed me and shared their cultural heritage with me. I learned to forage for wild herbs and teas, such as life everlasting and sassafras and to plant red peas, sugar cane, sweet potatoes, and garlic, and to harvest mullet, shrimp, seatrout, flounder, and red drum with hand-woven cast nets. My hosts were Julius and Cornelia Bailey, direct descendants of the formerly enslaved people of the remote island, and they treated me like their son, sharing their folkways, foodways, and home with me without hesitation or qualification. Together, Cornelia and I founded the annual Sapelo Island Culture Day Festival, which has continued to celebrate and educate about the importance of Sapelo's Geechee culture annually since 1995.

At that time, Cornelia—a noted storyteller and cultural and environmental activist—was writing her extraordinary memoir, *God, Dr. Buzzard, and the Bolito Man: A Saltwater Geechee Talks About Life on Sapelo Island*. Every morning, we enjoyed breakfast together—usually shrimp or mullet and grits—and then I walked from the Bailey home down the long, dusty dirt road, shaded by live oak trees. I visited the community's other Geechee elders and artisans: famed sweetgrass basketmaker Allen Green, cast net maker Earl Walker, and boat builder Glasco Bailey. At the end of each day, I walked back to the Bailey homestead and helped Cornelia review the day's writing, which she inscribed in sweeping cursive longhand on big yellow legal pads before mailing them to her co-writer, Tena Bledsoe. Julius, whom we all called "Frank" after his father, would usually be preparing dinner: stewed clams, smoked mullet, roasted raccoon and sweet potatoes, or—if we were lucky—smoked pork ribs brined in Coca-Cola. More often than not we ate the perfectly simple, unctuous, dish of red peas and rice seasoned with red bay leaf, dried ground sassafras leaf, saltpork, and black pepper.

Reading Cornelia's handwritten narrative, I learned how her ancestors were brought to Sapelo Island by the brutal enslaver Thomas Spaulding to work without pay on his indigo, rice, and cotton plantation. I learned how slave traders stacked people like cordwood in ships on the harrowing voyage across the Atlantic Ocean where many died and were dumped in the sea. Cornelia's ancestors were specifically selected for their knowledge of rice cultivation learned in their homeland in Africa. They were the descendants of a prince named Bilali, a Muslim scholar who was the author of an important Islamic religious text that now is part of the archives at The University of Georgia.

During the final days of the Civil War, US General Sherman issued Field Order 15, setting aside 400,000 acres of the Georgia coast for the formerly enslaved people who had lived and worked the Lowcountry plantations, including Cornelia's ancestors. They had earned their land—far more so than the first British colonists, such as Thomas Spaulding and Pierce Butler, who received free land grants from the British Crown, whose emissaries had first seized or scammed it from indigenous people. From Cornelia, I learned that Field Order 15 was issued in part to assuage Sherman's guilt for callously allowing the massacre of over a hundred recently freed slaves at Ebenezer Creek, north of Savannah.

But the transfer of land never took place.

President Andrew Johnson reversed Field Order 15 immediately following President Lincoln's assassination and stole the promised coastal Georgia lands back from the Geechee people. Then, to build political consensus, Johnson delivered the land as a gift to the very traitors who had staged a bloody war against their own country, killing three quarters of a million soldiers and thousands of civilian men, women, and children. Nevertheless, Cornelia's ancestors and the other Gullah Geechee people along the coasts of the southeastern US worked to buy their land, pay their taxes, and build culturally-rich farming and subsistence communities, preserving their West African folkways, beliefs, traditions, language, and dialect.

Cornelia's and Frank's generation inherited their land on Sapelo from their ancestors along with the cultural traditions best adapted to sustain it. Geechee customs harmonize with the environment, contrasting directly with the industrial exploitation of chemical factories, monoculture pulpwood farms, and resort developments enveloping much of the rest of the Southern coast of the United States. Sitting at the kitchen table with Cornelia, listening to her talk, reading her autobiography in her looping cursive script—the rich, dark, evil, honest, hopeful history of my home region spilled out before me.

• • •

Like many twentieth-century Americans, I was tempted as a child by Margaret Mitchell's seductive work of propaganda, *Gone With the Wind*. Arguably, no single piece of literature has done more to distort our nation's history, particularly in the minds of white Americans. I distinctly remember when Ted Turner began rebroadcasting David O. Selznick's movie adaptation of the story in the late 1970s. My family huddled together in our living room in front of the old wooden cabinet that held our Zenith Floor Model television set, eagerly anticipating the gorgeously filmed Technicolor drama. Sitting cross-legged on the floor in my pajamas, I was captivated by Vivien Leigh as Scarlett O'Hara. No other character mattered. Gable's Rhett Butler was an unconscionable bully, and the other men and women seemed weak, overly refined, and inconsequential.

Scarlett was powerful, angry, ferociously feminine, and beautiful. She stands out among the first female fictional characters with whom

I identified as a young reader. I'd fallen for the charismatic title character in Lucy Maud Montgomery's *Anne of Green Gables* and with the curious Mary Lennox from Frances Hodgson Burnett's *The Secret Garden*, but Scarlett O'Hara was a different obsession altogether. My immediate infatuation with her made me blindly accept the grossly distorted historical narrative that runs through both the book and the film. It didn't matter that the characters of Black people didn't in any way resemble the Black people I knew. It didn't matter that the otherwise self-evidently gross injustice and criminal nature of slavery was whitewashed to paint a palatable backdrop for the indomitable Scarlett. It didn't matter that my parents had cautiously taught me that the cause of the Confederacy was wrong. Somehow, despite all of that, we all loved the film.

Through the prism of *Gone With the Wind*, the Confederacy was depicted as an honorable fight for "states' rights," rather than an obvious insurgency of greedy white supremacists attempting to form a government for the purpose of preserving and expanding the institution of slavery. It didn't matter that the founding documents of the Confederacy explicitly, emphatically, and unapologetically stated that the proposed nation was based on the fundamental principle of protecting and expanding the right of white people to enslave and profit from the labors of captive Africans and their progeny. It didn't matter that the Confederate Constitution specifically denied its member states the rights to outlaw slavery or withdraw from the Confederacy (so much for states' rights). As I sat in front of that screen with my family eating salty, buttery, stove-popped popcorn from a big wooden bowl, we all were temporarily seduced by the insidious vision of Margaret Mitchell's "Tara" and the false Confederate Lost Cause mythology of a bygone era when a noble white gentry lived ideal lives as benevolent land stewards in mutual appreciation with willing, happy slaves. What a pack of lies.

Since 2020, I've had the honor to support local grassroots efforts to combat such false Confederate narratives through a variety of different programs in our community of coastal Georgia. One of the most impactful has been what we call the "Justice Journey." Each summer, a bus of our local high school students travels throughout the South visiting sites that tell the stories of our region's true heroes. Through the Justice Journey, students from our community have visited the Equal Justice Initiative's (EJI) Legacy Museum in Montgomery and participated in the museum's immersive experience that chronicles the history of racial injustice beginning with the transatlantic slave trade and continuing though the ongoing period of racial terror lynching to the epidemic of mass incarceration. Among other places, students from our community have visited the Lorraine Motel in Memphis where the Rev. Martin Luther King Jr. was assassinated and sites in Birmingham where Bull Connor turned fire hoses and attack dogs on innocent child protestors and where the Ku Klux Klan bombed the 16th Street Baptist Church, murdering four young Sunday School students: Denise McNair, Addie Mae Collins, Cynthia Wesley, and Carole Robertson.

After returning from the Justice Journey, participating students turn their efforts throughout the school year toward making our community better for all who live here, repairing and improving our public housing, feeding our communities and families in need, and encouraging and helping people register to vote. Through my connection to the Justice Journey and these local work projects, I've learned from our students that it's not enough to just turn our backs on the false narratives of the past, but that we also must seek justice in the communities where we live in order to build a better future. These young students in our community are committed to following the late John Lewis' admonition to get in "good trouble, necessary trouble, and help redeem the soul of America."

RED HILLS

. . .

For a few seasons in my midtwenties, I lived and worked as a hunting guide on a large Southern quail hunting preserve consisting of over 20,000 acres of old-growth longleaf pine forest and thousands of acres of riverbottom swamps. There, I continued my education in generational land stewardship that I'd begun to learn on Sapelo. My immediate supervisor was an expert bird dog handler, horse trainer, and outdoorsman named Claude Frazier, who was a third-generation descendant of enslaved people whose ancestors had been forced to work on plantations in the area before the Civil War. Claude was a wise, generous man, whose patience with me was boundless. Together, we rode Tennessee Walking Horses over every square mile of the place that he called home. We followed English Pointers and Setters, searching for wild bobwhite quail seven days a week throughout the fall and winter seasons, and in the spring we hunted wild turkey using handmade wooden box turkey calls that Claude made himself.

Claude lived in the house of his birth there among towering longleaf pines. His father, Richard Frazier, was also born in the same home and was a world-renowned bird dog handler and quail hunter during what is known as the golden era of Southern bobwhite quail hunting in the 1950s and '60s. Richard's parents had been among the last generation born into slavery in the area. A stately portrait of Richard Frazier painted by famed outdoor artist Aiden Lassel Ripley hangs in the dining room of the hunting compound there on the preserve. Instead of an old Southern plantation house, the hunting compound there is a cluster of modest, century-old cedar shake cabins with rough cabbage palm trunks that frame small open porches.

Since 1906, the land there has been preserved by a northeastern family whose bachelor ancestor purchased it as a hunting retreat and who first engaged the Fraziers and other local families to help maintain the land as a nature preserve. For well over a century now, generations of the Frazier family and others have managed and stewarded the land, protecting, preserving, and nurturing it specifically as a natural haven for wildlife. In recent years, a conservation easement was donated by the land's owners to The Nature Conservancy, creating an irrevocable, legally binding covenant to preserve it as a refuge for wild plants and animals in perpetuity, ensuring the continuation of generational land stewardship by the Frazier family and others.

Similarly, the State of Florida has cooperated with Ted Turner to place a permanent conservation easement on Avalon. The old-growth longleaf pine ecosystem where Jimmy Carter, Dr. Hicks, and their friends fly fished for largemouth bass will be preserved forever. Numerous landowners like Turner, whose properties once were enslaved labor camps during the antebellum era, have taken steps to permanently protect vast areas of wildlife habitat through conservation easements. In addition to conserving these lands, many have also established stewardship funds, donating substantial resources to ensure the long-term management and preservation of these areas. Organizations such as The Nature Conservancy, the Orianne Society, Tall Timbers, and independent land trusts play a crucial role in this effort, working to study, protect, and preserve the fragile ecosystems of the Southern United States, such as the native longleaf pinelands in places like the Red Hills and the barrier island live oak forests along the coast in places like Sapelo.

. . .

Ironically, many of the old antebellum plantations—more accurately described as forced labor camps—have become the South's most important conservation and ecological research areas and often as a direct result of the longstanding stewardship of wealthy Northerners who purchased Southern land cheap after the Civil War or by enterprising twentieth-century New South entrepreneurs, like Ted Turner. My wife and I were married at a centuries-old hunting and fishing retreat called Cabin Bluff that sits on the mainland along the Cumberland River in the shadows of Cumberland Island—both Cabin Bluff and Cumberland now have become public nature preserves, together comprising over 60,000 acres of protected wilderness along the coastline of the southeastern United States.

Cumberland, the largest of the Georgia barrier islands, once was the site of an enslavement camp that produced prized long-staple Sea Island cotton, earning a scandalous fortune for the Miller family who partnered with Eli Whitney to produce the cotton gin. When I was in elementary school, we learned about Whitney's miraculous invention and how it transformed the world economy in the nineteenth century. What we didn't learn was how the cotton gin ushered in an era of human enslavement on an unparalleled scale, caused the mass deforestation of more than 100 million acres of Southern wilderness, and quickly depleted and degraded the otherwise fertile soil.

In the 1880s, steel magnate Andrew Carnegie bought the bulk of Cumberland Island and maintained it as an exclusive hunting and fishing retreat for his family and friends for the next one hundred years. When Jimmy Carter was Governor of Georgia in the early 1970s, he was fishing for speckled trout on the east side of the island in Christmas Creek when an island caretaker threatened him with a shotgun, instructing Carter to leave, apparently not realizing or caring that he was talking to the highest-ranking public official in the state. The caretaker shouted at Carter that Christmas Creek was strictly off limits to anyone other than Cumberland's wealthy landowners and their guests. Jimmy Carter could have pulled rank and had the man arrested on the spot. Instead, he found another place to fish for the rest of the day and thereafter promptly passed a law guaranteeing everyone the right to fish "any of the salt-water creeks, streams, or estuaries leading from the Atlantic Ocean or from the sounds, rivers, or bays surrounding the several islands" of Georgia and making it a criminal offense for anyone to obstruct or interfere with another person's God-given right to go fishing.

Cumberland Island now is a US National Seashore, and the island's wealthy owners have largely ceded ownership, management, and protection of the fragile ecosystem to the US National Park Service. Today, anyone can travel across the salt marshes on a daily ferry to enjoy Cumberland's immense maritime forest and wide barren beaches. Similarly, the nearby mainland hunting retreat, Cabin Bluff, where my wife and I were married, was acquired in 2021 by the state in a unique public-private partnership with various federal agencies, The Nature Conservancy, the Open Space Institute, and private donors and conservationists. Now, it is a 27,000-acre Wildlife Management Area called Ceylon, managed and operated by the Georgia Department of Natural Resources and open to the public for hunting, fishing, hiking, camping, and birdwatching.

...

Shortly before Jimmy Carter became governor of Georgia, the state similarly acquired and set aside all of Sapelo Island, except for the Geechee community of Hog Hammock, as a nature preserve. On the south end of Sapelo, the University of Georgia owns a research center that facilitates the study of marine and estuarine ecosystems and the effects of human activity and climate change. President Carter and his family retreated to Sapelo Island once in 1977, during the first year of his presidency, and then twice in the summer of 1980 as his term was winding down. Before that, he'd visited the island frequently as Georgia's governor. Dr. Hicks traveled over to Sapelo Island to join them on all of those trips. The first presidential visit just months after the inauguration was a happy time, almost carefree in comparison to the visits during the fraught final days of the Carter presidency.

In his diary, President Carter wrote that one morning in late May of 1977 during his first year in office, he went in a small boat from the north end of Sapelo with Dr. Hicks and White House legal adviser Charlie Kirbo over to neighboring Blackbeard Island to fish freshwater ponds there for bass and bream. Blackbeard Island is a National Wildlife Refuge; it has no residents. During the yellow fever pandemic of 1878, it served as a quarantine station. The crumbling red brick crematorium for disposing of infected bodies remains there today, slowly being enveloped by thick palmettoes and twisted wild grape vines. In his diary entry, Carter noted that he "caught the largest bream I've ever seen" that day and mentioned discussing with Hicks and Kirbo his frustrations and struggles with "big business, who are a greedy bunch."

After reading that note in the president's diary, I asked Carlton about the fishing excursion from Sapelo to Blackbeard and the giant bream they caught. It turns out that was an inside joke. Dr. Hicks remembers it was unseasonably cold that day and they had to borrow heavy jackets from the Secret Service. Only one fish was caught the whole day. President Carter caught it, and it was the smallest bluegill bream any of them had ever seen. Jokingly, President Carter smiled his signature toothy grin and held it up for Dr. Hicks to snap a picture.

Their two visits to Sapelo in the summer of 1980 proved a stark contrast to that earlier trip. During the Iran Hostage Crisis from 1979 to 1981, President Carter exhausted himself daily, working tirelessly for a diplomatic solution to the hostages' release. The Reagan campaign relentlessly used the hostages as a tool to attack the president, and at the same time President Carter neglected his own campaign by obsessively focusing on rescuing the hostages from daily abuse, malnourishment, and crippling isolation in Iran. Later, at least one political operative, Ben Barnes, confessed to his part in a covert plot by the Reagan campaign to lobby Middle Eastern leaders during the summer of 1980 to convince the Ayatollah Khomeini to hold the hostages until after the election was over in order to sabotage Jimmy Carter's presidency.

On one particularly tough day on Sapelo during that 1980 summer visit, Dr. Hicks and the president took a break and went out for a jog on the dirt roads and foot trails winding through Hog Hammock.

Dr. Hicks broke the silence and asked his worried friend, "Isn't there some way we can just send some special forces guys to go over and get those folks out of there?" But President Carter just kept jogging, seemingly lost in thought. Unbeknownst to Hicks, the president's military advisors had already planned "Operation Eagle Claw," a Delta Force covert mission to rescue the hostages. When three of the eight helicopters failed to make it to the first staging area, the mission seemed cursed. One helicopter was lost in a sandstorm, another cracked a rotor blade, and the third suffered hydraulic problems. Reluctantly, Carter ordered the rest of the team to abort the mission. As the remaining helicopters turned back, yet another helicopter crashed—killing eight US servicemen. President Carter never got over their loss, personally or politically. For the rest of his life, he grieved the lives lost that day in the failed mission under his command.

Later that summer, Ronald Reagan took the stage at Joe Lewis Arena in Detroit at the Republican National Convention to accept his party's nomination. Dr. Hicks and Rosalynn gathered around a small television set on Sapelo to listen to the newly-selected Republican nominee. Reagan eviscerated Carter, accusing him of failing "his direct, personal, and moral responsibility." He said Jimmy Carter had abandoned the nation and was "living in a land of make-believe."

Rosalynn and Dr. Hicks fumed, but Jimmy Carter had left the room before the speech even began. Nothing Reagan had to say could hurt him more than the deaths of the Delta Force servicemen and nothing concerned him more than the futures of the American hostages in Iran. Dr. Hicks later found the president seated at a small corner table that was covered with hooks, thread, deer hair, and feathers, bent over a vise tying trout flies.

• • •

During their visits to Sapelo, the Carters worshiped on Sundays at either the First African Baptist Church at the north end of Hog

Hammock (where a young Cornelia Walker Bailey was a member) or at St. Luke Baptist (just a stone's throw from the Baileys' home). As is the tradition in many rural churches in the South, the Hog Hammock community isn't quite large enough to support competing church congregations. So everyone worships together on alternating Sundays in the different churches.

I've spent many Sundays worshiping at both churches and visiting the historic church at Raccoon Bluff on the far north end of Sapelo. I don't know that I've ever felt more a part of a community of God than in those sacred spaces. On a rainy day in October 2017, we held Cornelia's funeral service at the First African Baptist Church before taking her body to be buried with her ancestors in Behavior Cemetery. The cemetery is located in a secluded section of woods at a high point on the south end of the island. Five years later, we buried her beloved husband, Frank, there beside her, under the moss-draped oaks where all their ancestors have been buried since the late 1700s.

Since Cornelia and Frank died, developers and wealthy vacation home buyers have besieged the Geechee community on Sapelo. Intent on monetizing the land there, outsiders relentlessly push plans to replace the country's last intact Geechee community not connected to the mainland. When I lived with the Baileys in the 1990s, Geechee descendants of the formerly enslaved people of Sapelo were the only residents of the Island other than marine biologists working for the University of Georgia and a few other state employees. By the early 2020's, newcomers accounted for more than half of the Hog Hammock community.

The Gullah Geechee Cultural Heritage Corridor is a federal national heritage area that runs from the North Carolina coast down through Georgia and South Carolina to northern Florida, recognizing the international significance of the West African cultural traditions historically associated with the 79 barrier islands within the corridor. Over the past half century, Gullah Geechee communities throughout the corridor have been replaced by vacation homes and resorts, often through unscrupulous land acquisitions, such as driving up property taxes to force tax sales and leveraging complicated heirs' property issues to separate families from their land. Vacation homes continue to be built and property taxes continue to rise, making it more and more difficult for Geechee residents of the barrier islands to preserve their traditional subsistence-based lifestyle and culture throughout the length of the corridor. Only a few vestiges remain of the Geechee communities that thrived on my native St. Simons Island when I was a child.

In the fall of 2023, developers and vacation homeowners finally said out loud what they apparently had been planning all along. With little warning, they proposed changes to the zoning regulations originally designed to preserve Sapelo's Geechee community. The proposal sought to ban all traditional Geechee subsistence farming and husbandry, including the raising of chickens, goats, and even hogs in historic Hog Hammock. They proposed and passed changes that will forever change the architectural character of the community and that could pave the way for hotels and marinas to crowd out the Geechee residents of Sapelo. Some of the new homeowners have applied for permits to construct docks across marshes where Geechee families historically collected clams and along the creek where church congregations have historically held outdoor baptisms. The message could not be more clear: The traditional Geechee way of life is directly in the crosshairs of those intent on converting Sapelo Island into a playground for the wealthy, rendering one of the South's most noble and unique living cultural histories nothing more than a distant memory.

. . .

Sunlight crests the treeline across the pond. Shadows of gnarled oak branches cast twisted patterns of shadows along the water's edge. A belted kingfisher chatters on his perch on an old cypress crag. It flicks its shaggy crest, anxiously jerking its head left and right in search of some aquatic prey below the water's surface. Diving from its perch, the kingfisher stretches its wings and hovers over the water.

You stare at your deer-hair popper bobbing on the surface. You jerk the fly line once, then twice, then once more. The fly gurgles and splashes, making a popping sound. Somewhere deep back in the woods, you hear a wild turkey gobble. You stop and lift your head to listen. It gobbles again. Then, just as you are about to lift the rod and pull the fly line out of the water to recast the fly, the surface explodes violently. The fly disappears beneath the splashing water. The fly rod bends in a quivering arch, and the fly reel spins as the furious fish takes out line, searching for deeper water.

CHAPTER EIGHT
BLUE RIDGE MOUNTAINS

CARLTON HICKS

Rainbow trout was our primary goal in April 2004 when we visited Cane Creek in the Blue Ridge Mountains of western North Carolina. Travelers included President Carter and Rosalynn, Wayne Harpster, Bob Wilson, and me. Rosalynn was the only one of the wives able to make it, and John Moores couldn't break away to join us either. Bob, a native North Carolinian, organized the trip. He'd been trying for several years to get our group to experience the cool mountain rivers and streams of the Southern Appalachians.

Bob first met the Carters as a volunteer project leader on their annual Habitat for Humanity home-building team, known as the "Jimmy and Rosalynn Carter Work Project." He has an engineering background and owned a dock-building and dredging business in Mooresville, North Carolina, which made him an excellent project manager. He planned and helped execute one of the most impactful Habitat builds the Carters ever did in 1997 in the Southern Appalachians. Sometime after that build, President Carter invited him to join us on the Taylor River for the first of many trips with our group.

Bob had never been fly fishing before that trip to Colorado. I could tell he was a bit nervous and feeling clumsy. While Bob had worked with the Carters on Habitat builds for several years, he'd never spent any time with them socially. I could tell he wanted to make a good impression and hopefully get invited back.

Fly fishing intimidates a lot of first-time anglers. I know I was a bit frustrated on my first outings all those years ago—taking casting lessons from the president in the swimming pool at Camp David and trying to cast on the little stream there (but mostly getting my line tangled up in the trees).

Contrary to popular belief, fly fishing isn't all about expensive tackle, difficult casting techniques, and guided trips to exotic locations. Truthfully, an observant, patient fly angler in a T-shirt, shorts, and old tennis shoes, fishing with a used rod and reel combo at the creek behind her house, will almost always outfish a blustering dude wearing the latest brand-name waders, boots, and vest and waving around a $1,000 rod at one of the most exclusive fishing lodges in the world. Bob didn't know it yet, but all he needed to gain confidence and enjoy himself as a fly angler was patience, humility, and the discipline and willingness to slow down and observe nature.

The next time I saw Bob was about a year later when President Carter invited him to join us at Spruce Creek. Bob and I bunked at the cabin up the river on the northeastern corner of the Harpsters' farm, while the president and Rosalynn stayed in their usual place at the main cottage downstream near the covered bridge. The plan was for us to fish the pools upstream and meet downstream later for meals and to talk about what we'd experienced that day.

That first morning, I was getting my gear together and having a cup of coffee when I realized that Bob had already been out on the stream for a while. There's a pretty little hole that always holds a bunch of nice trout right in front of the cabin, next to a small waterfall. I had mentioned to Bob the day before that that was a good place to fish. But as I looked out, I saw to my horror that he was wading there right in the middle of the stream, flipping his fly line back and forth in the air without any real purpose.

Of course, it's incredibly important to approach fish very carefully so as not to spook them, particularly on a clear stream like Spruce Creek. Spruce Creek primarily runs through open pastures, so there's very little cover around the stream, making it even more important to be stealthy. I have watched my co-author Jim Barger Jr. actually belly-crawl up to holes at Spruce Creek from a distance and make long casts while kneeling yards back from the bank to avoid detection. Jim rarely wears waders when we go to Spruce Creek because he almost never gets in the water, except at the edge to net and release a fish. But here was Bob walking right up the middle of the creek!

I walked down and called him over to talk. "Bob, two things are going to happen, and neither one of them is good. Number one, flipping the line back and forth like that is not going to catch a fish. It's probably going to just get you tangled up in the weeds where you'll break your leader and lose your fly. Number two, you're going to mess up this part of the creek for the rest of the day wading through it like that. The trout are going to be so spooked they'll just hide on the bottom of the hole at least until tomorrow, if not longer." Bob sheepishly climbed out of the creek.

I could tell he wanted to learn to fly fish properly but he just wasn't sure where to begin. Like most people, he'd probably learned everything he knew about fly fishing from watching Brad Pitt play Paul Maclean in the movie, *A River Runs Through It*. The movie is based on the autobiographical novella by Paul's brother, Norman Maclean, and is a classic piece of American literature and outdoor writing. While the movie is an excellent adaptation of the book, some of the fly-fishing scenes have taught a lot of people that the best way to catch fish is to wade into the middle of a stream and false cast back and forth as many times as you can. Maclean calls it "shadow casting" in the book, which is certainly very poetic, but also completely wrong. When Bob indicated he was willing to listen to my advice, I shared with him some things I had learned many years before from the legendary "Dean of Fly Fishing," George Harvey.

George Harvey was one of our country's most notable fly fishermen, angling instructors, and entomologists. His contributions to the art of fly fishing for trout are unparalleled. George was a long-time professor and head of physical education at Penn State, where he introduced the first-ever college course on fly fishing all the way back in 1938. Subsequently, he taught hundreds, probably thousands, of people how to fly fish.

A friend of the Harpster family through three generations, George joined us on many of our early trips to Spruce Creek, where the Carters and I also became good friends with him. George wrote numerous books on fly fishing and fly tying, and he developed many fishing techniques and fly patterns that are still used today. In fact, he's the person who first introduced Jimmy Carter to the black ant fly pattern that the president favored so much. George was very famous for the flies that he tied, and I still have several dozen that he tied especially for me. Over the years, I count myself as very fortunate to have absorbed a wealth of knowledge from George Harvey.

When I first started fly fishing, on one of my first trips to Spruce Creek, George took me aside and said, "I want you to go with me this morning. I'm going to show you some of the things you really need to know about catching trout." So, I did.

We went up the stream a bit, where no one else was, and George started showing me the proper way to walk on the side of the bank. Logically, you might think that casting is the most important thing you need to learn as a fly angler. But George Harvey said that wasn't so. He said that the most important thing you need to learn to catch trout is how to walk.

George bent over as far as he could, held his rod up in the air, and said, "Just walk right behind me, exactly as I am walking, and you'll catch fish." Hunching over like that lowered our profile so the fish couldn't see us as well. George walked like that so much that even when he wasn't fishing, he was almost always hunched over. It was terrible for his posture, I guess, but he sure caught a lot of fish.

I have always appreciated that George took the time to pass the knowledge he'd learned through a lifetime of experience on to me. I decided to pay it forward by passing on what I'd learned from George to Bob Wilson at Spruce Creek.

Since Bob had at least temporarily ruined the fishing hole in front of the cabin, I told him to follow me upstream a little way. "Let me show you how George Harvey taught me to walk beside the bank without getting into the river," I said.

I hunched over and held my rod straight up in the air, doing my best George Harvey impersonation. Bob dutifully followed right behind, mimicking me. I'm sure we would have made a funny sight for anyone who doesn't know trout fishing.

There's a bend in the creek up from that first hole that always holds trout. Every time we're up there, we always see trout. But the problem is that if you see them, then they've probably already seen you first! So, I told Bob, "Before we get up to the next hole, get behind me and I'm going to get down on my knees here and peek up and see if I can see what the fish are doing."

Before we even got to the bend, I could see a nice rainbow trout feeding. It was hiding in the eddy of a rock. Periodically, it would ease to the surface and sip a fly off the water before settling back down into the eddy. I eased up, hunched over gently, and made a couple of false casts to get the line out. I made a good cast just above that rock, and almost as soon as the fly hit the water, the trout rose and ate it. After we landed and released the trout—which was a pretty nice-sized fish—Bob said, "Yeah, I like that!"

We repeated our hunched-over walk to the head of the same pool. This time, I let Bob take the lead. He eased up stealthily like I'd shown him and made some really nice casts. He had a couple of good drifts, and before long, he caught his first Spruce Creek trout.

I like to think I was somewhat helpful in getting Bob to stoop-walk down the path to becoming a good angler. Our morning together, followed by years of experience and lessons from other folks like

President Carter, ultimately made him a solid fly fisherman. In fact, years later when we went to Mongolia, Bob caught the largest taimen in our group. When we were on the Ponoi River together in Russia, he caught the largest salmon.

Bob surprised us all on our 2008 trip to Spruce Creek when he brought along a friend, Ineke Van der Meulen. It was clear right away that he was pretty crazy about Ineke. Two or three years later, they married.

President Carter officiated the wedding in North Carolina. Right before he administered the vows, the president turned to Ineke with a mischievous grin and quipped: "Why in the world would you want to marry this guy?" But they seemed to be good for one another, and after that, Ineke became one of the regulars with Bob. I know the president was grateful for the tireless work Bob did on those annual Habitat work projects and he considered Bob and Ineke to be good friends.

. . .

For our trip to Cane Creek, President Carter, Rosalynn, and I met in Atlanta and drove together to North Carolina with the Secret Service. We stopped on the way at McDonald's for lunch, which was the Carters' custom.

During that pit stop, we talked at length about a controversy in Crested Butte, Colorado. This was an area near and dear to the Carters and my family as the little mountain town had been the launching point for many of our fly-fishing trips to the Taylor River and the Gunnison River's Black Canyon. In the late nineteenth and early twentieth centuries, Crested Butte became a mining town, famous for its rich deposits of silver, gold, coal, and other natural resources. But the community organized in the 1970s to stop mining for molybdenum ore at Red Lady Bowl up on Mount Emmons, a beloved, red-tinged high mountain basin that overlooks the town.

Crested Butte has always been a little different than other fancy resort towns like Aspen or Vail. It's more of an eclectic community made up of old ranchers, retired miners, Native Americans, hippies, ski bums, anglers, hunters, and other outdoor enthusiasts. In the '70s and '80s, they all came together to save Red Lady from being destroyed for its deposits of molybdenum, a trace mineral used in the steel smelting industry. Two decades later, the Bush-Cheney administration planned to quietly sell the same public land on Red Lady to a huge mining company for a pittance.

An antiquated 1872 mining law—designed to encourage westward expansion based on the tired old mantra of manifest destiny—gave the federal government the power to sell public land with proven mineral reserves to mining companies for $2.50 per acre. The prices apparently hadn't changed since the nineteenth century! The sale would not only defraud the taxpaying public, it would ruin the nature of the town we dearly loved.

Sitting in McDonald's, eating our cheeseburgers and fries and sipping Coca-Colas, I told President Carter and Rosalynn what was happening. Both were pretty upset about it. I explained that no one outside of Crested Butte seemed to care, so the deal was pretty certain to go through.

At that time, Tom Brokaw had a weekly news segment called "The Fleecing of America," which exposed ways in which the federal government propped up big business at the taxpayers' expense. The NBC news anchor was an enthusiastic fly fisherman who would certainly recognize the impact molybdenum mining would have on the community, environment, and water quality—adversely affecting the area's trout population. I also knew that President Carter had granted a number of coveted interviews to Brokaw, who would certainly listen to any of the president's suggestions.

I casually said, "It sure would be nice if Brokaw would highlight what's going on at Red Lady. They are basically giving our nation's public land away to enrich some big corporation, and it will never be the same." President Carter nodded and kept eating his cheeseburger. We finished our meals, left the restaurant, and got back on the road to Cane Creek. I don't think Red Lady came up again on that trip.

About three months later, Jenny and I came home to a blinking light on our telephone answering machine; this was back before cell phones made answering machines obsolete! We had just missed a call from the president. When I pressed the button, his familiar South Georgia drawl came on the machine and said, "Turn on NBC News."

I rushed and turned on the television just in time to watch Tom Brokaw discuss how America was being fleeced by the practical giveaway of Red Lady. I can't help but believe that Brokaw's exposing the shady deal played a big role in getting the Bush-Cheney administration to kill the transaction.

In April 2024, the Biden-Harris administration finalized 20-year protections for the entire region of Colorado known as the Thompson Divide—some 200,000-plus acres from the White River and Grand Mesa all the way to the Gunnison and the Black Canyon. Hopefully, that measure will safeguard Red Lady for at least the next twenty years, giving some comfort to the local ranchers, farmers, anglers, hunters, and others who fought long and hard to protect it. But twenty years is barely an eyeblink in geologic time. It wouldn't surprise me if Red Lady is on the chopping block again in another twenty years.

It's a good reminder that we have to be ever-vigilant in safeguarding our natural resources. Whenever there's an opportunity to turn a quick profit from our nation's environmental treasures, freeloading profiteers will be ready with their hands out, hoping to convert the wilderness into a lucrative investment. While passing environmental protection laws is important, it seems to me it's even more important to educate people about protecting the environment in their own best interest and in the interest of generations to come.

...

Our hosts for the North Carolina visit were Philip and Charlotte Hanes, respected conservationists in the Southern Appalachians. For years, Philip served on the boards of The Nature Conservancy and the

Southern Appalachian Highlands Conservancy, helping preserve over 125 million acres of wilderness worldwide and more than 70,000 acres right there in the Blue Ridge Mountains, respectively.

Together, the Hanes established and donated the land for North Carolina's beloved Stone Mountain State Park, a 14,000-acre public wilderness area, offering some of the state's best rock climbing on the large granite dome from which the park takes its name. Stone Mountain Park also contains an 1800s homestead where visitors can learn about that period of Appalachian life and culture and view artifacts from the time. Creeks and streams there provide excellent small-water fishing for native brook trout for those willing to hike into the more remote areas to find them.

The Hanes also preserved another 9,000 acres around Mount Mitchell, which is the highest peak in the Appalachian chain and the highest peak in the United States east of the Rockies. Mount Mitchell is one of the most visited sites in all of the Blue Ridge Mountains, offering unparalleled views on clear days as well as primitive camping sites for visitors and many miles of hiking and mountain biking trails.

In addition to their immense land conservation efforts, the Carters and I were fascinated to learn that Philip and Charlotte had dedicated much of their lives to issues of responsible land use and stewardship and how they sought to reverse the harmful effects of industrialized farming while empowering and enriching the lives of small-scale family farmers. Of course, as lifelong peanut and cotton farmers, the Carters always were extremely interested to hear about farming techniques and to swap stories about rural life. Farming was never very far from the president's mind. But unlike the Carters' comparatively small family farming background, Philip's family had founded and operated for the better part of a century one of the world's largest textile companies, Hanes Corporation, most famous for its signature underwear.

It's well-documented that the textile industry had an inglorious history of exploiting cheap labor in the rural South, particularly in the Carolinas, drawing people away from fields and into factories and converting small family farms into industrialized monoculture that depleted the soils and eventually left much of the landscape all but barren. Throughout the twentieth century, wildlife and human communities across the South were negatively impacted by industrialized cotton farming as well as by big tobacco farming and also by clear-cutting and planting and replanting fast-growing loblolly and slash pine trees for the paper and chemical industries. Factories to process cotton, tobacco, and pulpwood products sprang up everywhere, and many people who once worked on family farms found themselves stuck in dangerous, low-wage, long-hour shift jobs, disconnected from the land. At the same time, many of the same factories were polluting the air or poisoning the ground and often both. Small towns across the South suffered. Some died out altogether.

As head of the Hanes Corporation in the 1960s and early 1970s, Philip witnessed problems associated with industrialized monoculture firsthand and came to understand that there had to be a better way. He also recognized that generations of his family had built an extremely lucrative business through such exploitative practices and that it was his responsibility to change things. So, he completely reversed course. Philip and his wife devoted their lives to full-time philanthropy with a particular interest in restorative farming practices that could renourish the soils and provide a viable path forward for people to leave industrial jobs and return to their rural roots.

The Hanes became pioneers in the restorative farming movement, educating others on organic farming and free-range grazing methods that benefit the soil while at the same time helping family farmers increase profits, decrease workloads, preserve land, and create important habitat corridors for wildlife. The Hanes began spreading the gospel of regenerative farming in the mid-1980s, setting an example for others to follow at their farm, River Ridge Land & Cattle Company. Now those same methods have proven incredibly effective and even lucrative for many other twenty-first-century family farmers, while simultaneously conserving land, benefiting native flora and fauna, and creating much needed jobs in rural communities. Will Harris of White Oak Pastures in Bluffton, Georgia, not too far from the Carters' hometown of Plains, is one of the most vocal proponents of such regenerative farming methods.

Several young farmers where Jim and I live in coastal Georgia have adopted regenerative farming practices. Jim's lifelong friend, Matthew Raiford, is a world-renowned chef and fourth-generation African-American farmer. Matthew's great-great-great-grandfather, Jupiter Gilliard, was a formerly enslaved person who bought the family farm in our community in 1874. Matthew's James Beard-nominated cookbook, *Bress 'n' Nyam*, celebrates Gullah Geechee foodways and his family's farming heritage. Another of our local regenerative farmers in coastal Georgia is Brandon Chonko, affectionately known as "The Grassman." Brandon took a patch of scrub that had been depleted by decades of monoculture pulpwood farming and turned it into an oasis for free-range chickens, cattle, pork, and organically grown citrus. He delivers his meat and produce around the community in an old bus. Ironically, people line up in the parking lots of our local supermarkets to buy their groceries from Brandon.

Even as global climate change and species extinction close in on us, I'm very encouraged by younger folks like Brandon and Matthew, who eagerly embrace new and inventive ways to earn their living by nurturing nature rather than destroying it. I'm also heartened to realize that the Hanes' example of good land stewardship to benefit people, crops, livestock, and wildlife has spread across the Southern United States and beyond.

One of the great side effects of my friendship with the Carters has been to meet and learn from folks like Philip and Charlotte, who quietly go about the day-to-day business of helping people and preserving the planet. After our visit with them in 2004, the Hanes continued for many years to invite me to come back and fish again, and I regret that I wasn't ever able to return to spend more time with them. Phil passed away in 2011, but the work he did to preserve wilderness areas in the Blue Ridge Mountains and to jumpstart the sustainable farming movement will continue to impact people, wildlife, and the environment for generations to come.

...

Cane Creek is a diminutive winding waterway, flanked by rhododendron, mountain laurel, and other evergreens that had not yet begun to bloom when we were there—though I could imagine how the fragrant blossoms would perfume the air later in the spring and summer. While the creek itself was small, the fish were quite big, and they readily rose to a well-presented fly. We caught mostly rainbow trout, but I'm sure there were also some big brown trout lurking somewhere and also the occasional native brook trout. Even more than the fishing, though, my fondest memories from that trip to western North Carolina are the conversations the Carters, the Hanes, Bob Wilson, and I had about our shared interests and experiences. On the drive back home, the Carters and I again stopped at McDonald's for lunch and the three of us agreed to make plans to take the Hanes up on their hospitable offer to return for another trip in the future. But, unfortunately, we never did.

JIM BARGER JR.

Over the past decade, I have spent more time in the Blue Ridge Mountains of western North Carolina than in any other single place on earth except my native coastal Georgia. There is a place there known as "The Goathouse" that is our home away from home. It sits at the head of a mountain wildflower meadow in the middle of a wilderness area abutting a far corner of the Pisgah National Forest high above the West Fork of the French Broad River. Apocryphally, free-range goats once foraged the top of this mountain there in the early nineteenth century. Whether that story is true or not is anyone's guess, but the wildflower meadow there in front of The Goathouse now provides a haven for migratory birds and butterflies and a nesting area for wild turkeys.

The meadow was created when the beams and timbers for The Goathouse were cut and milled on-site from a few small acres of the ancient canopy of trees that otherwise shrouds the rest of the mountain and beyond into the hundreds of thousands of acres of adjacent national forest. Closely encircling the meadow, the remaining old-growth northern hardwood forest sprawls for miles and miles, towering with hemlock, spruce fir, tulip poplar, white pine, sourwood, mountain magnolia, birch, buckeye, beech, sugar maple, and a dense understory of mountain laurel, rhododendron, sassafras, doghobble, mountain fern, and a dizzyingly diverse list of other green leafy plants among whose dank shadows grows a sprawling kingdom of fungi: golden chanterelle, cinnabar chanterelle, ghost pipe, black trumpet, lion's mane, coral mushroom, chicken-of-the-woods, and the ever-elusive morel. The place is a dreamscape.

Drifting among the clouds in front of the south-facing Goathouse across the wildflower meadow are the blue-tinged crests of Frozen Mountain, Round Mountain, Six Mile Mountain, Laurel Fork Mountain, Chestnut Mountain, and Currahee Mountain, hiding innumerable cool shaded hollers in between. Much closer and to the west looms the long bald face of Toxaway Mountain. Turning northwest, the peaks become steadily higher: The Pinnacle, Needle Knob, Rich Mountain Bald, Sassafras Knob, Bald Knob, Bracken Mountain, and Mount Hardy. Looking out in front of The Goathouse south for 180 degrees from due east to due west, as far as you can see are blue mountain peaks. Too many to name. Too many to remember.

Behind The Goathouse, facing north, all you can see is nearly impenetrable forest stretching behind you before dropping down to the invisible river somewhere far below.

The Goathouse has no walls. It was built in the late twentieth century from materials gathered there, large granite boulders, and the timbers from trees harvested when the meadow first was cleared for native wildflowers as a feeding ground for hummingbirds, moths, bees, and butterflies. Where normally there would be exterior walls, The Goathouse has only screens to keep the legions of insects from coming inside. There is no recycled air there. Whenever you are inside, you are also always outside. That is its quintessential charm.

A high-pitched cedar shake roof with wide overhanging eaves keeps out the episodic storms that seem to regularly visit the mountain every afternoon and evening in the summer. Just under the pitched roof is a sleeping loft where the sound of falling rain pattering on the wooden shingles and scurrying through the big copper half-moon gutters and trickling down the copper loop chain into the French drain lulls you into the darkest of sleeps. The night sky is studded with stars so close you can reach out and touch them from your bed. Up in the loft, tucked beneath the sheets as the sun sets over Toxaway Mountain and then again in the early pre-dawn mist just before the sun rises over Rich Mountain, whip-poor-wills call loudly to one another and respond from the far side of the meadow.

The Goathouse has a working kitchen, running water, and a wood-burning fireplace with a stone hearth made from granite rocks gathered on site. It's a simple, rustic, elegant structure with everything you need to enjoy living in communion with nature on the top of a mountain, but nothing else. Down a short gravel path beneath a natural arbor of tree branches is the bathhouse, a traditional mountain dogtrot with two utilitarian bathrooms with showers on one side and a functional laundry and storage room on the other. Across the ceiling of the open dogtrot are hand-carved wooden fishing rod holders where fly rods hang, strung with leaders, tippets, and flies.

No nails were used in the construction of The Goathouse. Each of its large, heavy timbers is joined by traditional hand-cut mortise and tenon framing in the traditional Appalachian vernacular architectural style. Every detail was carefully designed and executed by Al Platt, the father of my longtime friend, Parker Platt. Parker and Al are brilliant architects from nearby Brevard, and Al originally conceived and built The Goathouse as a rustic retreat to share with his wife, Cindy, and their family and friends. It sits within a 300-acre nature preserve protected by a permanent conservation easement that he and his family donated to The North American Land Trust decades ago, which now is supported by the nonprofit Richland Trust, providing research and conservation projects there for rare, threatened, and endangered species such as the bog turtle, eastern hemlock, and the eastern hellbender—one of only three species of giant salamanders in the world.

Hellbenders can grow to be more than two feet long and weigh over 3 pounds. They are an indicator species for healthy cold water environments, and western North Carolina is one of the last places on earth where they are found in abundance. In the summer of 2024, researchers located sixteen individual hellbenders living in the one-mile stretch of the West Fork River just below The Goathouse. If you move stealthily along the river bank while fly fishing there, it isn't uncommon to come across one of the shockingly large hellbenders lazily resting on a rock or slowly creeping along the rocky river bottom in the cold clear water.

For years, the Platt family lent The Goathouse to my family for a few weeks each summer as a temporary escape from the excruciating heat and ever-growing crowds of tourists that take over St. Simons at that time of year. Al's son, Parker, and I have been good friends for over three decades since we first met as college kids through our mutual friend, Keith Hawk, who also was born and raised there in the Blue Ridge Mountains. The two families were close friends, and my friend Keith's father was the local obstetrician who delivered at least two generations of babies in that far western corner of North Carolina during the turn of the twentieth century. Dr. Hawk was known fondly as "The Honey Doctor" because he used local honey as an analgesic for his patients' surgical wounds.

When Cindy Platt died in 2013, The Goathouse seemed to become more of a burden to Al than a joy. So, together with some of our friends, we scraped together the money to buy, maintain, and share it with others just as the Platt family had shared it for those many summers with us. Because the screen structure is open to the elements, The Goathouse is only habitable during the temperate spring through fall months. But during that time of year, my wife Burch and I and our two children, James and George, spend as much time as we can there in that hidden, quiet wilderness, hiking, foraging for mushrooms, wild blueberries, blackberries, and wild strawberries—and fly fishing for rainbow, brown, and native brook trout.

It was there that I first began to appreciate pollinators, an interest Rosalynn Carter and I later discovered we shared. In the late spring and summer, the mountaintop meadow in front of The Goathouse is blanketed in blooms creating a patchwork of bright orange, warm yellow, pale blue, mint green, pitch black, deep violet, and snowy white against a blue backdrop of ancient mountain peaks rolling across the horizon. These mountains are among the oldest on earth. Once as high as the Himalayas, a billion years of erosion has rounded their peaks since first they began to form as the North American and African continents collided to temporarily create the supercontinent of Rodinia when microbes and single-cell organisms were still the only life forms on the planet.

Large portions of wilderness in this southwestern corner of Appalachia remain essentially in their natural state thanks to the single stroke of a president's pen. In 1916, Woodrow Wilson purchased 500,000 acres of wilderness for the United States to create the Pisgah National Forest, building on a wide-ranging environmental conservation plan designed and first implemented by President Teddy Roosevelt six years earlier. The environmental conservation ethic of Roosevelt, a Republican, and Wilson, a Democrat, later served to both inspire and enable Jimmy Carter to use his presidential power to enact some of the most lasting environmental measures in our nation's history, including the designation of over 56 million acres of wilderness for protection under Teddy Roosevelt's Antiquities Act.

During his presidency, Carter more than doubled the size of our national park system and created thirty-nine new national parks scattered throughout the country. He saved California's redwood forest and giant sequoias, national treasures that have stood strong for thousands of years but were threatened in the 1970s by unbridled adjacent clear-cutting. With the help of an extremely reluctant Congress, he established the Alaska National Interest Lands Conservation Act, preserving over 150 million acres of Alaskan wilderness, which had long been the target of and continues to be the envy of international industrial extraction corporations.

In the Blue Ridge Mountains, Jimmy Carter used his position first as governor of Georgia and then as president to save two of the region's most iconic river systems and watersheds: the Chattahoochee and the Chattooga. And it was his personal connection to these places that motivated him. The Chattahoochee, threatened in the 1970s by unchecked urban sprawl, was where Jimmy Carter initially learned to fly fish for trout, and the Chattooga was where he earned his considerable chops as a whitewater paddler. Jimmy Carter and American Rivers founder Claude Terry were the first paddlers to brave a tandem canoe descent of the Chattooga's notoriously treacherous Class IV Bull Sluice rapid. Thanks to the foresight and leadership of Presidents Roosevelt, Wilson, and Carter, the Blue Ridge Mountains of southern Appalachia were mostly spared the environmental exploitation that plagued other parts of the region.

Just as Wilson was establishing Pisgah National Forest, industrial extraction interests were greatly increasing their decades of exploiting and stripping the mountains farther north, wreaking havoc on the environment while displacing and poisoning the people who'd lived there in harmony with the mountains for centuries. Appalachian deforestation and mining peaked during the mid-twentieth century, centering primarily in Kentucky and West Virginia and recklessly destroying much of that portion of the ancient mountain range.

In his immortal 1971 song "Paradise," John Prine wrote about how the lush natural ecosystem of his Appalachian ancestors had been chiseled away piece by piece, loaded onto train cars, and hauled away tree by tree and rock by rock. If the melody and lyrics to that song don't immediately jump into your mind, then I suggest you put this book down right now and go listen to it all the way through. Then, listen to it again and again. The haunting beauty of the Appalachian wilderness contrasted against its cavalier destruction by corporate exploiters has inspired some of America's finest lyrical poetry by some of her most talented artists. Arnold Schultz, Bill Monroe, Ralph Stanley, Leslie Riddle, Jean Ritchie, Loretta Lynn, Dolly Parton, Patty Loveless, S. G. Goodman, Rhiannon Giddens, Tyler Childers, and a host of others have carried new and bygone songs from Appalachia out to the rest of the world. Sadly, however, much of the enduring art they have created serves as a memorial to the wilderness that the Appalachian region has lost.

...

Beneath Precambrian rock outcrops in the cool shade below The Goathouse, copperheads, black racers, timber rattlers, and large black rat snakes sleep peacefully. Monarch butterflies dance across the meadow, clinging precariously to stems of milkweed, slowly waving their orange and black wings, suckling at nectar, fueling themselves for the long journey ahead. They have traveled 2,000 miles to get here, and they have 2,000 miles to go. Below the dense blanket of flowers, a spotted turtle slowly crawls across the meadow. Dragonflies dart and hover. In Plains, Rosalynn planted a wildflower garden where she tended and nurtured nectar-rich wildflowers, including milkweed, the host plant of monarch larvae. Her favorites were also some of mine: blanket flower, coreopsis, purple coneflower, zinnias, butterfly weed, and blazing star. The butterflies that stop over in Plains on their biannual trip between Canada and Mexico, resting, gathering nectar, spreading pollen, and laying their eggs on milkweed in Rosalynn's garden, may very well be some of the same who visit The Goathouse later in their journey.

It's a pleasant thought, anyway.

The widespread use of pesticides on industrial farms has drastically reduced the once-abundant populations of native milkweed upon which monarch butterflies rely for reproduction and survival. Overdevelopment and the proliferation of non-native close-cropped grass lawns also have converted once abundant nectar-rich wildflower meadows into food deserts for all forms of wildlife—but particularly for pollinators. So, maybe it isn't so far-fetched to conceive that some of the last surviving monarchs would find these two discrete, carefully nurtured habitats essential to their survival even though they are hundreds of miles apart.

In 2020, the US Fish & Wildlife Service determined that populations of monarch butterflies had dropped so steeply that they had become a candidate for inclusion on the Endangered Species list. The decline in monarch populations is part of an alarming overall decline in pollinators and insects in general that threatens to upset the entire food chain and could drastically alter life on Earth as we know it. This is not hyperbole or false panic. Reproduction of every plant and animal on the planet is ultimately dependent in one way or another on the unsung miracle of pollination.

But in the meadow below The Goathouse, charms of ruby-throated hummingbirds hover and zip between the Technicolor landscape, darting among happy kaleidoscopes of Appalachian swallowtail butterflies and scattered eclipses of Appalachian azure moths feeding on the nectar of white flowering cobs of common black cohosh. Honey bees buzz so loudly around sourwood blossoms and budding sumac bushes that they sound like someone running a sawmill way off down in the holler. Fat green monarch caterpillars insatiably munching on milkweed leaves strip the plants down to their bare stalks, scattering mounds of tiny black balls of frass all over the ground. The unmistakable orange-and-black-winged adults are so thick in this little mountain meadow that it's nearly impossible to imagine a world without them.

. . .

This river has a voice of its own. Upstream, it emerges from a west-turning bend where an unusually large sassafras tree bows reverently over the bank, dipping bright green leaves into the cool, clear water like cupped hands in a baptismal font. Downstream, the river disappears around an east-turning bend over metamorphic and igneous striped boulders, frothing white, picking up speed, running away. On the far bank runs a straight-line seam of water. Twittering on the surface are emerging yellow drake mayflies, frantically paddling like little whitewater kayakers, desperately trying to take flight, awkwardly flailing wide wings on the open water. Every third or fourth one that drifts into view is swallowed by a brook trout that porpoises above the surface to devour it as the other yellow drakes triumphantly fly to freedom and then eventually descend again onto the river as spinners to be slurped beneath the surface by a gluttony of feeding trout.

Standing in the cold water, you squint at the delicate tippet in your hand as you struggle to thread it through the tiny eye of the hook of the Burnt Wing Yellow Drake fly pinched between your fingers. Casting it upstream into the middle of the seam along the far bank, you let it drift in the current, mending as it goes. After three long, steady drifts, you catch the first fish—a solid brook trout of fourteen inches that impudently flashes away, immediately disappearing to the stony depths of the river the second you release it. You carefully dry the fly, blowing on it to separate the feathers. Two more casts. Two more drifts. Another fish, identical to the other. Caught, released, gone again. Daylight fades. You struggle to see the battered fly as you dry it for the third time after the third fish. Or was it the fourth? They were all nearly identical in shape, size, take, and fight. They begin to run together in your mind, prematurely merging with the memory of every fish you've ever caught like this on a dry fly standing on a rocky stream bed as the water gurgles over your bare knees in the crepuscular light.

The fly doesn't float as well as it did at first. The threads around the hook are soaked, and the feathers remain damp no matter how many times you blow on them. You should have brought some dry shake or other artificial floatant, but you didn't. You try to dry the fly on your shirttail, but it's still wet. You consider tying on a fresh fly, but you know that in the dying light, your eyes won't be able to see clearly enough to thread the tippet through the eye of the tiny hook. You should have brought a headlamp, but you didn't. If you cast this fly again as wet as it is, it will just sink and drag and spook the fish. So, you hook the fly onto the first ferrule of the rod, loop the fly line tightly around the base of the reel, wade back out of the river, and climb up the bank, following the trail away from the river through the woods to the open pasture at the base of the mountain.

Blue ghosts and lightning bugs flicker eerie lights in the darkening mist. Whip-poor-wills whistle lonely staccato calls. The sun has receded behind the mountain. The moon has disappeared behind the clouds. You feel your way along through growing darkness. The heady scent of mountain laurel hangs heavy in the air. Behind you, the river's voice whispers softer and softer and softer and softer until, finally, you cannot hear it anymore. All that's left is the enduring buzzing of cicadas, the echo of your solitary footsteps treading the well-worn gravel path, and the melody of a sorrowful song playing on a repeating loop inside your head.

CHAPTER NINE
MONGOLIA

MONGOLIA

CARLTON HICKS

In September of 2013, we traveled to Mongolia to fish for giant taimen, the world's largest salmonid, the family of fish that includes all species of trout and salmon. It had long been a dream trip for the president since he'd first learned about the massive freshwater fish when the Carters had traveled to Mongolia about a decade earlier. In 2001, President Natsagiin Bagabandi invited Rosalynn and Jimmy Carter to tour the country and explore the idea of having The Carter Center assist with election monitoring, healthcare programs, and grassroots economic development. The president and the first lady fell in love with the country and its people and vowed to return. Since Wayne had fished for taimen before and was familiar with Mongolia, he joined the Carters in talking the rest of us into going with them. President Carter arranged the trip, and the whole group went except for Jenny and Marjorie, who decided to stay home.

Mongolia is a very long way from Georgia. We all flew commercially to Anchorage, Alaska, and transferred to John Moores' plane for the flight to Ulaanbaatar, Mongolia's largest city. As you approach Ulaanbaatar from the air, you get a fitting picture of the dual nature of the country and its history, culture, and economy. You immediately understand visually how the place is split almost down the middle, with modern high-rise buildings on one side and traditional nomadic "gers" on the other. Before going to Mongolia, I'd heard about "yurts," the traditional Mongol tent structures. Once there, we learned that the word "yurt" comes from the European mispronunciation of the word "ger," which simply means "home" in the Khalkha Mongolian language.

Mongolia had the world's fastest-growing economy while a third or more of its population proudly maintained a nomadic herding lifestyle, similar to how their distant ancestors lived a thousand years ago. Mongol culture centers on the grazing of livestock, including camels, horses, cattle, goats, and sheep. Sheep, in particular, play a central role in the day-to-day life of Mongol families. Mongolia is the world's largest exporter of cashmere wool, and the traditional Mongol diet consists mainly of meat, yogurt, cheese curds, and other dairy products.

Mongolia's democratic government and free-market economy were a little over two decades old during our 2013 visit, but the country was making unbridled economic gains due to its wealth of extractive natural resources like copper, gold, silver, and coal. Mongolia's economy stalled a few years after our visit, but it has rebounded some in recent years.

The challenge for Mongolia's leadership has been figuring out how to preserve the traditional herding way of life perfectly adapted to Mongolia's vast desert landscape while also transitioning to a twenty-first-century economy that embraces emerging technologies. One example of the collision of ancient and modern worlds that we experienced was staying in gers powered by solar panels.

When Rosalynn and President Carter visited the Gobi Desert in 2001, they stayed with a Mongolian family who had a television inside their ger powered by solar energy. This was decades before solar power took off in the United States. According to the Carters, the family's past experimentation with wind energy had failed because the desert windstorms ripped the blades right off the windmills.

Incidentally, the Carters were early adopters of solar energy. They put solar panels on the roof of the White House in the late 1970s, which Ronald Reagan later removed. After leaving the White House and returning to Plains, the Carters eventually built one of Georgia's first private solar farms on one of their old peanut fields, which now powers more than half of their hometown. The Carters' solar farm also serves as a University of Georgia research study on the effects of solar farms on biodiversity and potential ways to improve pollinator habitats in and around solar farms.

From Ulaanbaatar, we traveled in an old repurposed Russian military helicopter for a couple of hours across the desert and landed near the Eg-Ur River. We actually landed right in the middle of a wild marijuana field! Half a dozen or so gers had been set up for our accommodations alongside the river. Since our spouses weren't with us, Wayne and I shared a ger. I was quite impressed with the construction of the gers, which were both functional and homey.

The basic ger design hasn't changed much in 3,000 years. They are round structures made with wooden poles and lattice, which are wrapped in wool and felt for insulation against both cold and heat. An opening at the center top of each ger allows light to come in and circulates the air. The gers are always set up with the entrance door facing south to take advantage of sunlight. It only takes an hour or so to set up a ger, allowing for the nomadic Mongols to pack up quickly and easily when it's time to migrate to fresh grazing grounds.

Mongolian weather fluctuates dramatically. It warmed up during the day and got cold at night. It snowed one night while we were there, but by the end of the next day, most of the snow had melted. Our hosts were incredibly hospitable, intent on making us comfortable, almost to a fault. Each ger had a small wood stove inside, and our hosts vigilantly kept the fires lit for us. The problem was the gers were so well made and insulated with sheep wool that it got incredibly hot inside and often stayed hot long after the fire had gone out.

Each evening before going into the main communal ger for dinner, Wayne and I would close the damper and put out the fire to keep it from getting too hot in our ger. When we'd return, it would be sweltering again because someone had inevitably come in and taken the trouble to relight the fire for us. As a result, Wayne and I had difficulty sleeping. Most nights I had to get up in the wee hours and stand outside to cool off before going back to bed. They were such kind hosts that our only complaint was that they were a little too attentive.

...

Taimen are native to the rivers of Mongolia and to parts of Russia, Kazakhstan, and China. They have been extirpated from much of their native waters and are considered a vulnerable species by the International Union for Conservation of Nature, which advises the United Nations Educational Scientific and Cultural Organization (UNESCO) on the status of species and natural world heritage. Mongolia and parts of Siberia provide some of the last best habitat for taimen. But even in remote Mongolia, habitat depletion is an issue because of increased mining and the potential use of hydroelectric power, which can devastate river systems. Taimen are strictly freshwater fish that require moving water. They don't do well in manmade lakes or reservoirs.

Unlike some other salmonid species—like steelhead, Atlantic salmon, and the various species of Pacific salmon—taimen are not anadromous; they don't migrate between the ocean and freshwater rivers. Instead, they spend their entire lives in the rivers of their birth. They do travel within those rivers, swimming as far as fifty or sixty miles sometimes. That's why it's imperative that rivers like the Eg-Ur remain undammed and pristine throughout the entire watershed if taimen are to continue to thrive there. Mining of construction aggregate (sand and gravel) has become a growing part of the

Mongolian economy, posing a threat to this ancient species through the possible erosion of riverbanks, pollution, and runoff.

Fly fishing is the most important driver of taimen conservation efforts. Catch-and-release taimen fishing provides an ecotourism cottage industry in Mongolia that monetarily incentivizes habitat preservation and environmental stewardship. Protecting taimen, in turn, helps safeguard all of the plants, animals, and people that depend on the ecosystems where taimen live. Anglers have created conservation funds earmarked for preserving and studying taimen and their habitat. Many of the outfitters who arrange taimen fly-fishing trips have been instrumental in raising money and awareness for conservation projects. Even so, it is vital for anglers to use only single barbless hooks and to handle taimen as carefully as possible so they don't become too stressed before being released back into the river.

Another reason the species is vulnerable is that, despite their massive size, taimen have an incredibly slow growth rate. It takes seven years before a taimen reaches the age of sexual maturity and can begin to reproduce. Adult taimen, however, can live a very long time, reproducing year after year; thirty or more years is quite common, and larger taimen may live fifty years or longer.

Bob Wilson and his guide landed the largest taimen on our trip, which was forty inches long and likely over forty years old. President Carter landed a fish that was three feet long and hooked but lost several larger ones, including one that our guide estimated was four feet long. The huge fish leaped straight out of the water and into the air while the president was fighting it. That fish very likely had lived in the river for fifty years or more. As with every other fish that got away, we'll never know.

Most of the taimen our group caught were around thirty inches or shorter, which is still incredibly large for freshwater fish. It was tough fishing, though. We didn't catch a lot of fish, and we worked hard for the fish we caught. The president caught nine taimen over the course of the trip, averaging about one a day. That was more than anyone else on our trip, and he wasn't bashful about reminding us.

We fished primarily big topwater flies to mimic struggling baitfish, rodents, and small birds, all part of the taimen's regular diet. Our fishing was primarily done by wading, rather than casting from the boat. We'd wade out to about knee to waist deep and begin casting toward the middle of the river. We then let the fly drift downstream on a tight line with a slight jerking motion to give the fly action and entice the taimen.

As the apex predator in the river, taimen will eat just about anything they find. If it's alive and in the river, it's fair game for taimen. For the angler, it is far more important to get the fly where the fish can see it and give it motion. This is different from what we do with trout, which is called "matching the hatch," or picking the fly that most closely resembles the insects that are hatching on the water at that moment. With taimen, it doesn't really matter that your fly looks like other things taimen are feeding on. The fly that's most likely to prompt a strike is anything big and floundering in the flow of the water within the taimen's sightline.

We also caught another salmonid species abundant in the Eg-Ur that we'd never fished before. Lenoks, also known as "Manchurian trout," are much smaller than taimen, closer in size to the rainbow or brown trout that we catch in the United States. They are believed to be the oldest species of trout on the planet. The only salmonid that may be older is the taimen. Fossils of taimen have been carbon-dated to over 40 million years ago.

At the end of each fishing day, I was often ready to prop my feet up and relax a little. I had a bit of a head cold on that trip, which slowed me down as well. But the president was always anxious to explore and spend more time with the people. As always, he never wasted a minute.

One afternoon when we'd come in from the river, taken off our waders, and stowed our fishing rods, the president and Wayne grabbed a couple of shotguns. They drove off in an old SUV with one of our hosts, Odkuu Magsaruren, to hunt Daurian partridges, which are abundant in northern Mongolia. Sure enough, they came back a couple of hours later telling stories of walking through the wilderness and flushing large coveys of birds. We enjoyed a delicious dinner of roast partridge that night cooked by Odkuu's wife, Mogi.

One night after dinner, President Carter and Rosalynn joined a group of our Mongolian friends on a sort of moonlight nature safari to look for nocturnal animals. Over breakfast the following morning, they told us about all the animals they'd seen. Most had scurried away as the humans approached in the SUV: Siberian musk deer, corsac foxes, Tarbagan marmots, and all sorts of other animals that I can't remember. Then, before you could even put down your coffee, the president had his waders on and was ready to get out in the river again.

. . .

When we got back to Ulaanbaatar, President Carter flew to Southeast Asia to the nation of Myanmar instead of coming back with Rosalynn and me to Georgia. The Carter Center was just beginning to help Myanmar transition from a military dictatorship to a functioning democracy. The government invited The Carter Center to establish a permanent office in the capital city of Yangon in 2013, and it's still there today. Myanmar consistently ranks as a country with one of the worst human rights records in the world, so not many other nongovernmental organizations are willing to operate there. The Carter Center's initiative in Myanmar is one of many examples of how Rosalynn and Jimmy Carter bravely committed to promoting peace around the world. The Carters often told me that if any nation seeking democratic freedom and prosperity invited them to come, they would show up and do whatever was within their power to help.

JIM BARGER JR.

Just a few years after the Carters and their fishing buddies visited Mongolia, the United States entered into a strategic partnership with the central Asian democracy and ancient civilization, increasing and formalizing education exchanges, defense cooperation, and economic relations between the two nations. For most of the twentieth century, Mongolia had been a communist state, heavily influenced by the Russians to the north, who maintained a military presence in the country, and China to the south, who eyed Mongolia's relationship with the Soviets with distrust. In 1990, the Mongolian people performed one of the rarest political moves in all of human history—a peaceful revolution, resulting in a new democratic government, constitution, and a free market economy. While not a direct result of any specific US foreign policy, it's hard to imagine that Mongolia would have emerged peacefully as a democratic nation if the United States hadn't first normalized relations with China decades prior during Jimmy Carter's presidency.

• • •

President Carter announced that he had normalized US relations with China in 1978 after a series of secret negotiations that culminated in a formal agreement with Chinese Vice Premier Deng Xiaoping. It was a bold, decisive move that surprised and angered many Americans at the time, particularly right-wing hawks who saw the battle against communism as a zero sum game. But Carter's instincts proved correct over time as China steadily shifted toward a mixed market economy and became a trade partner with the United States and other nations around the world. China's emergence as an economic juggernaut was arguably inevitable because of its vast natural resources, human capital, and chilling willingness to exploit both to achieve economic advantage. But if Chinese gains had occurred untethered to the United States and other democratic nations, it's highly unlikely that we could have sustained the relatively peaceful relations enjoyed between our respective nations over the past half century.

While human rights in China remain an ongoing concern, normalization with the United States has seen a huge rise in quality of life for the Chinese middle class as well as expansion of freedoms and protections far beyond what had existed before. Without the agreement forged in 1978 between President Carter and then-Chinese leader Deng Xiaoping, it's hard to imagine that China would have stood by in 1990 and allowed Mongolia, one of its largest border nations, to peacefully transition from communism to democracy and enter into a strategic partnership with the United States. Even so, Jimmy Carter has continued to lament China's authoritarian communist political structure, which gives people no say in selecting their leaders. China's poor record of human rights, particularly with regard to the Tibetan and Uyghur ethnic groups, causes Carter grave concern, as does US indebtedness to China from the sale of treasury bonds to finance our nation's seemingly ever-expanding budget deficit.

After President Carter and Vice Premier Deng announced the bilateral agreement between their respective nations, the Chinese leader visited the United States in late January of 1978 at the president's invitation. During their negotiations, the two world leaders had become fond of one another. Even though they came from vastly different cultures and perspectives, President Carter genuinely came to appreciate Deng, who he said was "small, tough, intelligent, frank, courageous, personable, self-assured, friendly" and a pleasure to negotiate with. The American people also warmed to the Chinese leader, who famously donned a cowboy hat while visiting a rodeo and posed in pictures with 12-year-old Amy Carter to demonstrate that they were the same height.

Responding to the Carters' hospitality one evening at the White House during a state dinner, Deng leaned over and spoke quietly to his new friend, "Mr. President, you have helped achieve great things for the Chinese people, and I wonder if there is anything we could do in China for you," Carter recalled in his book *Faith: A Journey For All*. I imagine this must have felt almost like the old ubiquitous childhood question: If you could have any three things in the world, what would they be?

President Carter reflected and then responded, "Yes, there are three things that I would like: for your government to let people worship freely, to own Bibles, and for our missionaries to return." The People's Republic of China is officially an atheist state. Up to that point, religion and religious texts, such as the Bible, were illegal and considered contraband. Carter said that Deng "seemed surprised, laughed, and said he would reply the next day." The following morning, Deng told Carter that he had given the president's request great thought and that he would lift the ban on religion and religious texts. "On missionaries, however, he was adamant, saying they had exalted themselves and tried to change the culture of Chinese converts, and China would never again permit this to happen," Carter noted in his diary.

A few months after leaving the White House, Rosalynn and Jimmy Carter traveled to China as private citizens where they were greeted warmly everywhere they went. They were just beginning to conceive of what they might do with the rest of their lives and had no way of knowing that it would be the first of dozens of trips to China and its neighboring nations as part of their work with The Carter Center. They had no way of knowing that they would become far and away the most well traveled presidential couple in US history, visiting more than three-fourths of the world's nations together—eventually hiking to Mount Everest Base Camp in Tibet, sleeping in Mongolian gers on the banks of the Eg-Ur River, and climbing to the top of Mount Kilimanjaro in Tanzania. Those and many more adventures lay ahead of them.

However, on this first trip to China, they had a more humble goal. More than anything else, they wanted to attend a church service in a country that had forbidden religious worship for more than half a century. They weren't sure what to expect or if anyone would even show up. When they entered the sanctuary, the Carters were shocked at how crowded and well-attended the service was and how quickly the Chinese people had embraced their newfound freedom of religion.

Deng had at least partially made good on his promise to Jimmy Carter, establishing a new law guaranteeing freedom of religious beliefs with certain limitations and oversight and officially recognizing the major religions that had been historically practiced in China, including Buddhism, Christianity, and Islam. The Carters observed that "Bibles were plentiful." Rosalynn and Jimmy Carter made many more trips to China over the years in their work with The Carter Center as well as to China's border nations Mongolia, India, Pakistan, Nepal, Bangladesh, North Korea, and Myanmar. By 2018, China had become the largest publisher of Christian Bibles in the world, but it had also begun to exercise state oversight of worship services and to specifically ban and reportedly commit human rights abuses against religions the government deemed out of sync with traditional Chinese cultural heritage.

CHAPTER TEN
RUSSIA

CARLTON HICKS

We took two trips to Russia. The first was in 2004, to the Russian Far East near the Pacific Coast in the vast wilderness of the Kamchatka Peninsula on the Zhupanova River, where the largest rainbow trout in the world are known to live. We took the second trip ten years later to the Northwestern Federal District above the Arctic Circle on the Ponoi River east of the city of Murmansk for Atlantic salmon. The president and Rosalynn were on both trips, along with Wayne, Bob, and me. Jenny and Marjorie weren't able to come with us on either of the trips, but Bob's wife, Ineke, was there on the second trip when Bob caught the largest fish of any angler on the Ponoi that summer—a beautiful Atlantic salmon that weighed a whopping 23 pounds! John Moores and his first wife, Becky, were there in 2004. When we visited Russia a decade later, John's second wife, Dianne, was with us. They didn't fish while we were there; instead, they enjoyed the company, the scenery, and photographing the wildlife as they did on all our trips.

On both trips, the Russian officials were sort of intimidating when we went through customs. You could tell they weren't interested in interacting with us at all. If you smiled at them, they did not smile back. If you spoke to them, they did not speak back.

They just wanted to see your passport, and that was it. They would look at you, and then look at your picture. Of course, they knew exactly who the president was, but they made a show of scrutinizing his and Rosalynn's passports. Former presidents and first ladies are entitled to special diplomatic passports, which are black instead of blue like other US passports. Even so, they looked sternly at President Carter. Then, they looked at his passport. Then, they looked at him again.

The Russian officials kept our passports while we were there, which was a little unnerving. But that wasn't the first foreign nation that did that. In most of the places we went, the US Secret Service detail gathered up all of our passports and gave them to the local authorities who would keep them for us until we got ready to leave. However, the Russian officials took our passports themselves without a word and only returned them to us as we were leaving the country. Other than that, though, the Russian people treated us with incredible hospitality—with one exception.

On the second trip, while we were getting our gear off the plane and loading it into one of these old Soviet-era helicopters, President Carter asked the head of the Secret Service detail—who was going to stay in the city while we were camping on the banks of the Ponoi—if he could arrange for us to tour the Soviet nuclear submarine museum, which was located there at our port of entry in Murmansk. After our fishing trip, we learned that the Russian government had flatly refused President Carter's request. I guess they didn't want President Carter, a former nuclear submarine scientist under Admiral Rickover, snooping around in their museum. Then again, maybe it was just a snub to a former president who had taken a pretty hard stance against the former USSR during the Cold War—opposing their invasion of Afghanistan, supporting the Afghan rebels, issuing a grain embargo, and boycotting the 1980 Olympics in Moscow. Regardless, they denied the request for him to see the museum.

On both trips, we rode out to the wilderness camps in the back of old Mi-17s, Russian military transport helicopters. We sat on rough bench seats that ran down the side of the helicopters. All of our luggage was stacked in the middle and tied down with big straps.

On our trip to the Ponoi, it seemed like the whole stack of luggage and gear was going to fall over at any minute. In Murmansk, that old helicopter was so loaded down that I didn't think it was ever going to lift off the runway. The Russian pilot had to taxi down the runway and get a running start to lift off. After we got off the ground, it took forever to gradually get high enough to clear the airport. During the several hours that we choppered over the summer-thawed tundra, I had to put out of my mind the possibility of that old helicopter crashing and being lost in the vast Russian wilderness. We arrived safely at our camp on the river.

...

Our first visit to Russia was to the Kamchatka Peninsula, which sits off the coast of the Pacific Ocean in the far eastern corner of Russia, separated from the rest of the country by the frigid wilderness of Siberia. There are no overland routes in or out of Kamchatka—no roads, no railways—making it one of the most remote places on the planet. The only feasible way to get there is by boat or by air. We flew into the airport in Elizovo, which is really just an old military base outside of Petropavlovsk, the only city in all of Kamchatka. As we taxied on the runway, we could see dozens of Soviet-era MiG fighter jets with the big red tails on them. Each MiG had its own small, individual hangar, and each hangar had grass growing on the roof. From the air, it was impossible to see the hangars, and that's how they camouflaged their fighter jets.

The coastal city of Petropavlovsk has two sources of commerce: fishing and nuclear submarines. Petro, as it is called, was where the

Soviet Union had all of their Inter-Continental Ballistic Missiles (ICBMs) aimed at the US and Canadian west coasts during the Cold War. A proud statue of Lenin remains in the town square, but there was very little activity, commerce, or much of anything going on when we were in the city. From Petro, we rode in a refurbished Russian Mi-16 military helicopter that probably dated back to the time that the Carters were in the White House.

The Zhupanova River is on the far southern end of the Kamchatka Peninsula off the coast of the Bering Sea in the northern Pacific, home to towering volcanoes and the largest rainbow trout on earth. In other places, a rainbow over twenty inches unquestionably would be considered the fish of a lifetime, whereas on the Zhupanova that's pretty average. It's one of the few places in the world where you can hope to catch a wild rainbow trout of thirty inches or more, which is considered by many to be the holy grail of trout fishing.

Part of the reason for their immense size is that Kamchatka is one of the most unpopulated places left in the world and one of the most difficult places to get to, which makes for pristine, untouched habitat. There is no industry at all in the wilderness surrounding the Zhupanova: no mining, no dams, no factories. In fact, there is almost no human influence there at all. The only history is natural history. Everything there is shaped by the eons of evolution that predate humanity. Even the genetic strain of rainbow trout that live there is unique from all other strains of rainbows in the world, which is also one of the factors that may contribute to their unusually large size.

In many ways the Kamchatka wilderness through which the Zhupanova flows is reminiscent of southwestern Alaska. In fact, it's closer in proximity to the Aleutian Islands than to anywhere else. Brown bears and reindeer are abundant. Golden eagles, peregrine falcons, and other birds of prey common to North America prowl the air. Along the coast of the peninsula, many of the same shorebirds found along the Pacific northwestern coast of the United States also are present. When the helicopter landed at our camp there, the first thing we did was cover ourselves in bug repellent, because the mosquitoes there are huge and they swarm you relentlessly. We think we have mosquitoes in south Georgia, but they are nothing compared to the mosquitoes in Kamchatka. Once we were dripping with bug spray, we had the "bear talk," receiving instructions for what to do in the apparently likely event that we encountered a bear. We were given whistles to blow and told to make a lot of noise and holler—"Hey Bear! Hey Bear! Hey Bear!"—to chase them away.

We floated the Zhupanova for six days, camping at night at well-appointed, predetermined camps with wall tents, cots, and even hot water for showers. The chef and a sous chef followed along with us down the river in a raft that they used to carry all of the food we needed for the trip. They froze gallon water bottles to keep the food cold and so that we would have ice. As a result, we had cold water to drink, and also iced cold vodka! We started out floating, and we'd float every day, stopping along the way to wade and fish.

When we visited the Zhupanova River it had only ever been fished about a dozen times. It was amazing, because the fish seemed as if they'd never seen a fly. A new fly that was introduced to me was a mouse. Mouse patterns were supposed to be really good for the big rainbows, because you could skip them across the water and they were hard to resist for the really big fish who were accustomed to eating mice that either fell into the river or tried to swim across. I never caught one on a mouse fly, but other people did. I did catch plenty of big trout on more traditional flies, though.

One evening, as we were sitting around the campfire, I commented that with all the volcanoes in the distance I sure would like to see an eruption. Well, low and behold, a few minutes later I turned around and we all witnessed one of the volcanoes erupting. The next morning there was actually ash floating in the river and settled over our boats and gear. After that, I learned that it actually wasn't that surprising, because Kamchatka has probably one of the largest concentrations of active volcanoes anywhere. They actually call it "The Land of Fire and Ice" because it's fairly common to witness an eruption there even when the tundra is frozen.

We saw eight bears total, including full grown bears and young ones, most of which we saw from the boat. None of them posed any sort of danger to us until the last day. I was with a guide by myself in the first boat out. We'd gone on ahead of the others, and the salmon had just started spawning, moving up the river. The bears were all coming down to the river, looking to feed on the fatty, protein-rich salmon, and we saw one coming down the side of the bank directly toward our boat. The others that we'd seen during the trip would generally scamper away when they saw us or heard us, but this one just kept coming. As it got a bit closer, it became agitated and started shaking its head back and forth at us. My guide happened to be a bear hunter, and he had a shotgun with him that he loaded. Then, he stood up and clapped his hands at the bear, who took off running up the side of the hill and away. I asked him afterward if we were in any danger there, and he said that it wouldn't have taken many leaps for the bear to have been on top of us in the river, which was why he'd loaded the shotgun.

After that, we continued to float on down, and everyone else was floating twenty or thirty minutes or so behind us. Before long, I hooked a big trout—the biggest wild trout of my life. I didn't want to have to fight the fish from the boat, so the guide pulled over to the bank and let me out so that I could wade and fight the fish. Then, just as I was about to land the fish and remove the fly from its jaw and release it, everybody else passed by in their boats and paused to watch. So, it was perfect timing, and I loved it. The Carters and everybody else got a good look at the thirty-inch rainbow I'd just caught! Later on during the trip, the president returned to camp one afternoon telling about a thirty-one inch rainbow, which he'd caught. It just happened to be one inch longer than my big fish.

Most every time we ever fished together, he somehow always caught a fish that was just a little bit bigger than mine. We were always very competitive like that, and he always liked to stay just one step ahead of me. After our sixth day on the river, we ended up at a little cabin where we spent the night and traveled by helicopter again back to Petro and then home.

・・・

When we returned to Russia a decade later, we went to the opposite end of the country to another remote wilderness to fish for Atlantic salmon on the Ponoi River. As we had in Kamchatka, we camped along the river, but rather than traveling to different camps each night as we worked our way downriver, this time we stayed in a more permanent site, called Ryabaga Camp, from which we could go out each day to fish the different sections of the river. Each section we fished each day was equipped with a tent and a wood stove where we could warm up while the guides cooked lunch over an open fire.

In the evening back at Ryabaga Camp, we ate traditional Russian fare and gathered under the stars to enjoy the night sky and listen to the sounds of the river. President Carter and Rosalynn were particularly fond of a borscht stew of beets and vegetables and beef that the Russians served to us in rye bread bowls baked right there over the fire at the camp. Considering how deep into the wilderness we were, it was hard to believe how comfortable the accommodations were and how good the food was. The guides were great, also. And the fishing was some of the best we've ever had on any of our trips.

There were a total of sixteen anglers at the camp on the Ponoi that week, including the five who fished in our group. Together we caught 422 Atlantic salmon, which is an incredibly large number until you learn that the week prior over 800 salmon were caught and that our week was one of the lowest totals of the entire summer. The Ponoi is just so loaded with big, bright, healthy fish, most of which we released. The only time that we kept a salmon was if the fish was bleeding and not likely to survive. Then, the guides would quickly and humanely kill the injured fish, and we would eat it on the river cooked over the open fire for lunch.

Atlantic salmon are extremely strong, quite different from the Pacific salmon that you catch spawning in the rivers in Alaska. Atlantic salmon make both fall and spring runs back and forth from the ocean annually. Fall is the spawning run where the females lay their eggs to be fertilized by the males, and the young salmon—called parr—remain in the river for the first two years before migrating out to the ocean where they can live for several years before returning to the river for the first time. First-year migrants that return to the river are called grilse, and they can weigh 5 to 7 pounds and can put up a very aggressive fight. But grilse are nothing compared to the mature salmon that return back to the river twice each year and can weigh over 20 pounds. Conversely, Pacific salmon usually make one spawning run at the end of their lives, where they return to the rivers of their birth to spawn before they die at the end of their journey. Sometimes in Alaska, the rivers will be littered with the carcasses of spawned out salmon and become crowded with bears gluttonously feeding on the dead fish.

But on the Ponoi, the fish return to the ocean after they spawn and because they retain their strength and build additional strength with each migration, they are fierce fighters. On the Ponoi, as on many of our trips, we typically split up into pairs to fish each day. Wayne and I usually fished together, and the Carters usually fished together. Wayne and I both used the same single-handed fly rods that we are accustomed to fishing with, but the Carters used two-handed spey rods, which is a traditional casting rod that requires a specialized technique particularly adapted for Atlantic salmon fishing. But I just couldn't get the knack of it.

Spey rods are much longer and stouter than the typical single-handed rod and rather than false casting behind you to get the line out, you do a slow, gentle looping roll cast, which propels the line far out into the water, making it more proficient to cover the river, which is hundreds of feet across at some points. Spey casting is a graceful movement that is highly effective and beautiful to watch, but I never got the hang of it and never felt comfortable with it. Nevertheless, with the traditional single-handed fly rod, I caught more fish than I could hope to catch and could cast the line as far as I needed to. Both the president and Rosalynn became quite proficient at spey casting, though, and it was pleasing to watch them slowly waving those long rods and rolling the line in a large loop out across the wide river.

Because the camp on the Ponoi was up above the Arctic Circle, it only got dark there in the summer months for just a few hours each night. As a result, we often rested after lunch and fished again after supper. It wasn't unusual for us to still be out on the river long after midnight. President Carter was particularly anxious to get as many fishing hours in as he could. One night the president stayed out fishing until after 2 a.m. with Ilya Sherbovich, the avid Russian fly fisherman and dedicated salmon conservationist who owns and operates the camp. In addition to being an avid salmon angler, Ilya is also passionate about other species, particularly taimen. After our trip to Mongolia for taimen the year before, the president was anxious to ply him for his fly-fishing knowledge, and the two stayed out fishing and talking into the wee hours of the night. In 2021, Ilya landed and released the largest taimen ever caught on a fly, weighing over 114 pounds, on the Tugur River in the Russian Far East.

...

There are a handful of fish in the lifetime of every angler that are lost but never forgotten. The memory of losing them chases you in your dreams. For me, one of those lost fish was on the Ponoi. After the fish struck, it went straight downstream, and I was never able to turn it. I never even saw it. The fish struck; I set the hook; and it took off down the river. The guide quickly pulled up the anchor, and we started downriver following the fish in the boat as fast as we could as the giant salmon continued to strip line from my reel. We couldn't keep up with it, though, even chasing it in the boat. It took out all of the fly line and went deep into the backing before finally breaking me off. We never saw it. So, I don't know how big it was. The guide said it was a really big fish, possibly the biggest salmon of the season, possibly a river record. But we'll never know. As I reeled my line back in and looked at the frayed leader, I added it to the faded memories of every other fish that ever got away.

...

Years later when President Carter and I were sitting and reminiscing about all of our fishing trips together, I asked him which trip had been his favorite from beginning to end—and he said that it was our trips to Russia, and especially that trip on the Ponoi.

JIM BARGER JR.

As the Carters moved into the White House in 1977, the most pressing of all issues facing the world was the specter of nuclear war. Although the likelihood of global destruction has ebbed and flowed since the United States first dropped atomic bombs on Hiroshima and Nagasaki, ending World War II, one constant has remained throughout most of that time period: humans still possess the capacity to destroy the planet in a matter of minutes. The only thing preventing us from doing so is our mutual will to exist. More than forty years later, the distinct possibility of a nuclear holocaust still haunts and remains an ever-present threat to all humankind despite our apparent acclimation to the longstanding threat.

At ninety-four, Jimmy Carter wrote his last of thirty-three books, *Faith: A Journey for All*. He reflected on the immense weight the nuclear arms race placed on him and on his Russian counterpart, Soviet President Leonid Brezhnev, in the late 1970s. He recognized his sacred duty to avert a nuclear war as the single greatest responsibility of his lifetime:

> *The most important element of faith ever imposed on me, and on another person simultaneously, involved the threat of the total elimination of human life on earth by a nuclear war with the Soviet Union. My ultimate responsibility as President of the United States was to defend my country against a military attack, and I learned soon after my election that we and the Soviets had enough atomic weapons in our arsenals to destroy each other and that the resulting radiation and other collateral damage would kill most of the rest of the world's population. This was a constant haunting realization that dominated my conscious hours during my term in office.*

Jimmy Carter turned ninety years old the year that Rosalynn and he traveled with Dr. Hicks and their other fishing buddies to fish the Ponoi River in Russia. The Soviet Union had collapsed more than two decades prior, ushering in a deceptively sleepy peace between the former Cold War adversaries, Russia and the United States. But just a few months prior to the Carters' fishing trip in 2014, Russia invaded Ukraine's Crimean Peninsula at the direction of President Vladimir Putin, who apparently has never abandoned hope of rebuilding Russia to its former Soviet glory.

Russian troops stormed Crimea's parliament, dismissed the government, and quickly declared under a disputed referendum that Crimea would permanently be annexed into Russia. Thereafter, Putin moved additional troops into the Crimean Peninsula and along the Russian borders surrounding Ukraine and inside the nation of Belarus, setting the stage for a second invasion into Ukraine in 2022 and the escalation of the most significant and longest-running military conflict in Europe since the Second World War.

...

Jimmy Carter's first aspiration was not to be President of the United States, nor was it to be a successful Georgia peanut farmer. Instead, it was to be a nuclear scientist and military strategist. As a young naval officer in 1953, Carter spent two hours in a grueling interview with Admiral Hyman Rickover, who developed and oversaw the US Navy's fleet of nuclear-powered ballistic missile submarines. Rickover was notorious for selecting only people to join his team who held what he called "extraordinary potential." During the interview process, Rickover was known to make interviewees sit in chairs whose front legs had been surreptitiously shortened so that the potential candidates for the program were constantly struggling to stay in their seats as he grilled them with questions on a variety of subjects until they eventually ran out of answers.

Carter recalled that he fielded questions about naval history and battle tactics as well as about literature, country music, and opera before Rickover finally asked the question that changed Jimmy Carter's life forever. Even though the future president had graduated in the top 10 percent of his class at the prestigious United States Naval Academy, Rickover asked bluntly, "Did you always do your best?" Carter struggled with the question. It was the first thing the admiral had asked that had absolutely stumped him. If he was being completely honest with himself, Jimmy Carter knew the answer that he had to give was, "No, sir." He knew there'd been times as a student when he could have given more but just didn't. The admiral eyed him sternly. "Why not?" Rickover asked. It was the first question in the interview to which Carter didn't have an adequate answer. From that day forward, Jimmy Carter vowed to always give his very best. *Why Not the Best?* became the title to his 1976 campaign autobiography, and in 2020, author Jonathan Alter used the phrase for the title of the only full-life biography of the president, *His Very Best: Jimmy Carter, A Life*.

Perhaps it was his honesty or some other glimmer of potential that the stern admiral saw in him, but Jimmy Carter was selected to work on Rickover's team where he was trained in nuclear physics and became a senior naval officer supervising development of the nuclear-powered submarine, the *Seawolf*. Carter worked 80-hour weeks under Rickover, and at one point was tapped to be the first person to lead a team on a secret mission into a nuclear reactor outside of the United States. The objective was to repair damages that threatened to leak radioactive wastewater into an adjacent river system with potentially grave consequences on the unsuspecting nearby human population.

Carter and his team bravely donned anti-contamination suits that likely provided scant protection and made the repairs to the damaged reactor with only passing regard to the potential lasting effects the radiation exposure might have had on them. Untold numbers of people who were never even aware they were in danger were saved by Carter's actions that day. It was a quiet, unsung act of heroism for which Jimmy Carter never took credit, even though it almost certainly would have helped him years later on the campaign trail. Not long after the incident inside the nuclear reactor, Jimmy Carter's naval career was unexpectedly cut short when he was forced to return to Plains to take over the family farm after the death of his father, accepting an honorable discharge from the navy.

As he ascended from successful peanut farmer to state senator to governor and finally to US president, Admiral Rickover's nagging question always followed Jimmy Carter, urging him no matter the circumstances not to waste a minute of his life and in every instance to give his very best.

As the only US president with direct knowledge of and firsthand experience with nuclear technology, Jimmy Carter was uniquely positioned both to understand the gravity of the nuclear threat and to discern the most strategic ways to combat it. During his presidency, the Soviets had far greater numbers of missiles and deployed more missile tests than the United States, but Carter understood that the United States had far superior technology in both weaponry and delivery systems. Unfortunately, while Jimmy Carter's administration secretly developed sophisticated weaponry to stay ahead of the Soviets, he was unfairly criticized for shutting down expensive inferior programs by people who were ignorant of the more advanced classified weapons in development that Carter could not yet disclose.

During the 1980 presidential debate, Ronald Reagan attacked President Carter for killing the bloated B-1 bomber program, claiming that it harmed the United States in its negotiations with the Russians. But what Jimmy Carter knew and couldn't say was that there were serious questions about the combat capability of the B-1 which was unnecessarily draining billions of much-needed dollars from the military budget, while the far superior—yet highly classified—B-2 stealth bomber was already in development. In hindsight, the B-2 stealth bomber arguably was the single most influential weapon delivery system in helping the United States win the arms race against Russia and end the Cold War.

In late November after Reagan had defeated Carter, the two men met during the transition period, and Jimmy Carter explained to the president-elect about the advancement of the B-2 stealth bomber and why the obscenely over-priced B-1 was obsolete and a gross misuse of taxpayer dollars. But by then Reagan had hemmed himself in with his former criticism of Carter over shuttering the B-1. Influenced by extensive lobbying from defense contractors who stood to make massive profits, Reagan revived the B-1 bomber program even though he knew it was an enormous waste that never would be used for its intended purpose.

Jimmy Carter also enlisted peaceful means to win the arms race and fight the Cold War that continued to pay dividends for the nation long after he left office, even though most of his initiatives ultimately inured to the political benefit of his successors who had chided him for his obsession with human rights and peace. But by shifting US foreign policy away from propping up often brutal anti-communist regimes in favor of protecting human rights, Carter demonstrated to the world and more importantly to the people living in the Soviet bloc that the United States stood on higher moral ground during the Cold War. In his inaugural address, Jimmy Carter outlined the new path forward for the United States at home and abroad, based on a "quiet strength" that he believed should stem more from a "nobility of ideas" than from a display of military prowess:

> *To be true to ourselves, we must be true to others. We will not behave in foreign places so as to violate our rules and standards here at home, for we know that the trust which our Nation earns is essential to our strength.*
>
> *The world itself is now dominated by a new spirit. Peoples more numerous and more politically aware are craving, and now demanding, their place in the sun—not just for the benefit of their own physical condition, but for basic human rights.*
>
> *The passion for freedom is on the rise. Tapping this new spirit, there can be no nobler or more ambitious task for America to*

undertake on this day of a new beginning than to help shape a just and peaceful world that is truly humane.

We are a strong nation, and we will maintain strength so sufficient that it need not be proven in combat—a quiet strength based not merely on the size of an arsenal but on the nobility of ideas.

We will be ever vigilant and never vulnerable, and we will fight our wars against poverty, ignorance, and injustice, for those are the enemies against which our forces can be honorably marshaled.

To spread the message, Jimmy Carter invested heavily in the free press, expanding the reach of radio transmission into Soviet countries by supporting infrastructure for Voice of America and Radio Free Europe. People listening behind the Iron Curtain began to crave freedom and democratic representation and to become more and more skeptical of the oppressive Soviet regime, slowly shifting the USSR toward reform from within.

Perhaps the most important measure President Carter took toward avoiding a nuclear war was his negotiation of the second Strategic Arms Limitations Treaty (SALT II) with Soviet President Brezhnev, essentially agreeing to numerical equality of nuclear weaponry between their respective nations. Talks with the country had begun years earlier between President Lyndon Johnson and Soviet Premier Alexei Kosygin and continued between Nixon and Breshnev, who negotiated the first agreement. While SALT I demonstrated a willingness on both sides to avoid a nuclear holocaust, the first treaty produced few concrete measures that could be agreed upon; both Nixon and Breshnev recognized the need to continue negotiating toward a more robust agreement.

As Jimmy Carter entered office, establishing a second treaty was his highest priority. Carter and Breshnev jointly signed the bilateral SALT II agreement at a summit in Vienna in 1979. While imperfect, SALT II successfully governed specific limitations and guidelines for nuclear disarmament and remained operative right up to the point that the Soviet Union began to collapse in the late 1980s.

Carter caught political heat for SALT II both by dovish critics who felt that it didn't go far enough toward mutual disarmament (under the agreement, both countries maintained an arsenal large enough to destroy the other) and by hawks who believed that the treaty surrendered the United States' chance of winning the arms race. The US Senate never ratified Carter and Breshnev's SALT II agreement. Neither did their Soviet counterparts. It was eventually withdrawn for legislative consideration after the Soviets invaded Afghanistan.

Nevertheless, the agreement between Carter and Brezhnev was honored by both of their successors and was the foundation for the mutually assured deterrence between the United States and the USSR for the better part of a decade. Ronald Reagan sharply criticized Carter for SALT II on the campaign trail, but as president, he abided by it and benefited politically from the peace it provided. In 1986, in the twilight of his presidency, President Reagan finally withdrew from SALT II in a demonstration that was pure political theater—the treaty had expired by its own terms one year earlier.

. . .

As Jimmy Carter contemplated the potential risk and devastating consequences of a nuclear war with the Soviet Union during his presidency, he often pored over Russian maps of Soviet naval bases. His fingers inevitably landed on two places more than any other: the Kamchatka Peninsula on the northeastern coast of the Pacific and the far northwestern city of Murmansk along the Arctic coastline in the Barents Sea. These two Russian ports on either end of the country provided the Soviet Union with the most direct access for launching submarines to attack the United States with nuclear warheads from either the Atlantic or the Pacific borders.

In 2004, the Carters and their fishing buddies visited Kamchatka in pursuit of some of the largest rainbow trout on the planet in the Zhupanova River, which cuts through some of the last great untouched wilderness on earth. Ten years later, they returned to Russia to fish the Ponoi on the Kola Peninsula east of Murmansk in what is considered the world's most productive Atlantic salmon habitat. The two places that had been the source of the president's greatest fear during his days in the White House eventually became the locations where he forged his fondest fishing memories.

. . .

Although I've never been to Russia, I have substantial experience fishing for rainbow trout as well as Atlantic salmon and can attest that both the numbers and sizes of fish that Jimmy, Rosalynn, Carlton, Wayne, and Bob caught on those trips is astounding. It is a testament to the quality of the wild habitat, the conservation and stewardship efforts of the people who manage those fisheries, and the exceedingly low fishing pressures in those areas. What is even more astounding to me, however, is that President Carter turned eighty the year that he fished the Zhupanova and ninety the year that he fished the Ponoi. Three years his junior, Rosalynn was seventy-seven on the first trip and eighty-seven on the second.

It takes immense stamina and physical fitness just to travel to such distant locations, riding in the back of decades-old Russian military transport helicopters, casting heavy two-handed spey rods, spending long days in open drift boats, standing in cold waters, fighting fish that hit the fly so hard the line jars the rod in your hand like an unruly Labrador jerking on its leash. It can take ten minutes to an hour to fight a large Atlantic salmon and just as long or longer to land a trophy rainbow trout.

Between the two of them on the Ponoi, the Carters caught over fifty Atlantic salmon during a week of fishing, two of which topped 16 pounds. To put that in perspective, that means that over the course of a week as they both approached their ninth decade on Earth, the president and first lady each spent two to five hours per day in a remote wilderness fighting salmon, not to mention fighting the ones that got away and the numerous smaller greyling and sea trout that they also caught as well as the effort exerted each day repeatedly casting to fish that never took the fly.

CHAPTER ELEVEN
ALASKA

ALASKA

CARLTON HICKS
~

In 2017, our group went to Alaska. Originally, I'd tried to plan a trip for us to go to Cuba for bonefish and for the president and me to try again to achieve our goal of catching and releasing a permit. But I just couldn't make it work. The logistics proved impossible. Maybe if we'd gone just one year earlier, it would've been a little easier. During his eight years in office, President Barack Obama greatly eased travel restrictions to Cuba. He renewed diplomatic relations between the two acrimonious nations and reopened the American Embassy in Havana. Jimmy Carter was the only other US president since the Cuban revolution in 1959 to see the wisdom in thawing the hostility with our country's closest island nation. Not coincidentally, during both Carter's and Obama's terms, the US enjoyed unprecedented peace and cooperation with Cuba—a country that once had brought us to the brink of nuclear war.

In 1977, President Carter reached an agreement of diplomatic exchange with Cuba, providing for a US office inside the Swiss Embassy in Havana and a Cuban office inside the Czech Embassy in Washington. It was a creative first step that allowed our governments to maintain an informal dialogue over the years. President Carter's measures opened the door for Obama to normalize diplomatic relations between the former enemies forty years later. Soon after President Obama left the White House in 2017, however, the next administration slammed the door shut again, opting for a policy of obstinate antagonism instead of moderate peace.

After banging my head against a wall trying to make the Cuba trip happen, we decided to switch gears. If we couldn't fish the waters of Ernest Hemingway's *Old Man and the Sea*, we would answer Jack London's *Call of the Wild*. One of President Carter's most memorable fishing trips happened in 1985 when he took his then 9-year-old grandson, Jason Carter, on the Copper River, which runs from the Wrangell Mountains down to the Gulf of Alaska. Just the two of them went alone. They fished for a week together deep within the Alaskan wilderness on what is perhaps the best river in all of North America for catching trophy rainbow trout. President Carter reminisced often about that trip. He told many stories from that trip over and over again, and I never got tired of hearing them.

President Carter caught his first thirty-inch wild rainbow on the very first day of his trip with Jason in 1985—unquestionably the most memorable fish of his lifetime. The president's heart leaped when the fish jumped clear out of the water and he realized just how large it really was. It took over an hour to finally get it in the net, and at times it took out all of the president's fly line and over 100 yards of backing. The giant rainbow measured nine inches around the girth and weighed 12 pounds. It was an old male fish with a hooked lower jaw that curved up under its nose. With trembling hands, the president released the fish from the net and watched it peacefully swim away. A replica of that thirty-inch rainbow trout hangs on the wall of his office at The Carter Center. As he watched that big fish disappear back into the Copper River, he felt sure he'd never catch another trout that big again. Decades later, on our trip to Kamchatka, he caught another wild rainbow over thirty inches long. Most anglers never even hope to catch a wild thirty-inch rainbow trout in their lifetimes. President Carter caught two.

The grandfather and grandson had many adventures together on that trip. From the plane, they watched beluga whales feeding on king salmon in the ocean near the mouth of the river. In addition to fly fishing for trout, they cast large silver-spoon lures with conventional spinning tackle for northern pike that they roasted in aluminum foil over an open fire and ate for dinner under the Alaskan night sky. They had a close encounter with a grizzly bear one day. After spotting the bear coming toward them, the president carefully maneuvered to stay between the bear and his young grandson, who watched carefully, remaining calm and still just as his grandfather had taught him. President Carter locked eyes with the big bear, unmoving, before it finally turned, disinterested, and lumbered away up a nearby hillside. One evening while fishing alone, the president saw a solitary gray wolf make its way across the tundra. It climbed up a rocky ledge where it lay down and curiously watched from a distance as the president continued to fish. Then, it continued on its way.

After hearing all of those stories over the years, I knew that if we couldn't get to Cuba, then there was probably no place the president would want to return to more than Alaska's Copper River. Both Rosalynn and the president came. We celebrated the Fourth of July on the banks of the river. Three days later we celebrated the Carters' 71st wedding anniversary. Their eldest son, Jack, turned 70 while we were there, so the Carters called and wished him a happy birthday. It was a week of celebrations. The Carters' son Chip and daughter-in-law Becky came with us on that trip. Jenny came, too. Bob Wilson also came and brought his son-in-law. To get there, we flew on a commercial flight to Anchorage and then boarded a smaller plane to fly south along the Kenai Peninsula before hopping in a seaplane with all of our gear and flying northeast straight up the Copper River where we landed on a lake and took our gear up to the remote cabin that became our home away from home for the week.

Something that struck me right away on that trip was my first realization that the Carters were finally beginning to show signs of their advanced age. It shouldn't have come as a surprise. President Carter was a few months away from turning ninety-three. Rosalynn was a few weeks from ninety. Less than two years prior to our trip, the president had survived a four-month battle with advanced melanoma that had metastasized to his liver and brain. It should have killed him. That he was even on the trip at all was a miracle. When they first diagnosed the cancer, doctors gave him just a few weeks to live. Rosalynn and he began to prepare for his funeral and notify their children and close friends. I remember getting that call. It hit me like a punch in the gut. But despite his terminal diagnosis, the president decided to battle cancer as he'd always battled everything else: head-on. He elected to undergo radiation treatment and volunteered to try a new drug therapy that, in theory, would unleash the full power of his body's own immune system to fight the cancer. And it worked. President Carter's miraculous recovery excited the oncology world. It reignited interest in cancer research, increased cancer philanthropy, and gave hope to people with cancer all over the world. I'd always looked up to him a bit like a wiser, stronger, tougher older brother. But after his defeat of terminal cancer, he seemed almost invincible to me.

I was a little taken aback when I saw the toll that our long day of travel and changing planes had on him. I shouldn't have been, but I was. I think it was the first time in all of our years together that I would describe the president as fatigued. Normally, on our trips even if we got there late in the day, the president would want to go out to the water and fish for a little bit or at least do some scouting. But on this trip, he needed to rest. Even so, in the morning, Rosalynn and he were among the first ones up and the first ones to put their waders on after breakfast and head down to the river. He'd always been like that on our trips: the first one up in the mornings and the first one out on the water. He was usually the last one to come in at the end of the day as well. He was always moving, full of focused energy. If he wasn't fishing, he was tying flies. If he wasn't tying flies, he was birdwatching. If he wasn't birdwatching, he was somewhere deep in conversation with someone about the native flora, fauna, the local people, and their history and culture. He was always particularly interested in their farming methods.

On our trips around the world, Rosalynn and he often went into the villages or towns to meet people where they worked; they visited with people in their homes, schools, churches, restaurants, or bars—wherever they happened to be. Rosalynn and the president were always intent on engaging with people, making new friends, and expanding their knowledge of new places. One of President Carter's mantras has always been that you should try to learn one new thing every day. He has stuck to it religiously all these years. Think about that for a second. The publication of this book is set to occur during the month of the president's 100th birthday. That's 36,500 days and 36,500 new things.

• • •

On one of his first casts that first morning, a giant rainbow rose and took the president's fly, running downstream. My guide and I were coming behind in the boat just as he hooked the fish, and you could hear the reel screaming as the fish stripped away the line. Before long, the fish took the president deep into his backing. I could tell right away that it was going to be a big fish, maybe even close to that big fish that he caught on his first day on the Copper River with Jason more than thirty years before. Because I'd noticed the president becoming tired the day before, I wondered if he'd have the stamina to fight the fish all the way to the net.

But I shouldn't have. The excitement of hooking the fish invigorated him, and he was up to the challenge. Over the years, he'd also learned different techniques about fighting fish, how to keep a deep bend in the spine of the rod near the butt section to put pressure on a fish, how to turn a fish's head in opposite directions from where it wants to go in order to tire it out quickly using horizontal pressure. The faster you can get a fish to the net, the less likely you are to stress the fish and cause it harm. After about thirty minutes, the fight was over. The fish was a gorgeous twenty-six-inch rainbow with a deep red stripe running the length of its body. It wasn't quite as big as the big fish he caught with Jason all those years ago, but it was close.

As the president leaned in to get a picture of the fish, I noticed that the Secret Service agent with him leaned in behind him and very gingerly placed his hands just above the president's hips to steady him and make sure he didn't fall in the water. That was the first time I'd ever seen anything like that on our trips. I had always known the president to be so strong and self-assured that I would never have imagined him needing or accepting any assistance up to that point. President Carter and Rosalynn had been very independent anglers all the years I'd known them. They never even let a guide or other person touch their fly rods while they were fishing, particularly if they had a fish on.

Sometimes novice or youth anglers require help casting, setting the hook, or landing a fish. Even with some intermediate anglers who shouldn't need help, I have on a few occasions seen guides cast the fly, set the hook, and fight the fish for a little while until it gets tired before handing the rod to their client for them to reel the fish in and snap a picture. But that would have been absolutely unheard of with the president or first lady. I honestly hate to think how President Carter or Rosalynn would react if a guide tried to help them bring in a fish. They might let a guide net a fish and even help hold a fish up for a picture and put it back in the water for them if it's the safest, most effective way to release the fish without overly stressing and harming it. But they would never let anybody help them cast to or catch a fish. It may be hard to imagine a 93-year-old cancer survivor standing in the middle of a river in a vast open wilderness and catching a giant rainbow trout like that, but he did it. That's all I can say. He did it. I saw it. If you look back over his lifetime and all the extraordinary things he accomplished, it's really not that hard to believe.

At the end of our week on the Copper River, we flew back the same way we came but in reverse. We took a float plane out of the camp and downriver. Then, we boarded an old single-engine turboprop passenger plane back to Anchorage, where we planned to spend the night in a hotel and fly home by commercial plane back to Georgia the next day. We were all pretty tired and ready to go to bed, but we were also hungry. So, we decided to have dinner at a pizza place the Secret Service agent picked out. And something remarkable happened while we were there.

The restaurant was crowded, packed mostly with younger people and families. There were women in hospital scrubs and more than a few men who looked like they'd just finished a full-day shift at a mill, maybe at an oil rig, or driving a truck, the primary industries in Anchorage. The serving staff all bustled about with big pizzas over their shoulders and pitchers of beer. It was loud with all the many conversations going on and music on the radio. At first, we thought we might be able to get by without anyone recognizing the Carters. Then, I noticed a few people casually getting up, walking by, and eyeing us before going back to their tables and whispering to one another.

When the Carters were in the White House, they'd been determined to preserve the Alaska wilderness. But the oil and timber companies were dead set against Jimmy Carter. It was just another example of the old adage, "No good deed goes unpunished"—which could apply in many ways to his entire presidency. President Carter suffered constant abuse throughout his presidential term from the Alaskan contingent. During his one visit to Alaska while in office, people lined up to jeer at him. The politicians and the lobbyists ran a pretty strong propaganda campaign against him, falsely convincing many hardworking people that the Carter Alaska Lands bill was going to take their jobs; the federal government was meddling in places it didn't belong. It didn't seem to matter that it was really just outside corporations seeking to line their shareholders' pockets who were amplifying that message with the help of high paid lobbyists and public relations consultants.

But all those years later on our way home from the Copper River, our little group was just tired and wanting to peacefully enjoy our pizza and a cold beer and go to bed. The last thing we wanted was to draw attention. Looking around the room, Rosalynn said, "Most of the people in here probably weren't even born when we passed the Alaska Lands bill. I wonder if they have any idea what Jimmy sacrificed for them." The president just kept eating his pizza.

Suddenly, a few people stood up and looked over at our table. They started clapping. Then, a few more stood up and started clapping. More people stood until everyone in the room was on their feet clapping, whistling, and cheering during an impromptu standing ovation for Jimmy Carter that lasted several minutes.

It brought tears to my eyes and to Rosalynn's eyes, too. I looked over at her, and her lip was quivering as she tried not to cry. Jenny teared up. I think we were all moved. The president looked around the room, smiled, and waved. I could tell the gesture was really good for him. You could see it in his face. A few people came up to the table to shake his hand. Before we left, the president went back into the kitchen and visited with the cooks, the servers, the dishwashers, and the rest of the restaurant crew. It was a fitting end to a long saga and a resounding answer to Rosalynn's question. The following day, we got up early to catch our flight back home to Georgia.

JIM BARGER JR.

Jimmy Carter's dogged determination to protect the Alaskan wilderness may very well prove to be his most enduring legacy.

Since Dwight D. Eisenhower, every president had struggled to define and implement land use practices in Alaska, balancing the interests of the many varied human stakeholders. Carter's position was comparatively simple: let nature take its course. Implementing that strategy, however, turned out to be incredibly difficult and contentious. President Carter made safeguarding the Alaskan wilderness a top priority early in his time in office. "I paid close attention to this extremely complex issue during my entire term," he reflected in annotations to his diary years later. "It provoked intense struggles among the state government, private landowners, Indians, Inuits, hunters, fishermen, timber interests, environmentalists, the oil industry, and their highly paid lobbyists in Washington."

The pages of his presidential diary are littered with descriptions of frustrating and ultimately fruitless meetings he conducted in the White House throughout his term confronting Alaska Senators Ted Stevens and Mike Gravel and others who vehemently opposed Carter's efforts to safeguard Alaska's wild spaces. "The two senators were aligned with oil and other commercial interests, and I was determined to set aside large areas for forestry, parks, and wilderness areas," he explained. There was little room for compromise between the two factions. While Jimmy Carter ultimately won the legislative showdown over the fate of Alaska that since has paid unsurpassed dividends for the state and the nation, in the short term his relentless determination to preserve the Alaskan wilderness proved to be just one more factor that set the political power structure in Washington against him and helped doom his chances of reelection.

At the end of his term in 1980, Carter finally succeeded in defying the powerful oil and gas lobby by establishing the Alaska National Interest Lands Conservation Act, preserving over 150 million acres of wilderness for posterity. No president before or since has come anywhere close to protecting as much land, more than 30 percent of our nation's wilderness. The achievement came at a high political cost and the effort dragged through his entire four years of office, drawing passionate responses from otherwise historically disenfranchised supporters and conversely from extremely powerful detractors who were accustomed to getting their way. Native Americans gathered in droves in the nation's capital to support President Carter's efforts. In a sacred ceremony, the Tlingit tribe welcomed the president as an honorary member into the Raven/Beaver Clan, renaming him "Haa Hoo Woo," a traditional title describing a chief who protects the natural world.

But back in Alaska, angry opponents of the president's conservation efforts who hoped to profit from untapped Alaskan oil reserves hung and burned Jimmy Carter in effigy. When President Carter traveled to the Lorraine Motel in Memphis in 1978 to place a wreath at the sight where the Reverend Martin Luther King Jr. had been assassinated ten years earlier, Alaska Congressman Don Young retorted that Jimmy Carter's proposed Alaskan lands bill was a violation of his constituents' human rights, comparing it to the oppression MLK fought in the Jim Crow South. In the summer of 1979, Carter made plans to stop and "see my friends" in Alaska on his way to Japan for the G7 Summit, to which one advisor dryly quipped, "Well, that won't take long." The president's visit was greeted by protestors and a chilly reception from Senator Stevens, who claimed that Jimmy Carter had "declared war on Alaska." Senator Gravel didn't show up at all. "I presume he only goes back to Alaska on election year," Carter jotted in his diary that day. As *Air Force One* touched down in Anchorage, one of Jimmy Carter's aides jokingly presented him with a mule driver's whip in case he needed "to whip somebody's ass." The following year, at the state fair in Fairbanks, people paid to throw bottles at pictures of Jimmy Carter or the Ayatollah Khomeini; the pile of glass shards under Carter's picture by the end of the fair was noticeably higher than Khomeini's.

Today, the Alaskan wilderness preserved by Carter is widely considered to be one of our nation's greatest assets, an area of global significance not unlike the Amazon rainforest, providing a baseline ecosystem for wildlife populations, sequestering carbon, and mitigating the ongoing warming of our planet and the mass extinction of species. Jimmy Carter's commitment to preserving the Alaskan wilderness not only demonstrated his long-term strategy for environmental stewardship in that state, but it also was a continuation of his consistent commitment to the preservation of natural spaces throughout his lifetime that can be traced back to his earliest moments in politics.

As a young state senator, Jimmy Carter supported the passage of Georgia's Coastal Marshlands Protection Act, a seminal piece of legislation that protects Georgia's 100-mile coastline. He was a charter member of the Georgia Conservancy, and he created the Georgia Heritage Trust, protecting—among many other wild spaces—the ancient stand of native cypress at Lewis Island near the Altamaha Delta that contains some of the oldest living trees in the country dating back to the Early Middle Ages. He prevented the Flint River from being dammed, ultimately safeguarding the entire watershed from its farthest reaches in north Georgia all the way down to Florida's Apalachicola Basin and the Gulf of Mexico.

During his four years as governor, Carter vetoed numerous applications to drain Georgia swamps, protecting one of the state's most vital but unsung natural resources, the freshwater wetlands. His efforts first as governor and later as president safeguarded the Chattahoochee River from its headwaters in the Southern Appalachians down to metro Atlanta, where it was in danger from contamination by proposed sewer lines and unchecked urban sprawl. He designated the Chattooga River as a wild and scenic river, safeguarding the river from damming and preventing development along all fifty-seven miles of the river. These weren't just sweeping acts by a remote politician sitting behind a desk, either. Jimmy Carter spent countless hours fishing the Chattahoochee, and he and friend Claude Terry were the first people ever to tandem canoe the harrowing white water of the Chattooga's Bull Sluice rapid.

During his four-year presidency, Carter designated 56 million acres of wilderness for protection under the Antiquities Act. The only president to protect more land in that manner was Teddy Roosevelt, who originally signed the Act in 1906. Carter's example inspired future presidents George W. Bush and Barack Obama to expand use of the Antiquities Act to the world's oceans, together preserving over half a billion acres of marine habitat. President Carter established our nation's Superfund, which continues to mandate cleanup of hazardous waste sites throughout the country in the ongoing fight for environmental justice and has saved untold numbers of lives of Americans who otherwise would have been poisoned by toxic contamination. He more than doubled the size of our national park system, created thirty-nine new national parks scattered throughout the country, and passed the Surface Mining Control & Reclamation Act to prohibit mining within or adjacent to our national parks. Carter saved California's redwood forest and giant sequoias, national treasures that have stood for thousands of years but were threatened in the 1970s by unbridled adjacent clear-cutting.

Jimmy Carter was among the first world leaders to consider the impending threat of climate change. He signed the National Energy Act and established the Department of Energy, the two most critical ongoing initiatives to diversify our nation's energy supply and prioritize alternative fuel sources. Long before discussions of climate change had become mainstream or were on the agendas of world leaders or even many scientists, President Carter commissioned studies of the issue which produced prescient warnings. One of those reports created during his first year in office entitled, "Release of Fossil CO_2 and the Possibility of a Catastrophic Climate Change," caused him grave concern and led to his commissioning the "Global 2000 Report to the President." The report predicted the effects on the planet by the year 2000 if climate change went unaddressed and was intended to be used by Carter and future administrations. Forty years before the United Nations Paris Climate Conference came to the consensus that global temperatures needed to be capped at 2 degrees Celsius, President Carter's "Global 2000 Report" made the same recommendation.

Addressing the nation in 1977, Jimmy Carter attempted to lay out both the problem and the solution. "We must not be selfish or timid if we hope to have a decent world for our children and our grandchildren," he said. Using exhaustive data and facts, he outlined ten guiding principles in addressing climate change that balanced economic growth, conservation, environmental protection, and cooperation among government, corporate, and individual interests. He set seven specific achievable goals, prioritizing conservation while establishing petroleum reserves and making specific reductions in energy demands, gasoline usage, and oil imports. He set goals for alternative fuel development and usage, calling for improved insulation on new construction of buildings and solar energy usage for over two million American homes.

"We simply must balance our demand for energy with our rapidly shrinking resources," he said. "By acting now we can control our future instead of letting the future control us." No succeeding president referenced the "Global 2000 Report" after Jimmy Carter left office. Although President Obama made significant strides toward addressing climate change, his successor rolled back those efforts and broke the legally binding promises the United States had made to almost 200 other nations that our country would reduce our greenhouse gas emissions.

Despite pushback and tepid reception for the issue politically, President Carter passed legislation to encourage the research and use of alternative fuels and even led by example by installing solar panels on the roof of the White House. After the Carters vacated the presidential residence, Ronald Reagan eventually had the solar panels removed, and his chief of staff told the press the panels were "just a joke." Criticizing Carter's environmental measures on the campaign trail, Reagan falsely denied the harmful effects of coal, gasoline, and other pollutants, bizarrely claiming that "80% of nitrogen oxide pollutants in the air come from trees." During his eight-year tenure, Reagan cut funding for alternative energy research by two-thirds, and his failure to heed Carter's warnings doomed the country to rely on fossil fuels and remain beholden to oil-rich nations in the Middle East. At the same time, the earth steadily continued to warm, and sea levels steadily continued to rise.

President Carter's environmental efforts were part of his lifelong commitment to a world he believed both mysteriously created by a watchful God and also the complex product of billions of years of evolution, shaped by and shaping the humans and other creatures inhabiting it. At ninety-four, Jimmy Carter expounded in *Faith: A Journey for All* on his unique perspective on the interplay between human and natural history gleaned from nearly a century of direct observation, intensive scientific study, and critical examination of his personal religious faith informed by his daily search for guidance and wisdom in the Christian Bible:

> *We know that evolution is a global process, usually progressive, that results from the adaptation of living organisms to natural selection and sudden mutations. I believe it has been God's plan to evolve human beings, and that after thousands of centuries we now find ourselves uniquely endowed with an understanding of who and what we are and have the knowledge and freedom to help shape our own destiny.*

President Carter anguished over our abuse of the planet; yet with his signature optimism tempered by realism, he maintained hope and faith in its resilient potential. "I am confident that the earth itself will remain basically the same, continuing to shape the lives of its owners, for good or ill, as it has for millennia," he wrote in *An Hour Before Daylight*. Jimmy Carter's unparalleled environmental legacy has stood firm for more than half a century, helping safeguard the earth for future generations despite relentless attacks by politicians and profiteers who would treat the earth as a temporary commodity for immediate gain.

CHAPTER TWELVE
YUCATAN

YUCATAN

CARLTON HICKS

We took our last fly-fishing trip out of the country in April 2018. After the Alaska trip the year before, I emailed and asked, "Mr. President, would you like me to go ahead and put together another trip for us this year?" Never one to waste words, President Carter replied succinctly, "Yes, maybe closer." After all our years together, I understood his message to mean, "Not as far as Alaska, please." The travel from the previous year's trip had taken a lot out of him.

Despite being in his nineties and having survived brain cancer, President Carter remained extraordinarily physically fit for his age. His mental acuity remained far superior to that of anyone I'd ever known. He was still sharp as a tack. Nevertheless, I realized how hard the extended travel had become for him, especially the long flights and days spent in and out of airports and overnights in hotel rooms in connecting cities. Just getting to some of these far-flung international locations sapped the strength and energy he needed to enjoy the fishing.

It occurred to me that saltwater fly fishing in the Caribbean or Central America might offer exciting adventures without the long flight times. I knew the president and Rosalynn had enjoyed some trips to the Bahamas for bonefishing. He had also gone saltwater fly fishing in the British Virgin Islands with his friend Jack Crawford, Georgia's former game and fish commissioner. And, of course, we'd had great times fishing for bonefish together in Venezuela and Honduras. But I also knew he'd never caught the most elusive fish in all of fly fishing: the permit.

Catching a permit remained an unfulfilled item on our bucket lists. We had hoped to catch a permit during our trip to Honduras in 2010, but both came up empty-handed. I'd wanted to get us a shot by going to Cuba, but I couldn't make the logistics work to get us there. Relatively few people have accomplished the feat of catching a permit on the fly, which is well-known as one of the hardest achievements in all of fly fishing. If we were ever going to do it, now was the time. I don't want to say that time was running out on us, but it was running out on our chance to catch a permit on the fly! It's a feat that many of the most experienced anglers take years and even decades to achieve, with many more never accomplishing it at all.

The greatest achievement in all of fly fishing is to catch the "grand slam," which consists of catching a bonefish, a tarpon, and a permit, all on the fly—and for the purists, all in the same day. One of the best places to pursue a grand slam is in Ascension Bay. This area in the southern part of the Yucatan Peninsula has large concentrations of bonefish, both resident and migratory tarpon, and some of the most productive permit waters in the world.

The permit is by far the hardest of the three fish in the grand slam to catch on the fly. Bonefish can be extremely stealthy, and big tarpon are arguably the most difficult to fight, catch, and release. But the permit is notoriously picky; they won't even give you a chance to fight them because they rarely eat a fly. The president and I had both caught many bonefish over the years as well as a fair number of tarpon. Neither of us had ever caught a permit, though, and the urge to do so was nagging both of us.

A travel agency specializing in saltwater fly fishing confirmed that our best bet for permit was Ascension Bay. Getting there was an adventure in itself, but the president was pleased with the three-hour nonstop flight from Georgia, a far shorter flight time than it took us to get to Alaska. We flew into Cancun, Mexico, and drove about an hour and a half south. A large portion of the ride was on an incredibly bumpy one-way road through dense jungle to the Sian Ka'an Biosphere Reserve. There, a local boatman took us in a traditional wooden panga on about a one hour trip through mangrove flats and open bays to the very end of the inland waterway and the sleepy coastal village of Punta Allen.

As I chatted with the president on the trip, I said, "My first goal is for you to catch a permit, because I know you've never caught one." I quickly added, "My second goal is for me to catch a permit, because—as you know—neither have I!" I knew my comments would stir his competitive nature. The president doesn't like to be outfished by anyone. The only person who was possibly more competitive was Rosalynn. Of course, Rosalynn was an outstanding angler who often caught more fish and the largest fish of any of us, including the president. While he was always quite proud of his wife's fly-fishing skills, President Carter still didn't like for anyone to outfish him. He was fond of boasting that he could usually outfish Rosalynn—but only if he fished twice as long as she did!

Unfortunately, Rosalynn couldn't join us on this last trip. She had not been feeling well and wasn't up to it. The upside was I had more time to fish with the president. Normally, Rosalynn and he shared a boat when we were saltwater fly fishing or doing freshwater float trips for trout. Or, if we were hiking or wade fishing somewhere, they would generally wander off to be together alone. Sometimes, you'd find them just lying on the beach with hats over their eyes holding hands, napping. Of course, we all spent time together in the evenings, preparing dinner, cleaning up, or sitting around and telling fishing stories.

On this last trip, the president and I fished together every day. I will always cherish the days we spent together on the panga out in the wide expanse of Ascension Bay. We often sat silently, searching the water for fish, and wondering whether the other person was concentrating solely on the fishing or thinking of something else. It thrilled me to watch him cast to a school of bonefish that were dipping their noses into the sand in search of crabs. We knew at any moment that a fish burrowed in the sand might strike, send a reel screaming, and zip across the flat.

Time together on a flats skiff can be both exciting and pretty mundane. Usually, if not out wading, you take turns fishing from the bow of the skiff and get to watch each other fish and see one another's successes and failures. When you aren't fishing, you're just eating sandwiches under the hot sun, looking up at the seabirds circling in the sky. But those are special times, too. We talked not only about fishing but also all that we'd been through together, the good times and the hard times. We covered all that the president accomplished during his time in office and in the years that followed. It was a privilege to spend those moments with him.

Sometimes we talked about the difficulties he faced as president and the obstacles that had been put in his path. He was more contemplative about those things than I ever was. He sought to learn from them, and with the benefit of time, he was forgiving about them. He wasn't one to dwell on or fume on past failures or frustrations. And he wasn't the type to harbor grievances, either. On the other hand, as his friend, I still hold grudges over wrongs his political opponents committed, which is all part of the game of politics, I guess. Some things that happened back then went too far for me. They didn't just hurt President Carter and his political agenda but also fundamentally hurt the nation and its citizens and undermined our democracy.

There is policy, and then there is character. People should be able to differ and change their views on policy, but character should never be compromised. I believe no other leader of this country has had greater character than President Carter, which makes it all the more frustrating that his political opponents compromised their character to undermine him.

For instance, I could never get President Carter to explicitly discuss it, but there's no doubt in my mind that he always believed that the Reagan administration negotiated a deal with Iran to continue to hold the hostages until after the election in 1980 so that Carter would appear feckless and so the electorate could be swayed in Reagan's favor. I certainly believed that all along. I pressed the president about it a number of times, and the closest he ever came to openly discussing it with me was to tell me to read a book called *October Surprise: The American Hostages in Iran and the Election of Ronald Reagan*. In the book, Columbia professor and Middle East expert Gary Sick, who served on the US National Security Council under Ford, Carter, and Reagan, recounts how Reagan's eventual CIA director, William Casey, devised a plot during the months running up to the 1980 election to prolong the imprisonment of the hostages to help Reagan sink Carter.

It's pretty hard to fathom that anyone would betray their own country like Casey and his minions did and allow those fifty-two American hostages to continue to languish as political prisoners in Iran just to persuade people to vote for their presidential candidate. Eventually, the weight of what they had done became too much to bear for at least one of the men involved. Right after President Carter was admitted to hospice in the spring of 2023, lifelong political operative Ben Barnes had a crisis of conscience and confessed his part in the scheme to Peter Baker, a reporter for the *New York Times*. Barnes described how at Casey's behest, he and John Connolly—a former Texas Democratic governor who switched parties and became a titan of the Republican establishment and key advisor to Nixon and Reagan—traveled throughout the Middle East in the summer of 1980 to meet with Arab leaders and persuade them to urge Iran not to release the hostages before the US election.

"History needs to know that this happened," Barnes admitted in the article. "I think it's so significant and I guess knowing the end is near for President Carter put it in my mind more and more. I just feel like we've got to get it down some way."

When I read those words in the *New York Times*, I was shocked that someone in Reagan's camp finally came clean. Of course, with all of the political scandal and intrigue these days, I don't think it even raised many eyebrows even though it is one of the most astonishing admissions of disloyalty to our nation—encouraging a foreign country to hold American citizens hostage! The day after Baker's article ran in the *New York Times*, though, the world seemed to just move on to the next news cycle. No one from the Republican Party even bothered to deny it or apologize.

Every generation has its political scandals, I guess, and the future generations just move on to the next scandal. To me, Barnes' admission confirmed my long-held suspicions and made me angry all over again. Surely it angered President Carter, too, but if it did he never said so to me. And I gave him plenty of opportunities, because I harped on it a lot. I guess that he'd learned over the years not to allow the past to disturb him. And, of course, his Christian faith mandated not only that he forgive his enemies but also that he actually love them—something I remain very conflicted about myself.

Those American diplomats were forced to live blindfolded in isolation for over a year, and US soldiers died trying to rescue them. Now we know for certain that people conspired with our nation's enemies to prolong the hostage crisis to sabotage the Carter presidency. There has actually been an open confession. I'm sorry if that is something that I find nearly impossible to forgive. On top of that, they lied about it for almost half a century and were never held accountable. It still makes my blood boil. You hear the phrase "Never forget" bandied around a lot. Well, I will never forget that Republican political operatives were complicit with our enemies during the hostage crisis in Iran. I was tempted to call the president and ask him what he thought of Barnes' confession, but I didn't.

...

President Carter usually steered our conversations to more positive things like his work with The Carter Center to eradicate infectious diseases. I remember when he first told me that Rosalynn and he planned to address the scourge of guinea worm, a crippling disease that infected millions. It seemed like an insurmountable task. When the Carters learned that the disease was preventable, they made it their goal to eradicate it. It's mind-boggling to me that my friends saw a problem that seemed unfixable, set out to fix it anyway, and ended up saving millions of lives.

As an optometrist, I've always encouraged the president's interest in eye health. When he was in the White House in 1978, I was honored to stand beside him in the Oval Office as he signed the annual proclamation designating the first full week in March as "Save Your Vision Week." Later, I listened to him passionately tell me how Rosalynn and he were working with The Carter Center to address the tens of millions of cases of river blindness in the world and how they also provided healing treatment for millions of cases of trachoma, an infectious eye disease caused by flies that burrow into the eyelids. Once infected, the eyelids become inverted and essentially sand away the cornea every time the eye blinks. It is one of the leading causes of blindness in the world and is excruciating for those who suffer from it. In rural areas like where the Carters and I grew up in Georgia, trachoma was quite common. It primarily affects people in the Southern Hemisphere today, and The Carter Center is determined to eradicate it everywhere.

President Carter and I often discussed the importance of regular eye exams and how they can lead to early detection and prevention of a host of health problems, from visual impairments to heart disease and diabetes. The Carters and I shared a common belief that access to health care, including preventable medicine, is a basic human right that should be available to everyone everywhere. While many people like me profess those beliefs, the Carters put their beliefs into action. I was the president's and first lady's optometrist for most of their lives and can attest that while their eyes aged, their shared vision never faltered. Their vision of a world where nations peacefully coexist, where governments are accountable to the people, and where preventable diseases are eradicated was their legacy and gift to all of us.

. . .

One night, after a long day of fishing out in Ascension Bay while having dinner back at the lodge in Punta Allen, President Carter just blurted right out of the blue to everyone, "I'm going to speak at Liberty University." There was absolutely no transition in the conversation at all, and we were all quite taken aback. Someone had just finished telling a fishing story of some sort and there'd been a slight lull in the conversation. I guess it had been something on the president's mind that he'd been waiting for the right time to share with us. "President Falwell asked me to come speak there and give the graduation address."

"What?!" I said.

John Moores looked at me. He and I raised our eyebrows at the president as if to say, "Have you lost your mind?"

"No," the president responded, receiving our unspoken protestation loud and clear. "They've invited me to speak and they're gonna let me speak on any subject I want to—so I'm gonna take them up on it."

For Jimmy Carter to agree to deliver the commencement address at Liberty University was like Daniel going into the lion's den. Only President Carter wasn't being thrown in like Daniel; he was going in willingly. Televangelist Jerry Falwell Sr., who founded Liberty University, was Jimmy Carter's polar opposite, even though they both supposedly lived by the strict tenets of the Bible. If that isn't proof that people bring their own interpretations to religious texts, then I don't know what is. Falwell built his entire empire championing Jim Crow laws and railing against desegregation. His whole conception of the ironically-named Liberty University was to perpetuate segregation in education. This is the man who infamously called the 1964 Civil Rights Act the "Civil Wrongs Act." Even after eventually desegregating his privately-owned schools, Reverend Falwell simply redirected his venom toward people based upon their gender or sexual orientation, taking particular aim at women and what he believed should be their limited role in society and limited access to health care. Falwell had always been highly critical of President Carter, particularly for affirming equal rights for LGBTQ+ people.

Now, all these years later, President Carter was casually telling us that he planned to speak at the college Falwell had founded, the same place that had given a standing ovation to Donald Trump a year earlier. I couldn't believe it! But the more I listened to President Carter explain why he was going, the more I realized, as always, that I shouldn't have been surprised. That was exactly the type of thing he would do, that he'd always done. Of course he would relish the chance to speak to an auditorium filled with people on the opposite end of the political spectrum and try to win them over.

A few weeks after our trip to the Yucatan, President Carter gave the commencement address. When I had the chance to read the president's remarks later, it all made sense. He was gracious, of course, but he led by recalling to the students that in the 1970s he'd received troves of angry letters from Liberty University students and professors lambasting him for actions he took as president, everything from "my giving away our Panama Canal, or forming what they considered to be an unnecessary new Department of Education, or normalizing diplomatic relations with the communist government of China."

Then, he told them about his background as a child of the Depression in the segregated South, the only white boy among his group of Black friends. He recalled how he felt that "the only ranking among us then was who could run fastest, had just caught the biggest fish, or could pick the most cotton in a day." He talked about his college years at the Naval Academy and his experience as a nuclear physicist on submarines. He told the evangelical audience about his experience going door-to-door in 1968 in Lock Haven, Pennsylvania, and Springfield, Massachusetts, and sharing his faith as a Baptist missionary with a Cuban-American named Eloy Cruz who was assigned to be his partner on those missions. Cruz taught him the simple statement he tried to live by for the rest of his life. "I try to have two loves in my heart," said Cruz. "One love is for God, and the other love I have in my heart is for the person who happens to be in front of me at any particular time."

He told them that the biggest challenge he faced while president was "the great disparity in wealth between the richest people and those who still worked for a living with their families." And he explained that it has only gotten worse. "Right now, for instance," he said. "Eight people (six of them Americans) control more wealth than the poorest 3.5 billion—half of the world's total population." Then, he ticked off the litany of problems the world faces, chief among them human rights, the abuse of women and girls, skyrocketing imprisonment here and around the world, the environmental devastation and exploitation of the earth, the renewed threat of nuclear war, and the division of all of the world's major religions that have proven powerless to address the problems we face.

I'm pretty sure those weren't the types of things the audience had heard the year before from Donald Trump. Most of us live in an echo chamber these days and never sit respectfully and listen to someone speak hard truths that we don't want to hear. Who was going to remind these young graduating students from Liberty University of their duty to address issues of equity, poverty, and justice if not Jimmy Carter?

"Despite all these challenges that I've already outlined, maybe to your discouragement," he said, "as a Christian, I believe that the ultimate fate of human beings will be good, with God's love prevailing." Then, he ended by telling them that they had a choice that no one could take from them and that no one could make for them:

> *Everyone decides: 'This is the kind of person I choose to be.' We decide whether we tell the truth or benefit from telling lies. We're the ones that decide: 'Do I hate? Or am I filled with love?' We're the ones who decide: 'Will I think only about myself, or do I care for others?' We ourselves make these decisions, and no one else.*

• • •

I don't think any of us realized then that our time in the Yucatan would be our last trip together. We had good fishing every day in Ascension Bay. We caught an awful lot of bonefish, but no tarpon, and no permit. Most of the permit that we saw were on the surface. President Carter casted to them but never hooked one. He never even got them to follow or show any interest. They just spooked and ran away or ignored his fly altogether. I didn't catch a permit, either, but I did hook one briefly that I never saw. My guide took me to an area of the bay where we casted to permit in deeper water, not up on the flats. He could see the fish in the darker depths, even though I couldn't see it. The guide told me when and where to cast, and I did exactly as he said. Sure enough, I got a strike. I never saw the permit, though—only felt it on the line for just a second or two before it broke off an eighteen-pound leader and was gone.

JIM BARGER JR.

Jimmy Carter never caught a permit. In late spring of 2018, at the age of ninety-three, he traveled to the remote waters of Ascension Bay in the Southern Yucatan on what would be the last angling adventure of his lifetime. The trip's primary purpose was stalking the most wary, the most finicky, and pound-for-pound, the most challenging fighting fish of the saltwater shallows.

Sight casting to a permit without spooking it, fooling the fish into eating a handful of feathers tied together to approximate a small sand crab, properly setting the hook in the permit's extraordinarily tough jaw, and then fighting the angry fish to hand is an extremely low-probability aspiration. Most anglers never even try. It's the mountain climber's K2, the distance runner's Barkley Marathons, the thru-hiker's Appalachian Trail, the birdwatcher's Big Year. For even the most skilled and experienced angler at peak fitness and ability, catching a permit on the fly is often a losing proposition.

A. J. McClane, author of *McClane's New Standard Fishing Encyclopedia*—the eponymous 1,156-page tome many consider to be the definitive word on all things angling—spent four years fly fishing for permit on the famed flats near Deep Water Cay in the Bahamas back in the 1970s. McClane was a pioneer of saltwater fly fishing and an expert fly caster, known to have been among the first to perfect the double-haul cast. This involved making pulls with the line hand on both the back and forward cast to increase line speed and shoot the fly line at great distances with tight loops. Effortlessly and with uncanny accuracy, McClane was consistently able to cast ninety feet of fly line, plus an additional eight feet of leader, and twenty or more feet of backing, with gear that is considered practically primitive compared to twenty-first-century fly rod and line technology. Of course, it should go without saying that he also had an encyclopedic knowledge of tackle, rods, reels, fly lines, fly leaders, tippets, fly designs, knots, fish habitat, tidal influences, weather patterns, and ichthyology in general. If anyone was qualified to catch a permit on the fly, it was A. J. McClane. During his first four years of fly fishing for permit around Deep Water Cay, one of the most productive saltwater habitats in the world, he landed only two.

In his fifth year of hunting for permit there, McClane spotted a large shadow drifting across a long white sand flat. He quietly slipped out of his boat and began to stalk the unsuspecting fish, hunched over to keep from being seen, steadily cutting the distance from 150 yards down to his casting range of around 100 feet, ever careful not to spook it. Quietly, he peeled line from the reel, made just one backcast, double-hauled, and shot the line out in front of the large fish. His tiny crab fly dropped softly into the water. He gave it a few quick strips before lifting the rod and sinking the hook into the jaw of a massive permit that immediately began to run like hell.

Water sprayed in violent white lines behind the big permit as it ripped across the flat with McClane high-stepping after it. It was a large, mature fish, likely weighing 30 to 40 pounds. The fight covered some half a mile and took almost an hour, with the fish dragging the weary angler all over the flat. The permit finally frayed the leader against some rough coral heads and broke free, leaving McClane with nothing but a limp line in his hands. Drenched in sweat and saltwater, quivering from a mix of adrenaline and exhaustion, the weary angler smiled and said, "If we caught every one of these [permit] we hooked, we'd never fish for them."

That's a permit fly angler for you. They cherish epic failure as much or perhaps even more than they relish success. The very reason that some of us love to fly fish for permit is because we expect to fail most of the time. Maybe it's also because permit can't be caught on a fly without a bit of luck. Fortune. Providence. Whatever you want to call it. Sometimes when you're standing on the bow of a skiff looking out over a vast open sea under a sweltering sun, you feel God shining down on you. Nobody deserves to catch a permit on the fly. No matter how skilled you are. Every permit ever caught was a gift from heaven.

Jack Samson, longtime editor-in-chief of *Field & Stream* when it was still in its heyday of being the most widely-read and influential outdoor magazine in the world, caught a permit on the fly on his very first try. Obsessed thereafter, he spent the next ten years chasing permit with a fly rod before he caught his second. In 1996, after almost thirty years of fly fishing for permit, Samson published the first book on the subject, authoritatively titled *Permit on a Fly*. My copy is heavily dog-eared and full of pencil notations. The blurb on the back says:

> *It takes a certain type of fly fisherman to fish for permit: It takes one who doesn't mind not catching fish. It takes a saltwater fly rodder who can spend days, weeks, and months on the flats in the broiling sun and whipping wind—with very little chance of reward.*

Not exactly subject matter that is going to appeal to a wide variety of readers or a book likely to fly off the shelves. Samson's *Permit on a Fly* has been out of print for twenty-eight years. The book devotes an entire chapter to the waters of Ascension Bay—where Dr. Hicks and President Carter had their last adventure together in 2018. Yet, at the time of its publication, Samson confessed that after many trips to those permit-rich waters south of Punta Allen, he had yet to catch a permit there.

It would take another two decades before anyone else would gather enough information or take the time to write another book solely dedicated to all the aspects of fly fishing for permit. Jonathan Olch published his two-volume treatise, *A Passion for Permit*, in 2016. Olch has spent the better part of fifty years traveling to the far reaches of the globe in search of permit, and his book takes up more pages on the subject of fly fishing for this single species than A. J. McClane wrote in his massive encyclopedia covering every type of fishing for every type of fish in the entire world. Astoundingly beautiful, obsessively researched, and thoroughly comprehensive, Olch's textbook is destined to become a collector's item. And, like Samson's *Permit on the Fly*, it likely won't see a second printing. This is the nature of fly fishing for permit: It only appeals to a strange, select, obsessive few, most of whom are flagellants.

So, why would Jimmy Carter—who had spent almost fifty years trying to shake the sting of his failed 1980 presidential reelection campaign—again court failure and everlasting disappointment by ending his otherwise storied angling career trying to catch a fish that was almost certain to elude him? He could have chosen many more likely adventures for his last fishing trip, ones that would have offered near-certain success coupled with soul-stirring nostalgia as he reflected on his life as the longest-living president in United States history.

President Carter could have revisited the Soque River in North Georgia where he'd caught countless trophy-sized trout. He could have returned to the waters of his childhood to cast popping bugs to redbreast sunfish on Choctahatchee Creek, happily reminiscing about his beloved friend Rachel Clark, the sharecropper who helped raise him in the Depression-era South and who was the "finest fisher" he'd ever known. He could have gone to the Okefenokee Swamp as he did on trips with his father and their fishing buddy, Lem Griffis, who told tales of catching "so many fish they had to haul in water to fill up the hole left" by the void.

All of these high-probability experiences were within safe striking distance of his home in Plains. Instead, approaching 100 years old and just a few years after battling brain cancer, President Carter chose to travel thousands of miles, braving near impenetrable jungle, before venturing into a vast aquatic wilderness in a small panga skiff after a fish he knew was nearly impossible to catch.

It's tempting to surmise that President Carter's choice to chase the elusive permit as his final quarry was an indication that he'd come to the enlightened conclusion that catching fish isn't the point of fishing. Outdoor writer and environmentalist Michael Baughman tells a story in his classic steelhead fishing book, *A River Seen Right*, of encountering an elderly fly fisherman on the North Umpqua River in Oregon. As Baughman watched from a high bank, the old man raised two nice steelhead from the upper end of a clear pool only to miss both fish and watch them swim away. Afterward, the old man showed Baughman the flies he'd been using and how he'd clipped off the points so that they could only elicit strikes with no way of hooking or catching the fish that rose and tried to eat them. Confused, Baughman asked, "Why did you do that?" Loosely paraphrasing Thoreau, the seasoned angler mused thoughtfully, "I think it was in *Walden* where he wrote that a lot of men fish all their lives without ever realizing that fish isn't what they're after."

There is truth in the proposition that beneath the angler's almost pathological desire to catch and release fish is a deeper need for an otherwise indecipherable connection to the natural world—connection that transcends the pursuit, capture, and release of an individual specimen. Over time, repeated meaningful outdoor encounters become like a drug feeding a healthy addiction to nature that inevitably manifests in both a zealous conservation ethic and an ardent naturalist aesthetic. On the other hand, it's a bridge too far to conclude that catching fish isn't the goal of the exercise. Catching fish is everything.

In 1974, counterculture journalist Hunter S. Thompson went on an ill-fated, multi-day, cocaine-fueled, acid-tripping, alcohol-soaked pseudo-fishing adventure in the Yucatan. In characteristically blunt terms, Thompson wrote, "The whole idea of fishing, it seemed to me, was to hook a thrashing sea monster of some kind and actually boat the bastard." He proceeded to skip out on his large bar and hotel tabs, run from the Mexican police, and catch a plane from Monterrey to Washington, D.C. to cover Richard Nixon's impeachment trial.

A few months later, Thompson improbably became an early enthusiast of Jimmy Carter. He was bowled over by a speech Governor Carter gave in Athens, Georgia, extemporaneously referencing Bob Dylan's "The Lonesome Death of Hattie Carroll" and taking imprudent potshots at an audience of powerful lawyers and king-makers. Carter railed about "the inadequacies of a system of which it is obvious you're so patently proud." Thompson, who said he "knew next to nothing about Carter at the time and that was all I wanted to know," was in attendance by happenstance; he was part of the press corps following Senator Ted Kennedy, whose subsequent 1980 presidential primary challenge contributed to President Carter's reelection defeat. Carter wasn't well-known outside of his home state at that time and had been invited to offer what his hosts at the University of Georgia Law School expected to be innocuous remarks celebrating "Law Day." They thought Carter would politely introduce Kennedy and quickly sit down.

Instead, he lectured the self-congratulatory group of established attorneys, judges, professors, and political power-brokers about judicial corruption, social injustice, and prisons crammed with people Carter said "ought not to be there." Thompson, half-drunk on Wild Turkey disguised as iced tea, could hardly believe it. "What the hell did I just hear?" he whispered to one of Kennedy's entourage. "He said his top two advisers are Bob Dylan and Reinhold Niebuhr," came the bewildered response. Thompson sobered up enough to run out to the car and get his tape recorder. By the time he got back, Jimmy Carter "was whipping the crowd about judges who took bribes in return for reduced sentences, lawyers who deliberately cheated illiterate Blacks, and cops who abused people's rights." The staid crowd was less than pleased, to put it mildly. "They had not come there to hear lawyers denounced as running dogs of the status quo," a memory Thompson relished years later.

Perhaps as astounding as the content of the speech was the fact that Carter hadn't prepared his remarks; he spoke off the cuff about what was lying heavily on his heart that day. The only reason we have any record of what Carter said was because Thompson—even with a head full of bourbon—had enough presence of mind to stumble out to his car for his tape recorder. Carter's description of the insidious corruption of power and the moral imperative to subvert privilege in favor of equity was both timely and prescient and his exact words that day bear repeating because their relevance has not changed:

> *In general, the powerful and the influential in our society shape the laws and have a great influence on the legislature or the Congress. This creates reluctance to change because the powerful and the influential have carved off for themselves or have inherited a privileged position in society, of wealth or social prominence or higher education or opportunity for the future.*
>
> *Dr. Martin Luther King Jr., who was perhaps despised by many in this room because he shook up our social structure that benefited us and demanded simply that black citizens be treated the same as white citizens, wasn't greeted with approbation and accolades by the Georgia Bar Association or the Alabama Bar Association. He was greeted with horror. Still, once that change was made, a very simple but difficult change, no one in his right mind would want to go back to circumstances prior to that juncture in the development of our Nation's society.*
>
> *I don't want to go on and on, I'm part of it. But, the point I want to make to you is that we still have a long way to go. In every age or every year, we have a tendency to believe that we've come so far now, that there's no way to improve the present system. I'm sure when the Wright Brothers flew at Kitty Hawk, they felt that was the ultimate in transportation. When the first*

atomic bomb was exploded, that was the ultimate development in nuclear physics, and so forth.

Well, we haven't reached the ultimate. But who's going to search the heart and soul of an organization like yours or a law school or a state or nation and say, 'What can we still do to restore equity and justice or to preserve it or to enhance it in this society?' You know, I'm not afraid to make the change. I don't have anything to lose.

Thompson was so enthralled by the speech that he played his recording of it to anyone who would listen. "I have never heard a sustained piece of political oratory that impressed me more than the speech Jimmy Carter made on that Saturday afternoon in May 1974," he recalled in *The Great Shark Hunt: Strange Tales from a Strange Time*—high praise considering Thompson spent the better part of his writing career critiquing political speeches for *Rolling Stone*. "Jimmy Carter had a few serious things on his mind that day," Thompson recalled, "and he figured it was about time to unload them, whether the audience liked it or not." Hunter S. Thompson saw in Jimmy Carter what most people close to him already knew—what the caricatures of the grinning peanut farmer and Sunday School teacher failed to portray: Jimmy Carter's personal Jesus was as much or more the angry man who kicked the money changers out of the Temple as he was the "prince of peace." After years of following his political career and getting to know Carter more intimately, Thompson later described the former president as someone who would "eat your shoulder right off" to accomplish his ambition.

This observation of Carter's ruthless tenacity seems to offer a clue as to why, even in a private personal pursuit like fly fishing, he would set his sights on achieving something that most people consider unattainable. Jimmy Carter delighted in upsetting norms, defying odds, and attempting things people believed he couldn't or shouldn't do, even if he knew there was a likelihood of failure. He was more comfortable facing the specter of failure and attempting to defy it than taking the easy route, and he was accustomed to people doubting him. When he told his own mother that he was going to run for president, she famously responded, "President of what?"

...

Fly fishing for permit is a metaphor for Jimmy Carter's entire life. Unless success was uncertain—unlikely, even—Jimmy Carter didn't seem to be interested. Repeatedly, Carter opted to seek unlikely outcomes, demonstrating that he was more than willing to try something if failure was not only a possibility but a probability. His first bid for governor of Georgia failed. His second bid for governor was destined to fail—until it didn't. His bid for president of the United States was destined to fail before it even got started—until it didn't. Convincing the Senate and the House of Representatives to give the Panama Canal back to the Panamanian people was like trying to cast 100 feet of fly line into a 20-knot headwind to a single nervous, notoriously uncatchable fish, under the cover of heavy clouds, with lightning striking the horizon. And yet, he did it. Thanklessly and against his own political interests, he did it. Because it was the right thing to do, and in so doing he avoided untold bloodshed and death that never fully materialized because of the treaties Carter negotiated that are now all but forgotten by the ordinary citizens across the Americas who all have benefited from them for half a century. Historians and commentators at both ends of the political spectrum now almost universally agree that while Carter took heavy criticism for the move at the time, the Torrijos-Carter Treaties are among the most important US foreign policy achievements of the twentieth century.

The Camp David Peace Accords, bringing lasting peace between Egypt and Israel and greater stabilization to a region plagued by discord since the dawn of civilization, was the crowning foreign policy achievement of his presidency. Everyone expected Carter's efforts at brokering a deal between Egyptian President Anwar Sadat and Israeli Prime Minister Menachem Begin to fail. According to Jonathan Alter's 2020 biography of Carter, former Secretary of State Henry Kissinger even called and warned Jimmy Carter "that presidents should never negotiate personally, because they expose themselves to unnecessary failure."

All the talk of failure just caused Carter to dig in deeper. Speaking of the naysayers, he later wrote, "I slowly became hardened against them and as stubborn as at any other time I can remember." Carter eventually brokered a peace that has lasted nearly half a century and is the longest-running peace treaty among nations in the Middle East in recorded history. It earned Sadat and Begin the Nobel Peace Prize.

Quoted in Alter's book *His Very Best*, Begin said all the credit should go to Carter, who never gave up, even though the goal often seemed impossible, with failure lurking around every corner. He said the Camp David Accords should have been named the "Jimmy Carter conference . . . . The president took a great risk for himself and did it with great courage. I think he worked harder than our forefathers did in Egypt building the pyramids."

Later, Carter would credit the three men's shared faith in one God, even as they came from the often-warring religious traditions of Judaism, Christianity, and Islam. "We finally got an agreement," he said, "because we all shared faith in the same God—we all considered ourselves sons of Abraham." Then, he quoted Jesus' Sermon on the Mount: "Blessed are the peacemakers, for they shall be called children of God."

As an incumbent US president running for reelection in 1980, the odds should have been highly in Jimmy Carter's favor. At that point in US history, only six other previously-elected incumbent presidents had failed to win reelection. Yet, Carter not only failed, he suffered a humiliating defeat by an embarrassing margin. Faced with a dismal US economy, an aborted rescue attempt of US hostages in Iran, a direct challenge by Ted Kennedy's political machine in the Democratic primary, and Ronald Reagan's charismatic campaign, which courted evangelicals and employed the Southern Strategy of leveraging racial fear and tension to turn a large portion of Carter's political base against him—Jimmy Carter's failure to win a second term appears in hindsight predestined.

But the failure that should have defined him, didn't. Instead, Jimmy Carter turned his sights on other unlikely aspirations: ending homelessness, eradicating tropical diseases, and ensuring fair democratic elections that reflect and enact the collective will of the people around the world. In 2002, more than twenty years after losing the presidency, Carter became only the third US president (after Teddy Roosevelt and Woodrow Wilson) to be awarded the Nobel Peace Prize. The committee recognized him "for his decades of untiring effort to find peaceful solutions to international conflicts, to advance democracy and human rights, and to promote economic and social development." Carter remains the only one-term president and the only ex-president to win the Nobel Prize after losing the presidency.

In his 1988 book *An Outdoor Journal*, Carter outlined his philosophy as a fly angler. "There should be a relative scarcity or elusiveness of the game or fish, and not too much disadvantage for the prey in that particular habitat, so that both skill and good fortune will be necessary in achieving your goal." He coveted unlikely challenges and had no fear of failure, accepting it as a natural and frequently expected result of trying.

By its very nature, fishing is mostly an exercise in trial and error, and fly fishing for permit is mostly an exercise in just plain error. "I have often spent many hours without any success whatever, either because I did not encounter any game or because bad luck or my lack of skill led to failure," he wrote. "These experiences, still enjoyable despite the results, only enhance the pleasure of my times of success," Carter reflected. "Even in the best of times, there is an element of difficulty, doubt, discomfort, disappointment, and even danger involved. Success, when it comes, must be uncertain."

Jimmy Carter understood that failure is the best teacher and that fear of failure is the wellspring of regret. In his book *Sources of Strength: Meditations on Scripture for a Living Faith*, Carter confronted the notion of failure not just in fly fishing but in every aspect of a life well-lived. "Failure is a reality; we all fail at times, and it's painful when we do. But it's better to fail while striving for something wonderful, challenging, adventurous, and uncertain than to say, 'I don't want to try because I may not succeed completely.'"

EPILOGUE

JIM BARGER JR.

At daybreak, the horizon is shrouded in clouds, and hidden behind them rises the sun. Chachalacas cackle back and forth high up in royal palms, boisterous as chickens squawking at storms. The smell of dark coffee mixes with the roasted cornmeal scent of simmering chilaquiles, the sharp smokey smell of fiery chilies, and the homey aroma of frying eggs. Sitting on the palm-thatched patio, looking out across Ascensión Bay, you open your fly box and sift through your flies. Del Brown crabs, epoxy crabs, Puff the Magic Dragons, McCrabs, velcro crabs, and permit crab flies by other silly names as well as a whole host of beautifully tied tarpon flies—cockroaches, toads, black deaths, gurglers—their ungraceful names contradicting their beauty as elegant portraits of baitfish sculpted from feathers, thread, and fur. A light rain patters the sand. Under the shroud of clouds, the day holds little promise. Winds blow in from the southeast. A tropical depression is forming to the north in the Gulf of Mexico.

But fortunes can change in an instant.

Everything was perfect the day before. You walked out from under the thatched roof of the modest lodge, across the sand, and into the surf. You handed your seven- and nine-weight rods to guide Carlos, along with an eleven-weight just in case you happened onto some migratory tarpon. The seven-weight was rigged for bonefish and the nine-weight was rigged with a permit crab.

By the time the old wooden panga skiff whirred across the open water toward the mangrove islands of Gayo Culebra, clouds that had been high in the sky at daybreak had settled over the horizon. The water was cyan. The sky cerulean. Painted across it—not in the typical arc but in a straight paintbrush stroke—was a rainbow. Deep in the mangroves, baby tarpon bubbled and rolled. Nesting frigatebirds stretched their long black wings and bobbed their heads in a prehistoric mating ritual. Magnificent frigatebirds are a miracle oddity of evolution—giant sea birds that can't get wet without endangering themselves to the point of drowning. Lacking the oily coating of other pelagic birds to protect their feathers from water, frigates spend weeks and months at a time aloft riding wind currents—even sleeping in the sky using an innate autopilot system that dates back fifty million years to the Eocene era. They feed primarily on flying fish caught midjump and on the prey they steal midair from other birds.

Newton's Third Law of Motion—that what goes up, must come down—does not apply to the frigatebird. They are built for the sky, with high aspect ratio wings spanning eight feet across, and forked tails that help them turn on a dime. The only time you can reliably find frigatebirds roosting is in the mating season. The males stake out territories on mangrove islands like the Culebra cays, where they fill the large gular air sacs at their throats like red balloons, stretch their massive wings as if seeking embrace, and point their long black beaks into the sky. Attracted females land in front of the males and mimic the posture as the two bob their beaks wildly to the heavens.

"Sábalo," said Carlos. "La Niña."

You grabbed the eleven-weight rod, eased up onto the bow of the boat, and began looking for rolling tarpon. The large, mature migratory fish are not likely to be found here back in the mangroves.

EPILOGUE

But baby tarpon, weighing anywhere from 20 to 50 pounds, thrive here and provide a challenge all their own. When hooked in this setting, immature tarpon run for the shadows. It can take all the strength in your body to fight them from the inevitable tangled mess of roots where they're almost certain to break the tippet and run free.

You stripped line from the reel into a neat pile on the casting deck of the bow. Made one quick rollcast pulling the fly into the air behind you. Followed with one quick backcast loading about thirty feet of fly line and then one false cast before shooting about fifty feet of fly line and leader out to the edge of the mangroves and landing the fly gently in the rippling water where a baby tarpon had just lazily rolled to the surface to swallow air. Then, you made nice, long, slow and steady strips to keep the fly moving near the fish as long as possible. It felt good to make your first cast of the trip and to watch the action of the pulsating feathers tied to the stainless hook swimming exactly, and also nothing like a baitfish, through the clear green water.

"I'd probably eat that if I were a tarpon," you thought to yourself.

But nothing followed the fly. The water settled back to a slight chop from the prevailing southeastern wind and made a muffled slapping sound against the side of the wooden panga. Carlos poled the skiff quietly around the mangroves. After about thirty minutes of searching without success, you reeled up the line, stowed the rod away, and sat on your hat. Carlos started the engine and steered the panga toward the grassy flats of Punta Hualaxtoo where the big permit are known to school. The tide was low and coming in, a good omen that you'd find schools of permit coming up onto the flat to feed. Carlos cut the engine. The silence that settled over the open sea quickly began to overtake the fading echo of the outboard inside your head.

You picked up the permit rod, and Carlos climbed up onto the poling platform. He began to gently push the panga across the grassy flat, leaning heavily against the long carbon push pole. You stared out across the water, looking for shorebirds that might indicate the location of baitfish. You scanned the water for any disturbance. The sun was hypnotic. You fought off daydreams.

"Palometa," whispered Carlos. "Elles estan a la una." Big permit. At one o'clock.

You turned slightly to your right and began scanning the water. Finally locating the school of at least a dozen large permit 200 yards out and moving back to your right. Carlos climbed down from the poling platform into the water. He motioned for you to hand him the rod and follow. The water was warm and nearly waist-deep. You bent over, lowering your profile, and stalked behind Carlos obediently. It was hard to see anything on the surface with your sightline so close to the water level and the glare of the sunlight rippling on the chop of the windswept water. After wading steadily for a hundred yards or so, you began to wonder if Carlos could still see the permit or if he was just wading blindly, hoping. Surely he didn't see the fish anymore. You couldn't see the fish anymore. And you were good at spotting fish. Not as good as Carlos, but there was no way he still had eyes on the fish either. They must have moved out into deeper water.

"Do you still see them?" you asked.

"Sí," Carlos answered. "Coming to us. Get ready."

Quickly, you stripped the line off the reel, preparing to cast. Carlos grabbed the loose fly line floating in the water and kept it from getting tangled in the current around your waist. You finally spotted the school coming directly at you about a hundred feet away and closing the distance. Gently, you rolled the slack line from the water and made two false casts before double-hauling and shooting the line eighty feet directly in front of you. You let the crab fly settle to the sand without stripping it and watched as the lead fish—a large permit, maybe 30 pounds or more—flashed at the fly.

Remembering not to strike at the bite as you typically would with other saltwater fish, you gently lifted the rod as the permit sucked the fly past its rubbery lips and bit down as it would crush a small crab.

EPILOGUE

Only this wasn't a crab. When the hook pierced the mouth of the fish, the permit streaked away angrily to your right, ripping the line out of your fingers, sending the reel whirring and the rod bowing and pulsing. Three long tugs on the fly line, and you strip-set the hook into its jaw. Other permit in the school peeled off to your left and right, several streaking right past you.

"Qué padre!" Carlos shouted, clapping you on the back. You turned to look at him and grinned. The fish was still running to deep water, and you began to follow it, wading across the flat with Carlos trailing behind you. But suddenly, the line went slack. What happened? Surely the knot didn't fail. There was no way the tippet had broken. Maybe the fish was still on the line and running back to you? You reeled as fast as you could to take up the slack, but it quickly became apparent that the fish was gone. As you reeled in the line, you felt the fly pulsing easily. And when you saw the fly dancing freely in the clear green water against the backdrop of the white sand, you knew for certain the permit had somehow thrown the hook.

You turned back to shake your head at Carlos, but he was bent over and pointing excitedly off to your left. Less than fifty feet away, the school of permit had returned, or another school had appeared. Within seconds, they would cross in front of you. Rattled, you awkwardly rolled the fly up out of the water and began stripping line back off the reel, false casting as quickly as you could before laying the line in a heap in front of the approaching school. In long rapid strips, you took the slack out of the miscast line just as the first fish in the school passed over the fly that was resting like a crab in the sand. The long thin black dorsal fins of the permit sliced through the water. Blood pounded in your head. You knew there was no way you'd get a second chance, that you didn't deserve a second chance. But as the last fish in the school passed over the fly, it dipped its head down toward the sand, popped its tail out of the water, picked up the fly, and ran with it.

This permit looked as big or bigger than the first. Again, you gently lifted the fly rod and felt the strength of the fish as it turned and rushed violently away with the fly. You stripped hard again, determined to set the hook properly in the permit's jaw this time. This fish would not get away; it was a gift from heaven you were determined to catch. Your mind flashed ahead to the coming moment when you would grab the worn-out fish by the caudal peduncle between its round body and crescent moon tail. Cradling it, you would look into its bewildered eyes, remove the fly from its jaw, and rock it back and forth in the water to oxygenate its gills before releasing it and watching it sink freely, disappearing back into the vast ocean wilderness.

The rod jerked up and down, arcing as the fish continued to run. A moment of pure redemption and unconscious joy. Then, the rod went slack again. This time you knew immediately it was all over for good. The fish was gone. Like the first, this second permit had mysteriously eluded you, leaving you standing waist-deep in a vast sea of green—no longer wondering what had just happened but wondering, like so many times before, whether it had even happened at all. High overhead, the giant wings of a magnificent frigatebird stretched a black silhouette against the impossibly blue sky, tilting its swallowtail in the wind; and then it, too, was gone. And all around, in every direction, as far as you could see, there was nowhere for your eyes to find rest except upon the far horizon.

JIMMY CARTER

Blackbeard Island National Wildlife Refuge, coastal Georgia, 1977. President Carter, Dr. Hicks, and White House Legal Advisor Charlie Kirbo fished all day and only caught this one small bream, which Carter wryly described in his diary as "the largest bream I've ever seen."

During the 1980s and early '90s, Hicks and the Carters fished the Taylor River in Colorado, often with friends and fellow conservationists Ann and Perkins Sams, Leigh Perkins of the Orvis Company, and Johnny Morris, founder of Bass Pro Shops.

Rosalynn and Jimmy Carter. Photo courtesy of The Carter Center.

In the spring of 2020, President Carter gave his beloved bamboo fly rod to his fishing buddy Dr. Hicks, after COVID-19 made it inadvisable for the Carters to make their annual fly-fishing trip to friend Wayne Harpster's dairy farm in Spruce Creek, Pennsylvania. Since then, Barger and Hicks have returned often to Spruce Creek, where they have taken turns catching trout with the president's rod and with flies tied by the president. Spruce Creek was a particularly important place for the Carters as a retreat during the presidency, and it was the place where they gathered with family to begin planning their post-presidency lives and work. For nearly half a century, they returned to Spruce Creek annually with Hicks and family and friends. In the background of this photo, spanning the creek, is the covered bridge that Jimmy Carter and Wayne Harpster, both accomplished carpenters, built as a testament to their long-standing friendship. Photo courtesy of Jim Barger Jr.

In September 2013, the Carters and Hicks traveled with their fishing buddies to Mongolia to fish for taimen, the largest (and probably most ancient) salmonid in the world. They traveled to the remote Mongolian wilderness in a re-purposed Russian military transport helicopter, landing in a field of wild marijuana alongside the Eg-Ur River, where they were hosted by nomadic Mongolians in traditional gers, or yurts.

RIVERS & DREAMS

On their 2017 trip to Alaska with family and friends, nearly four decades after signing the Alaska Lands bill, President Carter caught one of the largest rainbow trout of his life when he was ninety-three years old.

RIVERS & DREAMS

Fishing at home in Plains: Jimmy Carter sent this picture to his friend Smith Bagley because it reminded the president of his fondness for napping on the lawn at the Bagleys' retreat on St. Simons Island, Georgia, where he held his pre-inaugural cabinet meetings and enjoyed fishing for speckled trout.

ACKNOWLEDGMENTS

CARLTON HICKS
~

I will forever be indebted to Wayne and Marge Harpster and their family for allowing us to visit beautiful Spruce Creek and for their friendship over the past forty-five years; to John and Dianne Moores, without whose friendship and generosity our group would never have been able to travel to many of the different countries; and to Rosalynn and Jimmy Carter for encouraging us to write this book. I'm especially thankful to my family: my wife, Jenny, who joined me on many of these trips and encouraged me to go when she was unable; my daughters, Molly and Holly, who became good fly-fishing buddies; and my grandsons, who have been excited to read about my many fly-fishing adventures. Finally, I'm thankful for my friend Jim Barger Jr., who suggested we write this book together. Without his exceptional talent as an author, this book would not have been possible.

RIVERS & DREAMS

JIM BARGER JR.

≈

For the experience of vicariously sharing in their journeys, conversations, adventures, and vision for a better world and for graciously inviting me into their home and for sharing the use of their spoken and written words referenced and quoted throughout this book, I'm grateful to Rosalynn and Jimmy Carter. The Harpster family members repeatedly opened up the cottage at Evergreen Farm on Spruce Creek to my family and me, where the conversations with Carlton, Wayne, and others that are the primary source material for this book took place. Their generosity and hospitality made this book possible.

Guides, outfitters, and fishing friends in places all over the world spanning my entire lifetime have contributed to this book through our shared experiences on the water. There are too many to list, but you know who you are—I love and appreciate you all. I would be remiss, though, if I didn't mention by name a few of my very closest fishing buddies: my father, Jim Barger Sr., who taught me how to cast a fly and who has logged more time on the water with me than anyone; my wife, Burch, who shares her life with me and has fly fished with me for more than two decades now across five continents; my sons, James and George, who have given me the pleasure of watching them grow as anglers and as young men; my nephew, Jon Phillip, who is a master fly tier; my law partner, Elliott Walthall, who for the past seventeen years has been my near-constant traveling companion as we have fished, foraged, hunted, hiked, camped, and practiced law together and who took up my slack at our firm while I worked on this book; and, of course, Dr. Carlton Hicks, who first took me to Spruce Creek and who through many conversations streamside told me his story of fly fishing with the Carters.

Among the friends and family who specifically contributed to this book in one way or another either through sharing information,

ACKNOWLEDGMENTS

proofreading, providing a quiet place to write, or through their encouragement are: Tina McElroy Ansa, Nicole Bagley, Ben Bucy, Alexia and Gray Borden, Chip Carter, Brandon Chonko, Scott Coleman, Jared DiVincent, Kacey and Gary Eichelberger, Emily Ellison, Demetris Frazier, Carolyn and Henry Frohsin, Kana and Michael Goldsmith, Beth and Bill Grubb, Jimmy Gunderman, Gina and Keith Hawk, Christi Lambert, Molly Hicks, Holly Karbo, Erin Wilt Parsons, Pam Pierson, Parker Platt, Janisse Ray, John Richards, Bailey Rountree, Manning Rountree, Susan Shipman, Bill Strother, Clay Strother, Jason Vaughn, Jazz Watts, Emily Walthall, Nancy and Bill Wood, and my nieces and nephews. I also gratefully acknowledge Bronwen Dickey, the estate of James Dickey, and Suzzana Tamminen of the Wesleyan University Press for granting permission to reprint an excerpt of "The Strength of Fields," the poem Dickey wrote and read for Jimmy Carter's inauguration on January 20, 1977.

For being my most effusive champions and so much more, I owe a lifetime of gratitude to my sister, Melanie Barger, and my mother, Mary Jane Barger.

For her deft hand as an editor and gentle pushback and insightful suggestions that greatly improved this book, I'm grateful to Alison Law. Finally, without the dedication of my friends at *The Bitter Southerner*, this would not be the book that it is: Thank you to E.A. Axelberg and Grace Polaneczky for their invaluable copy-editing and fact-checking support; Eric NeSmith, whose cheerful support is unwavering; Dave Whitling, whose creative design made this book aesthetically beautiful; and especially Kyle Tibbs Jones, my sister in arms, who has been my steadfast advocate and who first invited me into *The Bitter Southerner*'s vision of helping shape a better South and a better world.

NOTES & SELECTED BIBLIOGRAPHY

Chapter 1: Spruce Creek
"She'd smile..." Jimmy Carter, "Rosalynn," *Always a Reckoning and Other Poems*. Times Books, 1995, 130.

"I loved to watch Rosalynn fishing..." Jimmy Carter, *An Outdoor Journal*. Bantam Books, 1988, 101–2.

Chapter 2: Golden Isles
General history of Musgrove provided by Nicole Bagley, interview by author, July 8, 2022.

For a history of the Guale Preserve, see St. Simons Land Trust, "Guale Preserve," https://sslt.org/protected-properties-2/guale-preserve/.

Chapter 3: Rocky Mountains
For more information on Koinonia's history, see Dallas Lee, *The Cotton Patch Evidence: The Story of Clarence Jordan and the Koinonia Farm Experiment (1942–1970)*, 3rd ed. Wipf and Stock, 2011.

"stigma of charity..." Habitat for Humanity, "The Carter Project," https://www.habitat.org/carter-work-project.

"need something to do, Garth..." Carlton Hicks, interview by author, July 20, 2022. See also Benjamin Vanhoose, "Garth Brooks Got Called Out by Jimmy Carter for Taking a Break," *People*, November 1, 2019.

"I had not been aware of the water, but now I was..." James Dickey, *Deliverance*. Houghton Mifflin, 1970.

"The Strength of Fields" (selected stanza). James Dickey, *The Whole Motion: Collected Poems 1945-1992*. Wesleyan University Press, 1992. Reprinted with permission from the Dickey family.

Horatio Spafford, "It Is Well With My Soul (When Peace Like a River)," public domain.

Chapter 4: Argentina
"opened a new era of pleasure and friendship..." Jimmy Carter, *White House Diary*. Farrar, Straus and Giroux, 2010, 322.

Chapter 5: Venezuela
"black rushing river with the great trees..." Candice Millard, *The River of Doubt: Theodore Roosevelt's Darkest Journey*. Anchor Books, 2006, 280.

Chapter 6: Honduras
"doing the right thing..." Jonathan Alter, *His Very Best: Jimmy Carter, A Life*. Simon & Schuster, 2020, 378.

Chapter 7: Red Hills
See Matthew 19:21, New American Standard Bible ("Jesus said to him, 'If you want to be complete, go and sell your possessions and give to the poor'").

For more information about the Justice Journey or to see how you can implement the Justice Journey in your own community, see A Better Glynn, "A Better Glynn Presents: The Justice Journey," https://abetterglynn.org/initiatives/justice-journey.

"good trouble..." John Lewis, *Walking With the Wind: A Memoir of the Movement*, Mariner Books, 1999, 65.

"any of the salt-water creeks, streams, or estuaries..." GA Code § 27-4-283, 2023.

"caught the largest bream I've ever seen..." Jimmy Carter, *White House Diary*, 59.

"his direct, personal, and moral responsibility..." Ronald Reagan, "Republican National Convention Acceptance Speech," Ronald Reagan Presidential Library & Museum, https://www.reaganlibrary.gov/archives/speech/republican-national-convention-acceptance-speech-1980.

Chapter 8: Blue Ridge Mountains
"shadow casting..." Norman Maclean, *A River Runs Through It and Other Stories*. University of Chicago Press, 1976, 110.

For more on the flora and fauna of western North Carolina's Blue Ridge Mountains, see generally Linda Martinson, *Nature First: Living in the Southern Appalachians*. Messy Desk, 2023.

General history of The Goathouse and Richland Ridge provided by Parker Platt, interview by author, May 2024.

Chapter 9: Mongolia
"small, tough, intelligent..." Jimmy Carter, *White House Diary*, 283.

Deng Xiaoping pictured with 12-year-old Amy Carter. Jonathan Alter, *His Very Best*, 424.

"Mr. President, you have helped..." Jimmy Carter, *Faith*, 109.

"Yes, there are three things..." Ibid., 110.

"seemed surprised, laughed, and said..." Jimmy Carter, *White House Diary*, 284.

"On missionaries, however, he was adamant..." Ibid., 284–85.

Chapter 10: Russia
"The most important element of faith ever imposed on me..." Jimmy Carter, *Faith*, 8.

"Did you always do your best?" Jimmy Carter, *Why Not the Best?*, 57.

Reagan/Carter transition meeting. Jimmy Carter, *White House Diary*, 486.

"To be true to ourselves, we must be true to others..." Jimmy Carter, Inaugural Address, Washington, DC, January 20, 1977.

Chapter 11: Alaska
"I paid close attention to this extremely complex issue during my entire term..." Jimmy Carter, *White House Diary*, 49.

"The two Senators were aligned with oil and other commercial interests..." Ibid., 253.

"Congressman Don Young from Alaska said my protecting the Alaskan territories was a violation of their human rights..." Ibid., 264.

"see my friends..." Jimmy Carter, Remarks at Elmendorf Air Force Base, Anchorage, Alaska, June 23, 1979.

"I presume he only goes back to Alaska on election year..." Jimmy Carter, *White House Diary*, 334.

"to whip somebody's ass..." Ibid.

Jimmy Carter, Address to the Nation About Energy Problems, Washington, DC, April 19, 1977.

"just a joke..." Jonathan Alter, *His Very Best*, 4.

"80% of nitrogen oxide pollutants..." "Reagan, Spare That Tree," *Washington Post*, August 16, 1980.

"We know that evolution is a global process..." Jimmy Carter, *Faith*, 20.

Chapter 12: Yucatan
"History needs to know that this happened..." Peter Baker, "A Four Decade Secret: One Man's Story About Sabotaging Carter's Re-election," *New York Times*, March 18, 2023.

"Civil Wrongs Act." Max Blumenthal, "Agent of Intolerance," *The Nation*, May 16, 2007; for more context about the political climate at Liberty University during the time of Carter's commencement address under the leadership of Jerry Falwell Jr., see Megan K. Stack, "Can Liberty University Be Saved?" *The New Yorker*, April 28, 2022.

Liberty speech quotations from Jimmy Carter, Liberty University Commencement Address, Lynchburg, Virginia, June 4, 2018.

"If we caught every one of these..." Jack Samson, *Permit on a Fly*. Stackpole Books, 1996, 37.

"It takes a certain type of fly fisherman to fish for permit..." Ibid., jacket blurb.

"so many fish they had to haul in water..." Jimmy Carter, *An Outdoor Journal*, 29.

"I think it was in *Walden* where he wrote..." Michael Baughman, *A River Seen Right: A Fly Fisherman's North Umpqua*. Lyons & Burford, 1995, 68.

"The whole idea of fishing, it seemed to me..." Hunter S. Thompson, *The Great Shark Hunt: Gonzo Papers, Volume 1, Strange Tales from a Strange Time*. Simon & Schuster, 1979, 436.

NOTES & SELECTED BIBLIOGRAPHY

"the inadequacies of a system of which it is obvious..." Jimmy Carter, University of Georgia Law Day Address, May 4, 1974.

"knew next to nothing about Carter..." Hunter S. Thompson, *The Great Shark Hunt*, 455.

"What the hell did I just hear..." Ibid., 477.

"In general, the powerful and the influential in our society..." Jimmy Carter, Law Day Address.

"I have never heard a sustained piece of political oratory..." Hunter S. Thompson, *The Great Shark Hunt*, 474.

Matthew 21:12-13 and Isaiah 9:6, New American Standard Bible.

"eat your shoulder right off..." James Calemine, "Long Gone Gonzo: The Friendship of President Jimmy Carter & Hunter S. Thompson," James Calemine, June 17, 2019.

"that presidents should never negotiate personally..." Jonathan Alter, *His Very Best*, 393.

"Jimmy Carter conference... The president took a great risk for himself..." Ibid., 416.

"We finally got an agreement..." Ibid.

"Blessed are the peacemakers..." Matthew 5:9, New American Standard Bible.

"There should be a relative scarcity or elusiveness..." Jimmy Carter, *An Outdoor Journal*, 12.

"I have often spent many hours without any success..." Ibid.

"Failure is a reality; we all fail at times..." Jimmy Carter, *Sources of Strength: Meditations on Scripture for a Living Faith*. Crown, 1997.

SELECTED BIBLIOGRAPHY

While not a complete record of all the works and sources consulted during the writing of this book, this selected bibliography is a great place to make your first cast.

Alter, Jonathan. *His Very Best: Jimmy Carter, A Life*. Simon & Schuster, 2021.

Bailey, Cornelia Walker, with Christena Bledsoe. *God, Dr. Buzzard, and the Bolito Man: A Saltwater Geechee Talks About Life on Sapelo Island*. Anchor Books, 2000.

Baker, Peter. "A Four-Decade Secret: One Man's Story of Sabotaging Carter's Re-election," *New York Times*, March 18, 2023, A1.

Barney, Gerald O. *The Global 2000 Report to the President: Entering the Twenty-First Century*. Penguin Books, 1982.

Baughman, Michael. *A River Seen Right: A Fly Fisherman's North Umpqua*. Lyons & Burford, 1995.

Bryan, John, and Rob Carter. *America's Favorite Flies*. Charles Creek Publishing, 2017.

Carter, Jimmy. *A Call to Action: Women, Religion, Violence, and Power*, Simon & Schuster, 2014.

Carter, Jimmy. *A Full Life: Reflections at Ninety*. Simon & Schuster, 2016.

Carter, Jimmy. *Always a Reckoning and Other Poems*. Times Books, 1995.

Carter, Jimmy. *An Hour Before Daylight: Memories of a Rural Boyhood*. Simon & Schuster, 2001.

Carter, Jimmy. *An Outdoor Journal: Adventures and Reflections*. Bantam Books, 1988.

Carter, Jimmy. *Living Faith*, Times Books, 1996.

Carter, Jimmy. *Sources of Strength: Meditations on Scripture for a Living Faith*. Crown, 1997.

Carter, Jimmy. *White House Diary*. Farrar, Straus and Giroux, 2010.

Carter, Rosalynn. *First Lady from Plains*. Houghton Mifflin, 1984.

Dickey, James. *Deliverance*. Houghton Mifflin, 1970.

Dickey, James. *The Whole Motion: Collected Poems, 1945–1992*. Wesleyan University Press, 1992.

Garrison, Everett E., and Hoagy Carmichael Jr. *A Master's Guide to Building a Bamboo Fly Rod: The Essential and Classic Principles and Methods*. Skyhorse, 2016.

Kreh, Lefty, *Fly Fishing for Bass: Smallmouth, Largemouth, and Exotics*. The Lyons Press, 2004.

Larsen, Larry, *Peacock Bass Explosions*. Larsen's Outdoor Publishing, 1993.

Lee, Dallas. *The Cotton Patch Evidence: The Story of Clarence Jordan and the Koinonia Farm Experiment (1942–1970)*, 3rd ed. Wipf and Stock, 2011.

Lewis, John. *Walking With the Wind: A Memoir of the Movement*. Simon & Schuster, 1998.

Maclean, Norman. *A River Runs Through It and Other Stories*. Chicago: University of Chicago Press, 1976.

Martinson, Linda. *Nature First: Living in the Southern Appalachians*. Messy Desk Publishing, 2023.

McClane, *A. J. McClane's New Standard Fishing Encyclopedia and International Angling Guide*. Henry Holt, 1974.

Millard, Candice. *The River of Doubt: Theodore Roosevelt's Darkest Journey*. Doubleday, 2005.

Mitchell, Margaret. *Gone With the Wind*. Scribner, 1996.

Niebuhr, Reinhold, *The Children of Light and The Children of Darkness*. University of Chicago Press, 2011.

Prine, John, *Beyond Words*. Oh Boy Records, 2017.

Raiford, Matthew, with Amy Paige Condon. *Bress 'n' Nyam: Gullah Geechee Recipes from a Sixth-Generation Farmer*. Countryman Press, 2021.

Samson, Jack. *Permit on a Fly*. Stackpole Books, 1996.

Sick, Gary. *October Surprise: America's Hostages in Iran and the Election of Ronald Reagan*. Crown, 1991.

Thompson, Hunter S. *The Great Shark Hunt: Gonzo Papers, Volume 1, Strange Tales from a Strange Time*. Simon & Schuster, 1979.

Wilson, Edward O. *Half-Earth: Our Planet's Fight for Life*. Liveright, 2016.

Dr. Carlton Hicks first met the Carters in 1966 when he was just twenty-seven years old. Jimmy Carter was beginning his first campaign for governor of Georgia. Now, at eighty-four, Hicks shares his memories of more than half a century of friendship, campaigns, and adventures fly fishing around the world with Rosalynn and Jimmy Carter. In addition to volunteering on Jimmy Carter's two gubernatorial and presidential campaigns, Hicks served on President Carter's inaugural committee and as senior advisor and optometrist to the Carters throughout most of their adult lives. Together with his wife of sixty-two years, Jenny, and their fifth Weimaraner puppy, Slate, Hicks lives on St. Simons Island, Georgia, where he served as the community eye doctor for six decades.

Jim Barger Jr. is a native of St. Simons Island, Georgia. He is the author of "Ahmaud Arbery Holds Us Accountable," "The Untold Story of Hibiscus Grandiflorus," and "Unwavering" for *The Bitter Southerner*. He is a graduate of Furman University and holds an M.A. in Southern Studies from the University of Mississippi and a J.D. from the University of Alabama, where he is a longtime adjunct professor of law. A lifelong fly angler and former quail hunting guide, Barger has fly fished on five continents and traveled to thirty-five countries. He lives on St. Simons Island with wife Burch, their two sons, James and George, and their 11-year-old bird dog, Buster.

Jimmy Carter has dedicated his life to public service. As the 39th President of the United States, he negotiated the historic Camp David Peace Accords and the Panama Canal treaties. He demonstrated his unwavering commitment to the natural world by preserving over 150 million acres of wilderness, doubling the size of the US National Park System, and shepherding the passage of environmental protection laws that continue to safeguard America's natural and wild spaces. Together with Rosalynn Smith Carter, his wife of more than seventy-seven years, Carter personally participated in building more than 4,000 homes through Habitat for Humanity. The former president and first lady traveled the world through their work with The Carter Center, an organization whose mission is resolving conflicts, preserving democracy and human rights, preventing and eradicating diseases, and improving mental health care. In 2002, more than twenty years after losing reelection, Carter was awarded the Nobel Peace Prize for "his decades of untiring effort to find peaceful solutions to international conflicts, to advance democracy and human rights, and to promote economic and social development," making him the only US president ever to receive the prize for service to the world after leaving office.

BS publishing

JIMMY CARTER
Rivers & Dreams

Published by The Bitter Southerner, Inc.
Athens, Georgia

ISBN: 978-0-9980293-5-1

Permit painting on the front cover by Nick Meyer
Back cover photo by John Moores
Cover design by Dave Whitling

Designed in the South.
Printed in Canada.

© 2024 by The Bitter Southerner, Inc.
All rights reserved.